FISCAL YEAR 2015

BUDGET

OF THE U.S. GOVERNMENT

I0113335

OFFICE OF MANAGEMENT AND BUDGET

BUDGET.GOV

THE BUDGET DOCUMENTS

Budget of the United States Government, Fiscal Year 2015 contains the Budget Message of the President, information on the President's priorities, budget overviews organized by agency, and summary tables.

Analytical Perspectives, Budget of the United States Government, Fiscal Year 2015 contains analyses that are designed to highlight specified subject areas or provide other significant presentations of budget data that place the budget in perspective. This volume includes economic and accounting analyses; information on Federal receipts and collections; analyses of Federal spending; information on Federal borrowing and debt; baseline or current services estimates; and other technical presentations.

The *Analytical Perspectives* volume also has supplemental materials (formerly part of the printed volume) that include tables showing the budget by agency and account and by function, subfunction, and program. These and other tables and additional supplemental materials are available on the internet at *www.budget.gov/budget/Analytical_Perspectives*.

Historical Tables, Budget of the United States Government, Fiscal Year 2015 provides data on budget receipts, outlays, surpluses or deficits, Federal debt, and Federal employment over an extended time period, generally from 1940 or earlier to 2015 or 2019.

To the extent feasible, the data have been adjusted to provide consistency with the 2015 *Budget* and to provide comparability over time.

Appendix, Budget of the United States Government, Fiscal Year 2015 contains detailed information on the various appropriations and funds that constitute the budget and is designed primarily for the use of the Appropriations Committees. The *Appendix* contains more detailed financial information on individual programs and appropriation accounts than any of the other budget documents. It includes for each agency: the proposed text of appropriations language; budget schedules for each account; legislative proposals; explanations of the work to be performed and the funds needed; and proposed general provisions applicable to the appropriations of entire agencies or group of agencies. Information is also provided on certain activities whose transactions are not part of the budget totals.

ELECTRONIC SOURCES OF BUDGET INFORMATION

The information contained in these documents is available in electronic format from the following sources:

Internet. All budget documents, including documents that are released at a future date, spreadsheets of many of the budget tables, and a public use budget database are available for downloading in several formats from the internet at *www.budget.gov/budget*. Links to documents and materials from budgets of prior years are also provided.

Budget CD-ROM. The CD-ROM contains all of the budget documents in fully indexed PDF format along with the software required for viewing the documents. The CD-ROM has many of the budget tables in spreadsheet format and also contains the materials that were previously included in the printed *Analytical Perspectives* volume, but are now available on the internet.

For more information on access to electronic versions of the budget documents (except CD-ROMs), call (202) 512-1530 in the D.C. area or toll-free (888) 293-6498. To purchase the Budget CD-ROM or printed documents call (202) 512-1800.

GENERAL NOTES

1. All years referenced for budget data are fiscal years unless otherwise noted. All years referenced for economic data are calendar years unless otherwise noted.

2. Detail in this document may not add to the totals due to rounding.

3. Public Law 113-82, commonly referred to as the Military Retired Pay Restoration Act, was signed into law on February 15, 2014. The estimates in the 2015 Budget do not reflect the effects of this Act due to the late date of enactment.

Table of Contents

THE BUDGET MESSAGE OF THE PRESIDENT

To the Congress of the United States:

After 5 years of grit and determined effort, the United States is better positioned for the 21st Century than any other nation on Earth. We have created more than 8 million new jobs in the last 4 years and now have the lowest unemployment rate in over 5 years. Our housing market is rebounding. Our manufacturing sector is adding jobs for the first time since the 1990s. We now produce more oil at home than we buy from the rest of the world. We have cut our deficits by more than half since I took office. And for the first time in over a decade, business leaders around the world have declared that China is no longer the world's number one place to invest; America is.

We have made great progress, but we must do more to rebuild our economy on a new foundation for growth and prosperity. I believe that what unites the people of this Nation, regardless of race or region or party, young or old, rich or poor, is the simple, profound belief in opportunity for all—the notion that if you work hard and take responsibility, you can get ahead. That belief has suffered some serious blows. Over more than three decades, even before the Great Recession hit, massive shifts in technology and global competition had eliminated good, middle class jobs and weakened the economic foundations that families depend on.

Today, after 4 years of economic growth, corporate profits and stock prices have rarely been higher, and those at the top have never done better. But average wages have barely budged. Inequality has deepened. Upward mobility remains stalled. Even in the midst of recovery, too many Americans are working more than ever just to get by—let alone get ahead. And too many still are not working at all.

Our job is to reverse these trends. We need to return to an America where our success depends not on accident of birth, but on the strength of our work ethic and the scope of our dreams. That is what drew our forebears here. Opportunity is who we are. And the defining project of our generation is to restore that promise. It will not happen right away. But we must continue to strive toward that goal.

What I offer in this Budget is a set of concrete, practical proposals to speed up growth, strengthen the middle class, and build new ladders of opportunity into the middle class—all while continuing to improve the Nation's long-run fiscal position.

Earlier this year, thanks to the work of Democrats and Republicans, the Congress produced an agreement that undid some of last year's severe cuts to priorities like education and research, infrastructure, and national security. Recognizing the importance of that bipartisan compromise, the Budget adheres to the spending levels agreed to by the Congress for fiscal year 2015. But there is clearly much more we can and should do to invest in areas like infrastructure, innovation, and education that will create jobs, economic growth, and opportunity. So I am including in my Budget a fully paid for Opportunity, Growth, and Security Initiative that provides the Congress a roadmap for how and where additional investments should be made in both domestic priorities and national security this year.

We know where to start: the best measure of opportunity is access to a good job. With the economy picking up speed, companies say they intend to hire more people this year. And over half of big manufacturers say they are thinking of insourcing jobs from abroad.

We need to make that decision easier for more companies. Both Democrats and Republicans have argued that our tax code is riddled with wasteful, complicated loopholes that make it harder to invest here and encourage companies to keep profits abroad. Last summer, I offered a proposal to couple business tax reform with critical investments in infrastructure. This Budget includes that proposal, using the transition revenue that will result from a shift to a simpler, more efficient tax code to create jobs rebuilding our roads and bridges and unclogging our commutes and transporting goods made in America—because in today's global economy, first-class jobs gravitate to first-class infrastructure. At the same time, this Budget lays out how my Administration will continue to act on our own to cut red tape and streamline the permitting process for key infrastructure projects, so we can get more construction workers on the job as fast as possible.

We also have the chance, right now, to beat other countries in the race for the next wave of high-tech manufacturing jobs. My Administration has already launched four hubs for high-tech manufacturing, where we have connected businesses to research universities that can help America lead the world in advanced technologies. The Budget expands on these efforts by providing funding for five additional institutes, and, through the Opportunity, Growth, and Security Initiative, supports the goal I announced last summer of creating a national network of 45 of these manufacturing innovation institutes over the next 10 years.

We know that the nation that goes all-in on innovation today will own the global economy tomorrow. This is an edge America cannot surrender. That is why the Budget includes investments in cutting-edge research and development, driving scientific and technological breakthroughs that will create jobs, improve lives, and open new opportunities for the American people. The Budget's Opportunity, Growth, and Security Initiative will allow us to push our limits even further, supporting additional biomedical research at the National Institutes of Health that will help us fight Alzheimer's, cancer, and other diseases, climate research to develop climate change-resilient infrastructure, and agricultural research that will help increase agricultural productivity and improve health.

We also know that one of the biggest factors in bringing more jobs back is our commitment to American energy. The all-of-the-above energy strategy I announced a few years ago is working, and today, America is closer to energy independence than we have been in decades.

The Budget advances this strategy by ensuring the safe and responsible production of natural gas and cleaner electricity generation from fossil fuels. It creates new incentives to cut the amount of energy we waste in our cars, trucks, homes, and factories. It promotes clean energy with investments in technologies like solar and by expanding and making permanent the tax credit for the production of renewable energy. And it continues to strengthen protection of our air, water, land, and communities, and addresses the threat of climate change. Climate change is a fact, and we have to act with more urgency to address it because a changing climate is already harming western communities struggling with drought and coastal cities dealing with floods. That is why I directed my Administration to work with States, utilities, and others to set new standards on the amount of carbon pollution our power plants are allowed to dump into the air, and why this Budget advances new approaches to address the growing cost and damage from wildfires.

All of these efforts can speed up growth and create more jobs. But in this rapidly changing economy, we have to make sure that every American has the skills to fill those jobs. The Budget therefore invests in new efforts to drive greater performance and innovation in workforce training, including on-the-job training, apprenticeships, and other steps to equip workers with skills that match the needs of employers.

Of course, it is not enough to train today's workforce. We also have to prepare tomorrow's workforce by guaranteeing every child access to a world-class education. That is why the Budget builds on the progress we have made with new investments and initiatives to improve all levels of education, from early childhood through college.

Research shows that one of the best investments we can make in a child's life is high-quality early education. This year, we will invest in new partnerships with States and communities across the country to expand access to high-quality early education, and I am again calling on the Congress to make high-quality preschool available to every four-year-old child. The Budget also includes funding to provide access to high-quality infant and toddler care for more than 100,000 children, and supports the extension and expansion of voluntary home visiting programs.

Last year, I called on the Federal Communications Commission (FCC) to connect 99 percent of our students to high-speed broadband over the next 4 years. This year, the FCC is making a down payment on this goal by connecting more than 15,000 schools and 20 million students over the next 2 years, without adding a dime to the deficit. To ensure students receive the full benefit of this connectivity, the Budget invests in training for teachers in hundreds of school districts across the country.

The Budget also supports redesigning our high schools, helping them partner with colleges and employers that offer the college-level coursework and real-world skills to prepare students for college and careers. And it launches a new Race to the Top competition aimed at closing the achievement gap, so that all children get the high-quality education they need to succeed.

And we are shaking up our system of higher education to encourage innovation, give parents more information, and reward colleges for improving quality and reducing costs, so that no middle class student is priced out of a college education. Last summer, I directed the Department of Education to develop and publish a new college rating system that will identify colleges that provide the best value to students and encourage all colleges to improve. The Budget supports the development of that rating system and provides bonuses to reward colleges that improve educational outcomes for Pell Grant recipients. And to help more Americans who feel trapped by student loan debt, the Budget expands income-driven repayment options, allowing millions the opportunity to cap their monthly student loan payments at 10 percent of their income.

We also must do more to ensure our economy honors the dignity of work, and that hard work pays off for all of our citizens. Americans overwhelmingly agree that no one who works full time should ever have to raise a family in poverty. I have already acted by Executive Order to require Federal contractors to pay their federally funded employees a fair wage of at least $10.10 an hour. The Congress needs to go further and raise the minimum wage for all workers to that same amount. This raise will help families, and it will help the economy by giving businesses customers with more money to spend and by boosting productivity and reducing turnover. The Budget also invests in enforcement efforts to make sure workers receive the wages and overtime they have earned.

There are other steps we can take to help families make ends meet. Few policies are more effective at reducing inequality and helping families pull themselves up through hard work than the Earned Income Tax Credit (EITC). The EITC for families with children lifts millions out of poverty each year and helps about half of all parents at some point in their lives. But as a number of prominent policymakers, both progressive and conservative, have noted, the EITC does not do enough for single workers who do not have kids. The Budget doubles the value of the EITC for workers without children and non-custodial parents, and also makes it available to younger adult workers, so that it can encourage work in the crucial years at the beginning of a young person's career.

We also need to do more to help Americans save for retirement. Today, most workers do not have a pension. A Social Security check often is not enough on its own. And while the stock market has doubled over the last 5 years, that does not improve retirement security for people who do not have retirement savings. That is why the Budget builds on my proposal to create a new way for working Americans to start saving for retirement: the MyRA savings bond. To encourage new savers, MyRA requires a low initial contribution and guarantees a decent return with no risk of losing what you put in. Separately, the Budget also proposes to establish automatic enrollment Individual Retirement Accounts, offering every American access to an automatic savings vehicle on the job.

For decades, few things exposed hard-working families to economic hardship more than a broken health care system. With the enactment of the Affordable Care Act, we are in the process of fixing that. Already, because of the health reform law, more than 3 million Americans under the age of 26 have gained coverage under their parents' plans. More than 9 million Americans have signed up for private health insurance or Medicaid coverage. Because of this law, no American can ever again be dropped or denied coverage for a preexisting condition like asthma, back pain, or cancer. No woman can ever be charged more just because she is a woman. And we did all this while adding years to Medicare's finances, keeping Medicare premiums flat, and lowering prescription costs for millions of seniors. To continue this progress, the Budget fully funds the ongoing implementation of the Affordable Care Act.

We must always remember that economic growth and opportunity can only be achieved if America is safe and secure. At home, the Budget supports efforts to make our communities safer by reducing gun violence and reforming our criminal justice system.

Looking beyond our borders, the Budget responsibly transitions from the completion of our military mission in Afghanistan in 2014 to political and security support for a unified Afghan government as it takes full responsibility for its own future. When I took office, nearly 180,000 Americans were serving in Iraq and Afghanistan. Today, all our troops are out of Iraq and more than 60,000 of our troops have already come home from Afghanistan. With Afghan forces now in the lead for their own security, our troops have moved to a support role. Together with our allies, we will complete our mission there by the end of this year, and America's longest war will finally be over.

In addition to responsibly winding down our operations in Afghanistan, the Budget ensures we maintain ready, modern, and capable defense forces to address any threats we might face, including threats from terrorism and cyber attacks. It funds humanitarian and diplomatic efforts in Syria, supports transition and reform throughout the Middle East and North Africa, and advances our strategic rebalancing toward the Asia-Pacific region. It enhances stability and creates new markets for U.S. businesses with investments in Power Africa and promotes peace and security by supporting global health care and addressing climate change. And it strengthens oversight of intelligence activities and enhances the protection of U.S. diplomatic facilities and personnel overseas.

The Budget also ensures that we continue to meet our obligations to our troops and veterans who have given so much to our country. To deliver on this commitment, it provides significant resources to support veterans' medical care, help military families, assist soldiers transitioning to civilian life, reduce veterans' homelessness, and reduce the disability claims backlog so our veterans receive the benefits they have earned. It also introduces necessary reforms to our military compensation system, which our uniform military leadership called for, to ensure servicemembers and their families receive the benefits that they have earned while making sure that our military can invest in the training, equipment, and support that it needs.

In addition to making these critical investments, the Budget outlines the steps my Administration is taking to create a 21st Century Government that is more efficient, effective, and supportive of economic growth. Our citizens and businesses expect their Government to provide the same level of service experienced in the private sector and we intend to deliver. The Budget includes initiatives that will lead to better, faster, and smarter services, both online and in-person. It calls on Federal agencies to share services and leverage the buying power of the Government to bring greater value and efficiency for taxpayer dollars. It continues to open Government data and research for public and private sector use to spur innovation and job creation. And it invests in the Government's most important resource, its workers, ensuring that we can attract and retain the best talent in the Federal workforce and foster a culture of excellence.

The Budget does all of these things while further strengthening the Nation's long-term fiscal outlook. Over the last 5 years, we have cut the deficit in half as a share of the economy, experiencing the fastest period of deficit reduction since the demobilization following World War II. The Budget continues this progress, bringing deficits down as a share of the economy to below 2 percent by 2023 and putting debt as a share of the economy on a declining path.

Although we have seen a notable and significant decline in health care spending growth over the last few years, in part due to the Affordable Care Act, we know that over the long run, the growth of health care costs continues to be our Nation's most pressing fiscal challenge. That is why the Budget builds on the savings and reforms in the health reform law with additional measures to strengthen Medicare and Medicaid and encourage high-quality and efficient health care.

We also know that revenue has to be part of the solution to our Nation's long-term fiscal challenges. Given the aging of our population and the declining ratio of workers to retirees, we will need additional revenue to maintain our commitments to seniors while also making the investments that are needed to grow our economy and expand opportunity. The Budget secures that revenue through tax reform that reduces inefficient and unfair tax breaks and ensures that everyone, from Main Street to Wall Street, is paying their fair share.

Finally, if we are serious about long-term, sustainable economic growth and deficit reduction, it is also time to heed the calls of business leaders, labor leaders, faith leaders, and law enforcement—and fix our broken immigration system. Independent economists say immigration reform will grow our economy and shrink our deficits by almost $1 trillion in the next two decades. And for good reason: when people come here to fulfill their dreams—to study, invent, and contribute to our culture—they make our country a more attractive place for businesses to locate and help create jobs for everyone.

The Senate has acted to pass a bipartisan immigration reform bill that is worthy of support. It is time for the House of Representatives to finish the job.

We have made progress over the last 5 years. But our work is not done. This Budget provides a roadmap to ensuring middle class families and those working to be a part of the middle class can feel secure in their jobs, homes, and budgets. To build real, lasting economic security, we also need to expand opportunity for all so every American can get ahead and have a shot at creating a better life for their kids.

None of it is easy. America has never come easy. But if we work together, if we summon what is best in us, I know it is within our reach.

BARACK OBAMA

THE WHITE HOUSE,
    MARCH 4, 2014.

OPPORTUNITY FOR ALL

Thanks to the hard work and resilience of the American people, the economy and our Nation are moving forward. More than eight million private sector jobs have been created over the last four years, the unemployment rate is at its lowest level in over five years, and health care costs are growing at the lowest rate on record. For the first time since the 1990s, the manufacturing sector is creating jobs and we produce more of our own oil at home than we buy from the rest of the world. And for the first time since the turn of the century, CEOs around the world have declared that the United States is the number one place to invest.

Our economy is moving forward and businesses are creating jobs, but our top priority must be accelerating that growth while expanding opportunity for all Americans. For the last several years, manufactured crises in Washington have hindered, rather than helped, economic growth and opportunity. But earlier this year, Democrats and Republicans came together to produce a 2014 budget that invests in key areas of innovation, education, and infrastructure—investments that will help grow our economy, create jobs, and strengthen the middle class.

The President's 2015 Budget shows how we can build on that progress. By rewarding hard work with fair wages, equipping all children with a high-quality education to prepare them for a good job in the future, making sure a secure retirement is within reach, and ensuring health care is affordable and reliable, we can expand opportunity for all Americans. By fixing our broken immigration system, investing in our infrastructure, simplifying the tax code for businesses, and reforming our skills and job training programs, we can create jobs and achieve stronger and more inclusive economic growth. By cutting wasteful tax breaks for the wealthiest Americans and making common sense reforms to Government programs, we can manage our Government more efficiently and effectively, and continue to cut the deficit in a balanced way.

BUILDING ON ECONOMIC PROGRESS

The economy is moving forward as we continue to recover from losses sustained during the Great Recession. The economy has added private sector jobs for 47 consecutive months, for a total of 8.5 million jobs. In 2013 alone, private sector employment increased by 2.4 million jobs. Despite variances in month-to-month figures, the year-over-year changes indicate that the recovery has been durable even in the face of headwinds that have emerged in recent years from the Eurozone crisis and from self-inflicted wounds at home, such as last year's sequestration, Government shutdown, and uncertainty surrounding the debt limit.

There are encouraging signs emerging across industries. Domestic oil production is exceeding imports for the first time since 1995 and is at its highest level since 1989. Increases in domestic oil and petroleum production have helped to cut U.S. net imports of crude oil and petroleum products in half relative to the 2005 peak, reduce trade imbalances, and boost manufacturing. Manufacturing production has grown since the end of the recession at its fastest pace in over a decade, adding 622,000 jobs over the past 47 months. Since Chrysler and General Motors emerged from bankruptcy in mid-2009, the auto

Seasonally-Adjusted Private Sector Monthly Job Gain/Loss

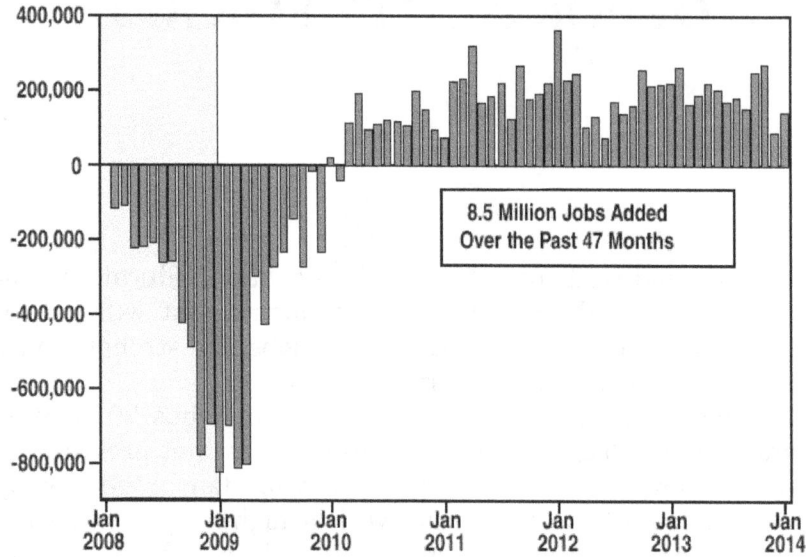

8.5 Million Jobs Added
Over the Past 47 Months

Source: Bureau of Labor Statistics.

industry has added 423,900 jobs, the industry's strongest growth since the 1990s. The housing sector is coming back, with housing prices, new home sales, and building permits up in 2013.

PROGRESS ON OUR FISCAL HEALTH

Under the President's leadership, the deficit has been cut in half as a share of the economy, representing the largest four-year deficit reduction since the demobilization from World War II. This progress is largely the result of increased economic growth, cuts to discretionary spending in the Budget Control Act (BCA), and the restoration of tax rates on the highest earners to 1990s levels in the American Taxpayer Relief Act.

The policies in the Budget will strengthen the recovery by making investments for the long

Annual Deficits as a Percent of GDP

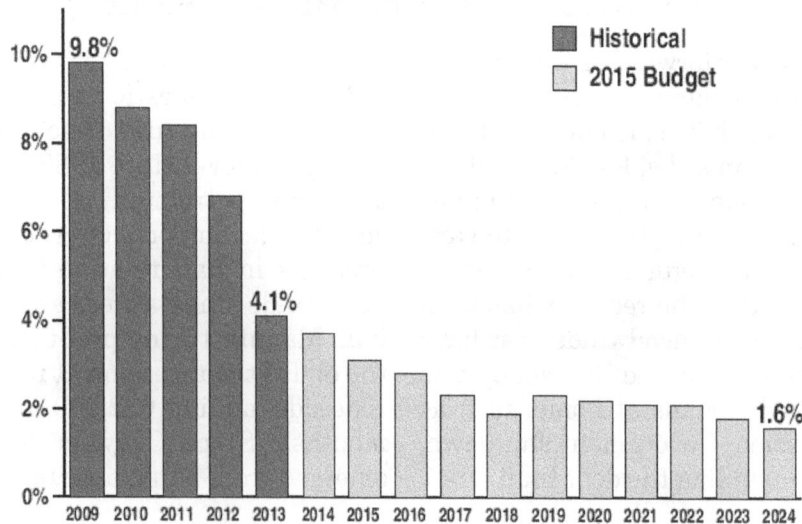

Historical
2015 Budget

9.8%

4.1%

1.6%

2009 2010 2011 2012 2013 2014 2015 2016 2017 2018 2019 2020 2021 2022 2023 2024

term, while continuing to bring our deficits down and putting debt on a declining path as a share of the economy. Under the Budget, deficits will continue to fall, declining to below two percent of Gross Domestic Product (GDP) by 2023, with the debt stabilized by 2015 and declining after that.

Over the long run, the largest single factor driving projected deficits remains rising health care costs. In the last few years, health care spending growth has fallen to the lowest levels since the Government started tracking these data in the 1960s. Data from the Centers for Medicare and Medicaid Services and the Bureau of Economic Analysis show that, from 2010 to 2012, health care spending grew at an annual rate of just 1.1 percent in real inflation-adjusted per capita terms, a small fraction of the 4.0 percent average annual rate over the first part of the last decade.

While some portion of the slowdown is attributable to the business cycle, evidence suggests that a substantial fraction is probably structural, meaning that it reflects factors more likely to per-

sist once the economy fully recovers.[1] One notable structural factor contributing to the slowdown is the Affordable Care Act (ACA), which is lowering costs and improving quality by reducing excessive Medicare payments to private insurers and providers, deploying new payment models that encourage more efficient, higher-quality care, and creating strong incentives for hospitals to reduce readmission rates.

This slowdown is already yielding substantial fiscal dividends. Compared with the 2011 Mid-Session Review, aggregate projected Federal health care spending between 2014 and 2020 has decreased by more than $1 trillion based on current budget estimates. If sustained, the slowdown in health care costs will also help boost employment and bolster wage growth as the job market strengthens, and will translate into higher wages and living standards over the long run. If even one-third of the recent slowdown con-

---

[1] This is the conclusion reached by multiple groups of outside researchers. For further discussion, see Council of Economic Advisers, "Trends in Health Care Cost Growth and the Role of the Affordable Care Act," November 2013, *http://www.whitehouse.gov/sites/default/files/docs/healthcostreport_final_noembargo_v2.pdf.*

Growth in Real Per Capita National Health Expenditures, 1960-2013

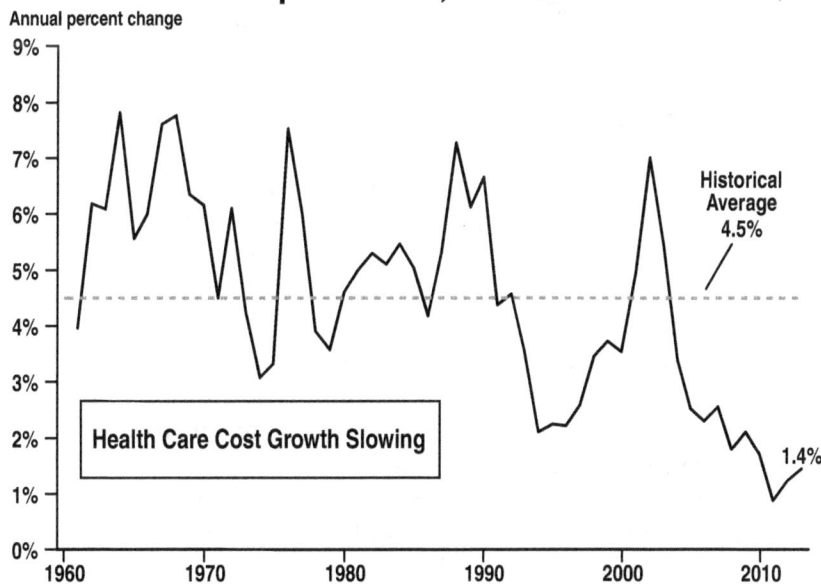

Annual percent change

Health Care Cost Growth Slowing

Historical Average 4.5%

1.4%

Note: Data for 2013 (1.4%) is a projection.

Source: Centers for Medicare and Medicaid Services, National Health Expenditure Accounts; Bureau of Economic Analysis, National Income and Product Accounts; and CEA calculations.

tinues, health care spending a decade from now will be about $1,200 per person lower than if the growth returned to its 2000-2007 trend—gains that workers will see in the form of higher wages and Federal and State governments will see in the form of lower costs.

The ACA will have a growing impact on reducing health care costs and improving quality in future years. The Budget builds on the savings and reforms in ACA with additional measures that will help ensure health care cost growth remains low and improve the quality of care.

HELPING, NOT HURTING, OUR ECONOMY

Over the past few years, Washington has lurched from one manufactured crisis to another, including sequestration, a Government shutdown last fall, and repeated threats to put the Nation in default by failing to raise the debt limit. These actions have created uncertainty for families and businesses around the Nation, put at risk our commitments to seniors, our military men and women, and the most vulnerable among us, undermined the Government's ability to serve the public, weakened economic growth, and wasted billions of dollars. These self-inflicted economic wounds must stop.

The Congressional Budget Office estimated that the 2013 sequestration reduced real GDP growth by about 0.6 percentage points in calendar year 2013 and cost 750,000 jobs. Private sector economists have estimated that the Government shutdown reduced the annualized growth rate of GDP in the fourth quarter of 2013 by 0.2 to 0.6 percentage points, and, during the shutdown, the Gallup Daily Economic Confidence Index fell to its lowest level since December 2011. A report by the Office of Management and Budget also highlighted other costs of the Government shutdown, including billions of dollars in lost productivity, reduced revenue for the Federal Government, and major disruption to Government services that the American people and the private sector economy rely on.[2]

---

[2] See: *http://www.whitehouse.gov/sites/default/files/omb/reports/impacts-and-costs-of-october-2013-federal-government-shutdown-report.pdf.*

ENACTING BIPARTISAN BUDGET AND APPROPRIATIONS ACTS: IMPORTANT STEPS IN THE RIGHT DIRECTION

In the immediate aftermath of the shutdown, the President called on both parties to return to regular order in Washington. The enactment of the Bipartisan Budget Act of 2013 (BBA) and the Consolidated Appropriations Act of 2014 (CAA) represents compromise between Democrats and Republicans and a positive step toward returning Washington to regular order and ensuring that fiscal policy is helping our economy, not hurting it.

While neither side got everything they wanted, the BBA took an important first step toward replacing the damaging sequestration cuts with sensible long-term reforms, including a number of reforms proposed in the President's 2014 Budget. The CAA built on the BBA to provide funding for investments in key areas of innovation, education, and infrastructure—investments that will help grow our economy, create jobs, and strengthen the middle class. It also supported our national security by providing the Department of Defense (DOD) with needed relief from the untenable sequestration cuts that were undermining military readiness. This bipartisan legislation provided appropriations for every agency in the Federal Government, enabling them to more efficiently and effectively serve the American people and bringing greater certainty to businesses and communities across the Nation.

THE PRESIDENT'S 2015 BUDGET

The BBA and the CAA were important first steps toward ending manufactured crises and replacing the damaging cuts caused by sequestration with long-term reforms. But they did not go far enough. In particular, while the BBA replaced half the discretionary sequestration cuts for 2014, it replaced just one-fifth of the scheduled cuts in discretionary funding for 2015. As a result, taking into account projected growth in programs such as veterans' medical care and other factors, the BBA non-defense discretionary funding levels for 2015 are several billion below the levels the Congress provided in 2014. They are also below 2007 funding levels adjusted for inflation, even though the need for pro-growth investments in infrastructure, education, and innovation has only increased due to the Great Recession and its aftermath.

Recognizing the importance of this bipartisan compromise, the President's Budget adheres to the spending levels agreed to in the BBA in 2015, and proposes difficult but necessary cuts and reforms to make room for investments in priority areas such as research, clean energy, early learning, and ending homelessness. But even with those tough cuts and reforms, the discretionary levels set by the BBA simply are not sufficient to ensure that the Nation is achieving its full potential in creating jobs, growing the economy, and promoting opportunity for all.

For that reason, the Budget also includes a separate, fully paid for $56 billion Opportunity, Growth, and Security Initiative. The Opportunity, Growth, and Security Initiative, which is split evenly between defense and non-defense funding, shows how additional discretionary investments can spur economic progress and strengthen our national security. It will help restore our global edge in basic research, provide funding to support preschool across the United States, and train teachers to take advantage of broadband technology in the classroom. It will invest in our communities through emergency response activities, juvenile justice programs, and expansion of Promise Zones, and will fund a national network of manufacturing institutes that will spur economic development. It will put people back to work, restoring our national parks, renovating veterans' hospitals, and building resilient infrastructure that will help our communities prepare for the effects of climate change. It will support partnerships between community colleges and employers to train workers for jobs that are in demand, including a bold new expansion of apprenticeship programs. It will also help us put a stop to short-sighted cuts to Government operations that compromise efficiency and effectiveness and cost money over the long run, such as growing deferred maintenance backlogs, sharp cuts to Federal employee training, and erosions in customer service at agencies like the Internal Revenue Service (IRS).

OPPORTUNITY, GROWTH, AND SECURITY INITIATIVE: SECURING OUR NATION'S FUTURE

The Budget's fully paid for Opportunity, Growth, and Security Initiative provides a roadmap for additional investments that will help secure our Nation's future.

NON-DEFENSE

The non-defense portion of the Initiative makes investments in six key areas. Below are examples of specific investments in each of these categories.

Education

- *Enhancing Early Childhood Education*—providing additional Preschool Development Grants to reach two-thirds of all States by 2015, laying a stronger foundation for Preschool for All;

providing access to high-quality early learning opportunities to a total of more than 100,000 children through Early Head Start-Child Care Partnerships; and supporting Head Start grantees in expanding their programs and investing in teacher quality, without reducing the number of children served.

- *Accelerating Improvements to K-12 Education*—providing 100,000 teachers in 500 districts with access to professional development to take greater advantage of the universal broadband provided through the ConnectED initiative; increasing investment in high school redesign to create additional innovative, career-focused high schools; and providing additional incentives, through Race to the Top, for States to bring the most successful K-12 reforms to the most disadvantaged schools to help close the achievement gap.

- *Making Other Invesments*—to ensure that all students have access to a high-quality education, from preschool to college.

Research and Innovation

- *Re-establishing Global Leadership in Basic Research*—providing 650 additional new National Institutes of Health (NIH) grants; increasing funding for an NIH Defense Advanced Research Projects Agency (DARPA)-like initiative that will invest in breakthrough medical research; and increasing NIH's contribution to the multiagency BRAIN Initiative (Brain Research through Advancing Innovative Neurotechnologies) that is helping to revolutionize our understanding of the human brain; developing and scaling new manufacturing technologies; investing in a thousand additional National Science Foundation grants to expand knowledge across disciplines and accelerate innovation across industries; and building a new biosafety research laboratory.

- *Advancing Clean Energy Research and Development (R&D)*—investing in applied research at the Department of Energy to accelerate the development and deployment of new energy efficiency and renewable energy technologies—such as higher-performing electric drive motors, batteries, and ultra-light materials and composites to enable electric vehicles to be as affordable and convenient as the gasoline powered vehicles we drive today; and technological advances to make renewable electricity as inexpensive and accessible as fossil-fuel based electricity.

- *Launching a Race to the Top for Energy Efficiency and Grid Modernization*—incentivizing States to make progress toward the goal of doubling American energy productivity in 20 years and toward modernizing their electricity grids, resulting in more cost-effective demand response, distributed generation, and improved grid reliability and resilience.

- *Making Other Investments*—to maintain U.S. global leadership in basic research and help transition our economy to a clean energy future.

Infrastructure and Jobs

- *Expanding Advanced Manufacturing and Investing in Regional Economic Growth*—investing in a national competition to establish 45 manufacturing institutes, positioning the United States as a global leader in advanced manufacturing technology; launching a new public-private "Scale-Up" fund to help firms with innovative advanced manufacturing technologies take them to scale; and investing in regional economic growth and competitiveness through grants to communities.

- *Developing Climate Resilience*—investing in research and unlocking data and information to better understand the projected impacts of climate change and how to better prepare our communities and infrastructure; helping communities plan and prepare for the impacts of climate change and encouraging local measures to reduce future risk; and funding breakthrough technologies and resilient infrastructure that will make us more resilient in the face of a changing climate.

- *Launching the National Parks Centennial Initiative*—helping launch a Works Progress Administration (WPA)-like effort to put thousands of veterans, youth, and others to work upgrading the National Park System for its 100th anniversary in 2016, along with similar improvements to national forests, refuges, and other public lands.

- *Modernizing the National Airspace System*—supporting the Federal Aviation Administration's NextGen initiative, a multi-year effort to improve the efficiency, safety, capacity, and environmental performance of the aviation system.

- *Supporting High Priority Medical Construction and Renovation Projects*—investing in the Department of Veterans Affairs (VA) construction and capital projects to improve veterans' services and meet increased demand at VA, as well as new Indian Health Service health care facilities to improve the health of American Indians and Alaskan Natives.

- *Promoting Financial Stability and Protection*—protecting investors, consumers, and taxpayers by providing additional funding for investigating and prosecuting the full spectrum of financial fraud and for implementing financial reform.

- *Making Other Investments*—to help rebuild our Nation's infrastructure, support small businesses in creating jobs, and spur economic development in communities around the United States.

Opportunity and Mobility

- *Expanding Opportunity in Distressed Neighborhoods*—through a combination of base and Opportunity, Growth, and Security Initiative funding, supporting 40 additional Promise Neighborhoods and 10-14 Choice Neighborhoods to improve educational outcomes and revitalize distressed neighborhoods.

- *Supporting Apprenticeships and Job-Driven Training at Community Colleges*—awarding grants to partnerships of community colleges, employers, and others to launch training for in-demand jobs, and doubling the number of apprenticeships in America over the next five years.

- *Improving Training and Employment Services*—increasing State and local capacity, including through greater innovation and performance incentives; targeting additional resources to populations that face significant barriers to employment; and reaching a total of 50,000 households in public housing with Jobs-Plus job training and financial incentives, an 1-based approach that has been shown to boost annual incomes by $1,300 on average. In addition, the defense portion of the Opportunity, Growth, and Security Initiative, discussed below, would provide funding for additional teens to participate in National Guard Youth ChalleNGe, an evidence-based residential training and mentoring program that has been shown to increase employment, education, and earnings for at-risk youth.

- *Encouraging States to Offer Paid Leave*—providing additional funding to help more States launch paid leave programs like those in California, New Jersey, and Rhode Island that have helped more than a million workers care for a new child or cope with a family member's illness.

- *Making Other Investments*—to increase economic opportunity and assist vulnerable populations, including incentivizing schools funded through the Bureau of Indian Education to introduce reforms that improve student outcomes; and additional funding for the Legal Services Corporation, which assists millions of low-income Americans each year with essential civil legal services in areas such as housing and consumer protection.

Public Health, Safety, and Security

- *Supporting Homeland Security and Law Enforcement*—investing in a reformed, risk-based approach to increase preparedness, mitigation, and emergency response to disasters and other threats in communities across America.

- *Making Targeted Investments in State and Local Justice Assistance Grants and Strengthening Public Safety*—funding a new youth investment initiative that will incentivize State efforts to increase the availability of alternatives to incarceration, reenroll youth back into school after confinement, and reduce ethnic and racial disparities in the juvenile justice system; and providing resources for bringing newly completed or acquired Federal prisons on-line.

- *Providing for the Public Health*—accelerating development of a universal flu vaccine.

- *Investing in Global Security*—funding foreign assistance programs that have a proven track record of fostering economic growth, reducing poverty, and improving health.

- *Leveraging Funds for Global Health*—making additional matching funding available for the Global Fund to Fight AIDS, Tuberculosis, and Malaria to encourage other donors to increase their pledges.

- *Making Other Investments*—in programs that are important to maintaining public health and safety at the local, State, Federal, and global levels.

More Efficient and Effective Government

- *Advancing Cross-Government Customer Service Initiatives*—combined with base discretionary funding, supporting IRS customer service improvements that will increase toll-free telephone service response rates from about 60 percent to about 80 percent; and funding SSA improvements to reduce wait times and enhance services for the public.

- *Helping Businesses Cut Through Red Tape*—supporting the National Inventory of Historic Properties to help expedite Federal permitting and get infrastructure projects off the ground; and making improvements to *Business.gov* and *Exports.gov*.

- *Investing in Federal Employee Training*—restoring cuts to Federal employee training to help train, retain, and recruit a skilled and effective Federal workforce, targeting investments in employee training to common, but high-impact areas such as customer service or information technology.

- *Making Other Investments*—to ensure that the Federal Government can meet its core responsibilities to the American public, now and in the future.

DEFENSE

The defense portion of the Opportunity, Growth, and Security Initiative makes investments in four key areas.

Key Weapons Systems Modernization

Consistent with the reductions in discretionary spending required by the BCA and the BBA, DOD has reduced or slowed down planned purchases of a variety of weapons systems and equipment over the last three years. The Opportunity, Growth, and Security Initiative would allow DOD to accelerate the schedules for developing and buying new or upgraded systems in order to ensure that the United States maintains technological superiority over potential adversaries. For example, the Opportunity, Growth, and Security Initiative provides enhanced resources for procurement of manned and unmanned aircraft, helicopters, ground vehicles, and communication systems. It also expands the R&D efforts that underpin all defense modernization programs.

Readiness Restoration

In 2013, significant reductions in funding degraded readiness throughout the Joint Force by requiring sharp cuts to training, maintenance, and support. For example, the Air Force had to ground 33 squadrons and reduce an additional seven squadrons to basic "takeoff and land" training for several months. Although the base budget provides the resources needed to continue gradually restoring readiness and balance, the Opportunity, Growth, and Security Initiative provides the resources to expedite progress by supporting increased activity at depot maintenance facilities around the Nation, greater training support, and increases in funding for fuel, spare parts, and transportation costs.

Nuclear R&D and Infrastructure

The Opportunity, Growth, and Security Initiative provides additional funding to support the infrastructure and human capital that underpin long-term, effective sustainment of the nuclear weapons stockpile and supporting enterprise. For example, the Opportunity, Growth, and Security Initiative allows the National Nuclear Security Administration to begin important facilities construction and deferred maintenance projects and to undertake several R&D projects to keep nuclear weapons safe, reliable, and effective.

DOD Facilities Improvement

Sequestration required significant funding cuts for DOD facilities, forcing the Department to defer some sustainment, restoration, and modernization (SRM) costs, as well as some military construction projects. The base budget provides the funds necessary to keep DOD bases, housing, and other facilities safe, secure, and operational, but not enough to avoid long-term deterioration. The Opportunity, Growth, and Security Initiative provides additional resources for SRM and construction at hundreds of DOD installations that will generate jobs and reduce future costs to replace buildings, roads, runways, and other facilities.

Importantly, the Budget also shows that this initiative is fully paid for, and easily affordable if the Congress is willing to enact a few common-sense spending and tax changes. Building on the model established in the BBA, the Budget outlines a specific set of mandatory spending reforms and tax loophole closers that would fully offset the cost of the Opportunity, Growth, and Security Initiative:

- **$28 billion in savings from common-sense spending reforms, including:**

  — *Reforming Federal crop insurance by reducing subsidies for overly generous coverage* ($14 billion). While the newly enacted Farm Bill made progress on curbing direct subsidy payments, it failed to adopt bipartisan reforms to the increasingly expensive Federal crop insurance program. The Budget proposes to reduce Federal subsidies for disproportionately subsidized plans that benefit wealthy corporate farmers and to reduce overpayments to private crop insurance companies.

  — *Reallocating spectrum to promote economic growth* ($5 billion). The Budget proposes to introduce new mechanisms to promote more efficient allocation of spectrum to high priority uses.

  — *Reforming the Transportation Security Administration (TSA) passenger fees to reflect the cost of aviation security* ($5 billion). While the Congress took steps toward better matching TSA fees with costs in the BBA, the Budget proposes to further reform these user fees to more closely reflect the costs of passenger screening and other aviation security services.

  — *Preventing Unemployment Insurance and Disability Insurance overlap* ($3 billion). The Budget proposes to prevent individuals from collecting Unemployment and Disability Insurance benefits for the same period of time.

- **$28 billion in savings from reducing tax benefits for multi-million dollar retirement accounts.** Tax-preferred savings accounts were intended to help middle class families save for retirement. However, under current rules, some wealthy individuals are able to accumulate millions of dollars in these accounts, substantially more than is needed to ensure a secure retirement. The Congress could pay for the remaining half of the Opportunity, Growth, and Security Initiative by enacting the President's proposal to prevent additional tax-preferred saving by individuals who have already accumulated tax-preferred retirement savings sufficient to finance an annual income of over $200,000 per year in retirement—more than $3 million per person.

When considering both base funding and Opportunity, Growth, and Security Initiative resources, the Budget provides a comprehensive and detailed plan for making investments that will drive the Nation forward. Without taking action, funding levels for 2016 and beyond will continue to preclude the investments needed to protect our Nation or enable our economy to achieve its full potential, since the BBA did not provide even partial sequestration relief after 2015. The Budget proposes to restore discretionary spending to a path that would continue to support economic growth, opportunity, and safety and security; these investments will also be paid for with a combination of reforms to mandatory spending programs and targeted tax loophole closers included in the Budget. Even so, under the Budget proposals, discretionary spending will fall to its lowest level as a share of the economy in more than 50 years.

MANAGING GOVERNMENT TO DRIVE FURTHER GROWTH AND OPPORTUNITY

At the same time, the Budget takes key steps to enhance the Administration's efforts to deliver a Government that is more effective, efficient, and supportive of economic growth. The Budget includes initiatives to deliver better, faster, and smarter services to citizens and businesses. The Budget advances the Administration's effort to modernize the infrastructure permitting process, cutting through red tape, allowing more construction workers on the job faster, and achieving better outcomes for our communities and environment. The Budget also expands the use of shared services between Federal agencies and strategic sourcing to leverage the buying power of the Government, bringing greater value and efficiency for taxpayer dollars. Further, the Budget continues to open Government data and research for public and private sector use to spur innovation and job creation. These and other key management initiatives are detailed in Chapter 2 of the Budget.

INVESTING IN JOBS, ECONOMIC GROWTH AND OPPORTUNITY

Creating jobs that pay good wages is the best way to grow our economy and the middle class. To compete in the 21st Century economy and make America a magnet for job creation and opportunity, we need to invest in American innovation, strengthening our manufacturing base, and keeping the Nation at the forefront of technological advancement. To ensure our energy security and address global climate change, we must continue to focus on domestic energy production, the development of clean energy alternatives, and the promotion of energy efficiency. The Budget therefore includes investments in advanced manufacturing, R&D, and clean energy and energy efficiency technologies.

Making America a Magnet for Jobs. The President is committed to making America a magnet for jobs and manufacturing so that we can create new opportunities for American workers.

Transforming Communities Into World-Leading Centers of Advanced Manufacturing. To support investment and accelerate innovation in U.S. manufacturing, the President has called for the creation of a national network of manufacturing innovation institutes across the Nation. Leveraging the strengths of a particular region, each institute will bring together companies, universities, community colleges, and Government to co-invest in the development of world-leading manufacturing technologies and capabilities that U.S.-based manufacturers can apply in production. Through a combination of base discretionary funds and the Opportunity, Growth, and Security Initiative, and building on the four institutes already launched and the five additional institutes expected to be launched in 2014, the Budget supports the President's goal announced last summer of creating 45 new manufacturing innovation institutes over 10 years, tripling the number originally proposed in the President's 2012 and 2013 State of the Union addresses.

Expanding SelectUSA to Attract Investment to Our Shores. In 2011, the President launched SelectUSA at the Department of Commerce, creating the first Federal effort to actively attract business investment in the United States. Building on the resources provided in the CAA, the Budget supports the President's proposal to significantly expand and enhance SelectUSA.

Investing in R&D. Scientific discovery, technological breakthroughs, and innovation are the primary engines for expanding the frontiers of human knowledge and are vital for responding to the challenges and opportunities of the 21st Century. We look to scientific innovation to promote sustainable economic growth and job creation, improve the health of all Americans, move us toward a clean energy future, address global climate change, manage competing demands on environmental resources, and ensure the security of the Nation. Science and engineering research is a valuable source of new knowledge that has driven important developments in fields ranging from telecommunications to medicine, yielding high economic and social rates of return and creating entirely new industries with highly-skilled, high-wage jobs.

Continuing our commitment to world-class science and research, the Budget provides $135 billion for R&D overall, while targeting resources to those areas most likely to directly contribute to the creation of transformational technologies that can create the businesses and jobs of the future. The base Budget increases R&D relative to the 2014 enacted levels, with over $5 billion in additional funding in the Opportunity, Growth, and Security Initiative to drive progress in key R&D priorities.

Advanced Manufacturing and Clean Energy Technologies. The Budget will support the development and scaling of new advanced manufacturing technologies, such as increasing research in the National Institute of Standards and Technology's labs and accelerating the transfer of new technologies from Federal labs to industry. The Budget will also increase funding for clean energy technology investment at the Department of Energy's Office of Energy Efficiency and Renewable Energy and Advanced Research Projects Agency—Energy, building on the Administration's success in reducing our dependence on fossil fuels, promoting energy efficiency, and doubling U.S. renewable electricity generation. Through the Opportunity, Growth, and Security Initiative, the Budget will support a new Energy Efficiency and Grid Modernization Race to the Top, which will incentivize States to modernize their electricity grids and to make progress toward the goal of doubling American energy productivity in 20 years.

Health Care R&D. The Budget, including the Opportunity, Growth, and Security Initiative, will support biomedical research at NIH, providing about 9,500 new NIH

grants that will help us better understand the fundamental causes and mechanisms of disease. The Budget will help us in the fight against Alzheimer's disease, cancer and other diseases that affect millions of Americans. The Budget will support the BRAIN initiative, which will help revolutionize our understanding of how the human brain processes, stores and retrieves information. The Budget will also allow for the development of a new health research program modeled after the DARPA program designed to fund innovative projects and accelerate the discovery of life-saving treatments and cures.

Agriculture R&D. The Budget includes funding for the Agriculture and Food Research Initiative competitive research program, supporting research in areas important to American agriculture: bioenergy, food security, water, obesity prevention, and food safety. The Budget also includes funding to support three multidisciplinary institutes dedicated to crop science and pollinator health, advanced biobased manufacturing and anti-microbial research. The Opportunity, Growth, and Security Initiative includes additional funding to support competitive research and the construction of a new biosafety research laboratory in Athens, Georgia.

Supporting Applied R&D by Reforming and Making Permanent the Research and Experimentation Tax Credit. The Research and Experimentation (R&E) Tax Credit is an important Federal incentive for research. But the R&E Tax Credit is less effective than it could be in spurring additional research because it is complicated and temporary. Currently, businesses must choose between using a complex, outdated formula that provides a 20 percent credit rate and a much simpler one that provides a 14 percent credit rate. The Budget would increase the rate of the simpler credit to 17 percent, which would make it more attractive and simplify tax filing for businesses. In addition, the Budget makes the basic and the simplified

R&E credit permanent to provide certainty and increase effectiveness.

Investing in Homegrown Clean Energy. In order to secure America's energy future and cut carbon pollution, the Budget invests in clean energy, improving energy security, and enhancing preparedness and resilience to climate change. These investments are critical components of the President's Climate Action Plan, bringing about a clean energy economy with new businesses, jobs, and opportunities for American workers.

Promoting Safe and Responsible Production and Use of Natural Gas and Cleaner Energy from Fossil Fuels. Our domestic natural gas resources are reducing energy costs across the economy—from manufacturers investing in new facilities to lower heating costs for families throughout the United States. The Budget invests in research to ensure safe and responsible natural gas production. The Budget invests in innovative approaches to cleaner fossil fuels, including advanced high-efficiency combustion engines and carbon capture and storage technologies from both natural gas and coal. The Budget also supports technical assistance to States and local communities to help ensure shale gas is developed in a safe, responsible way that helps build diverse and resilient regional economies that can withstand boom-and-bust cycles and can be leaders in building and deploying clean energy technologies. In addition, it helps States and localities improve the integration and utilization of natural gas in manufacturing and transportation.

Making Energy Go Further Across the Economy. Cutting the amount of energy we waste in our cars and trucks, in our homes and buildings, and in our factories will make a stronger, more resilient, and more competitive economy. That is why the President set a goal of cutting in half the energy wasted by America's homes and businesses with action aimed at doubling the economic output per unit of energy consumed in the United States

by 2030, relative to 2010 levels. The Budget takes a number of steps to help reach this goal, including: supporting the development of additional efficiency standards for appliances and buildings, expanding the Better Buildings Challenge to encourage greater energy efficiency in industrial and commercial buildings, improving energy efficiency in Federal buildings, improving energy data access for consumers and for Federal facilities through the "Green Button" initiative—under which utilities are establishing a standardized system allowing electricity customers to securely download their energy usage information—and supporting and encouraging the adoption of State and local policies to cut energy waste.

Investing in Energy Security. Over the President's first term, the United States cut oil imports by more than 3.6 million barrels per day, more than under any other President. In 2012, America's net oil imports fell to the lowest level in 20 years. To ensure that we continue on a path toward greater energy security, the Budget establishes an Energy Security Trust to help fund efforts to shift our cars and trucks off oil. This $2 billion investment over 10 years will support R&D in a range of cost-effective technologies—like advanced vehicles that run on electricity, homegrown biofuels, renewable hydrogen, and domestically produced natural gas—and will be drawn from revenues generated from Federal oil and gas development. The Budget proposes an extension of tax credits to support cellulosic biofuels and new tax incentives for medium- and heavy-duty trucks that run on alternative fuels like natural gas, and for the fuel infrastructure needed to deploy them. The Budget also includes reforms to promote responsible oil and gas development on Federal lands, including increasing funding at the Department of the Interior's Bureau of Land Management to support better permitting processes for oil and gas, renewable energy, and infrastructure, including the transition to an electronic, streamlined system for oil and gas permits.

Meeting the Challenge of Climate Change. The President's Climate Action Plan, which was released last year, builds upon the Administration's commitment to help address climate change by cutting carbon pollution in the United States in the range of 17 percent below 2005 levels by 2020. The Budget continues the Administration's significant progress toward reaching that goal by increasing available renewable energy, seeking achievable reductions in emissions through carbon pollution standards, and improving the energy efficiency of vehicles and major appliances. The Budget also supports efforts by Federal agencies to assist in local preparedness for climate change impacts, manage Federal lands to improve resilience, fund activities to create climate-resilient infrastructure, and develop better information, data, and tools to be used by decision-makers. The Budget strengthens U.S. global leadership on climate issues, encouraging international efforts to reduce carbon pollution and build global climate resiliency.

Making permanent and expanding the Production Tax Credit. In order to provide a strong, consistent incentive to encourage investments in renewable energy technologies like wind and solar, the Budget would, as part of business tax reform, make permanent the tax credit for the production of renewable electricity and reform it by making it refundable.

Addressing Growing Costs and Damage From Wildfires. The Budget proposes a significant reform to address wildfire suppression costs that have cannibalized forest health and rehabilitation programs and other priorities at the Department of Agriculture's Forest Service and the Department of the Interior. By creating a dedicated source of funding outside of the discretionary budget caps for wildland fire suppression, the Budget provides funding certainty in future years for firefighting costs, frees up resources to invest in areas that will promote long-term forest health and preservation, and maintains fiscal responsibility by addressing wildfire disaster needs through agreed-upon funding mechanisms.

BUILDING A 21ST CENTURY INFRASTRUCTURE

Building a durable and reliable infrastructure will create good American jobs that cannot be outsourced and will provide businesses with the transportation and communication networks our economy needs. The Budget includes significant investments to repair our existing infrastructure and build the infrastructure of tomorrow.

Eliminating Loopholes in Our Business Tax Code and Rebuilding Our Infrastructure. Last summer, in an effort to spur congressional action that would help our economy, the President offered a proposal to pay for investments in infrastructure by closing loopholes and reforming our business tax code. The Budget includes this proposal, which would use one-time transition revenue resulting from business tax reform to fill the Highway Trust Fund funding shortfall and make critical new infra-

structure investments as part of a four-year transportation reauthorization proposal. Meanwhile, reforming the tax code for businesses will also promote long-run growth, job creation, and competitiveness by cutting tax rates, simplifying the tax code, and eliminating inefficient provisions that distort companies' investment decisions.

Transportation Reauthorization. To spur economic growth and allow States and localities to initiate sound multi-year investments, the Budget includes a four-year, $302 billion surface transportation reauthorization proposal. By reinvesting the transition revenue from pro-growth business tax reform, the President's plan will ensure the health of the Highway Trust Fund for another four years and invest in a range of activities to spur and sustain long-term growth. The

President's plan to rebuild America will increase "fix-it-first" investment to repair and modernize our highways and bridges, while also modernizing our infrastructure by making new investments in transit, intercity passenger rail, and competitive programs. The President's plan will also provide Americans with affordable transportation options by increasing investment to expand new transit projects and maintain existing systems, link regional economies by funding the development of high-performance rail and strengthening Metropolitan Planning Organizations, and support American exports by improving movement within the Nation's freight networks. To help spur innovation and economic mobility, the reauthorization proposal will permanently authorize the competitive TIGER grant program to support projects that bring job opportunities to communities across the United States. The proposal will also advance the President's Climate Action Plan by building more resilient infrastructure and reducing transportation emissions by responding to the greater demand and travel growth in public transit.

Reforming Our Business Tax Code. The President believes that reforming our business tax code can help create jobs and spur investment, while ensuring a fairer and more equitable tax system that eliminates the loopholes that reward companies for moving profits overseas and allow them to avoid paying their fair share. In February 2012, the President provided a framework for how business tax reform could achieve these goals. The Budget builds on that framework with specific proposals to simplify and strengthen tax incentives for research and clean energy, to begin closing loopholes and eliminating special interest subsidies, and to begin reforming the international tax system. The Budget proposals would both prevent U.S. companies from shifting profits overseas and prevent foreign companies operating in the United States from avoiding the taxes they owe.

The President favors adopting these measures as part of long run revenue neutral business tax reform that would also cut the corporate tax rate to 28 percent—with a rate of no more than 25 percent for manufacturing—cut taxes for small businesses, and comprehensively reform tax subsidies and the international tax system. For this reason, the Budget does not count the net savings from the business tax proposals described above toward its deficit reduction targets, instead reserving them to help pay for business reform. However, the transition to a reformed business tax system will generate one-time, temporary revenue, for example from addressing the $1-2 trillion of untaxed foreign earnings that U.S. companies have accumulated overseas. The Budget proposes to use the one-time savings generated from transitioning to the new business tax system to fill the Highway Trust Fund shortfall and pay for the four-year transportation reauthorization proposal included in the Budget.

Boosting Private Investment Through a Rebuild America Partnership. To help further drive infrastructure investment, the Budget includes proposals aimed at enhancing the role of private capital in U.S. infrastructure investment as a vital additive to the traditional roles of Federal, State, and local governments.

Creating a National Infrastructure Bank. The President continues to call for the creation of an independent, wholly-owned Government entity to support increased investment in our Nation's infrastructure. A National Infrastructure Bank or similar financing entity with bipartisan support in the Congress will have the ability to leverage private and public capital to support infrastructure projects of national and regional significance. In addition, such an entity will be able to invest through loans and loan guarantees in a broad range of infrastructure, including transportation, energy, and water projects.

Enacting America Fast Forward Bonds and Other Tax Incentives for Infrastructure Investment. The Budget again calls for the creation of an America Fast Forward (AFF) Bonds program based on the successful example of the Build America Bonds program. AFF Bonds will attract new sources of capital for infrastructure investment—including from public pension funds and foreign investors that do not receive a tax benefit from traditional tax exempt debt. In addition, the Budget proposes changes to the Foreign Investment in Real Property Tax Act aimed at enhancing the attractiveness of investment in U.S. infrastructure and real estate to a broader universe of private investors.

Cutting Red Tape in the Infrastructure Permitting Process. In order to accelerate economic growth and improve the competitiveness of the American economy, the Administration is taking action to modernize and improve the efficiency of the Federal permitting process for major infrastructure projects. In August 2011, the President issued a Memorandum to add more transparency, accountability, and certainty into the permitting and review process. Since then, agencies have worked to expedite the permitting and review of 50 major projects, and have completed the review of 30 projects including bridges, railways, ports and waterways, roads, and renewable energy projects. In support of this effort, and as part of the President's Management Agenda, the Budget includes funding for a new Interagency Infrastructure Permitting Improvement Center housed at the Department of Transportation, which will lead the Administration's reform efforts across nearly 20 Federal agencies and bureaus. The Budget also supports an expanded, publicly available Permitting Dashboard that tracks project schedules and metrics for major infrastructure projects, further improving the transparency and accountability of the permitting process.

Launching National Parks Centennial Initiative. To mark the 100th year anniversary of the founding of the National Park Service in 2016, the Budget will fund a targeted effort to put youth, returning veterans, and other Americans to work restoring some of our greatest historical, cultural, and natural treasures. The Centennial Initiative, building on the President's America's Great Outdoors Initiative, would be one of the largest parks improvement efforts in the history of the National Parks System, helping to upgrade roadways, water mains, bridges, paths, and visitor services across the entire system, including some of the Nation's most famous sites, from Yosemite National Park to the Blue Ridge Parkway to Katmai National Park.

Conserving Lands for Current and Future Generations. The Budget builds on receipts collected under the Land and Water Conservation Fund (LWCF) Act by proposing $900 million annually to invest in conserving lands for future generations, supporting livable communities and creating jobs through a growing outdoor recreation industry. Since the passage of the LWCF Act almost 50 years ago, the need for this funding has increased due to population growth and land lost to agricultural, commercial, industrial, and residential development.

Making Permanent the Enhanced Tax Deduction for Conservation Easements. Combined with targeted reforms, making permanent the enhanced tax deductions for conservation easements will create certainty for America's landowners who willingly seek to ensure land and water conservation gains for future generations. It will also help stimulate the economy by ensuring working lands stay working, and guarantee recreational as well as hunting and fishing opportunities. The enhanced deduction will also help achieve a key goal of the President's Climate Action Plan by locking in a strong tool to help conserve land and water resources.

EQUIPPING EVERY AMERICAN WITH A HIGH-QUALITY EDUCATION AND THE SKILLS TO SUCCEED

Americans must be prepared with the skills and knowledge necessary to compete in the 21st Century economy. Expanding educational opportunities is critical to equipping all children with these skills and positioning them to succeed as adults. The Budget includes investments and initiatives to improve all levels of education, from early childhood through college, as well as significant new efforts to ensure our workforce has the skills needed by American businesses.

Enhancing Access to High-Quality Early Childhood Education. The Budget includes the Preschool for All initiative proposed by the President last year. This proposal calls for partnering with States to provide every low- and moderate-income four-year-old child access to high-quality preschool, while incentivizing States to expand those programs to reach additional children from middle class families and establish full-day kindergarten policies. These investments are fully financed by raising Federal tobacco taxes, which will also help to discourage youth smoking and save lives. In addition, building on funding provided in the CAA, the Budget invests discretionary funding in Preschool Development Grants, which, together with additional resources in the Opportunity, Growth, and Security Initiative, would reach two-thirds of States by 2015, laying a stronger foundation for Preschool for All. Additional funding in the Opportunity, Growth, and Security Initiative would also provide early learning opportunities to a total of more than 100,000 children through Early Head Start-Child Care Partnerships and support Head Start grantees in expanding program duration and investing in teacher quality. In addition, the Budget invests $15 billion in mandatory funds over the next 10 years to extend and expand evidence-based, voluntary home visiting programs, which enable nurses, social workers, and other professionals to connect families to services and educational supports that improve a child's health, development, and ability to learn.

Redesigning High Schools. The President has called for a comprehensive effort to rethink the high school experience, challenging schools to scale up innovative models that personalize teaching and learning for students, so that they receive the rigorous and relevant education needed to graduate and transition into postsecondary learning and adulthood. The Budget provides $150 million for a new program to redesign high schools to focus on providing students challenging, relevant learning experiences, and rewarding high schools that develop new partnerships with colleges and employers to help develop the skills students need for jobs now and in the future. This will build on $100 million provided through the Youth CareerConnect grant competition at the Department of Labor (DOL) to expand these models.

Connecting Schools and Training Teachers for the Digital Age. The President has called on the Federal Communications Commission (FCC) to take steps to connect 99 percent of American students to the digital age through next-generation broadband and wireless in their schools and libraries. The FCC is making a major down-payment on this goal—connecting more than 20 million students in 15,000 schools over the next two years—without adding a dime to the deficit. The Budget proposes $200 million for the ConnectEDucators program to ensure that students receive the full benefit of this connectivity by providing professional development and high-quality digital instructional resources to teachers to help them make effective use of these new resources. The Opportunity, Growth, and Security Initiative would add an additional $300 million to this initiative to provide a total of 100,000 teachers in 500 school districts across the Nation access to professional development.

Preparing Students for STEM Careers. Our Nation's competitiveness depends on our ability to improve and expand science, technology, engineering, and mathematics (STEM) learning in the United States. The Budget proposes a fresh Government-wide reorganization of STEM education programs designed to enable more strategic investment in STEM education and more critical evaluation of outcomes, leveraging Government resources more effectively to meet national goals. This proposal reduces fragmentation of STEM education programs across Government, and focuses efforts around the five key areas identified by the Federal STEM Education 5-Year Strategic Plan: P-12 instruction; undergraduate education; graduate education; broadening participation in STEM to women and minorities traditionally underrepresented in these fields; and education activities that typically take place outside of the classroom.

Making College More Affordable. The President has placed a high priority on making college affordable and helping Americans obtain a meaningful college degree. Beginning in 2009, the Administration has increased the maximum Pell Grant for working and middle class families by $1,000, to $5,730 in school year 2014-15, and created the American Opportunity Tax Credit, which helps more than 10 million students and families each year pay for college. Last summer, the President directed the Department of Education to develop and publish a new college ratings system that will identify colleges that provide the best value to students and encourage all colleges to improve. The Budget supports the development and refinement of the ratings system by investing in data initiatives or other necessary projects. The Budget also provides new College Opportunity and Graduation Bonuses to reward colleges for improving educational outcomes for low- and moderate-income students. The Budget includes an expansion of "Pay As You Earn" (PAYE) repayment options to all student borrowers, and reforms the PAYE terms to ensure that the program is well-targeted and provides a safeguard against raising tuition at high-cost institutions.

Improving Training and Employment Services. Helping workers acquire the skills they need to pursue in-demand jobs and careers is critical to growing our economy, ensuring that everyone who works hard is rewarded, and building a stronger middle class. The Budget's approach to skills and training is guided by the principle that all Federal investments should be designed to equip the Nation's workers and job seekers with skills matching the needs of employers looking to hire them into good jobs. The Budget proposes significant new investments at DOL to drive greater performance and innovation, through the Workforce Innovation Fund and Incentive Grants that reward States that succeed in serving workers with the greatest barriers to employment. Additional resources to support this effort, as well as to increase State and local capacity and provide targeted assistance to high-need populations, are made available through the Opportunity, Growth, and Security Initiative.

Investing in Job-Driven Training at Community Colleges and Apprenticeships. Through the Opportunity, Growth, and Security Initiative, the Budget invests in a Community College Job-Driven Training Fund at DOL. This Fund will offer competitive grants to partnerships of community colleges, employers, and others to launch new training programs that will prepare Americans for in-demand jobs and careers. The Fund will also support expanding apprenticeship opportunities. On-the-job apprenticeship training programs provide a robust path to middle-income jobs in many countries. The funds provided through the Opportunity, Growth, and Security Initiative will support doubling the number of apprenticeships in America over the next five years.

Helping Build the Skills of the Long-Term Unemployed. Although the unemployment rate has come down from its peak during the Great Recession, too many of our unemployed have been without a job for an extended period of time, which can lead to a deterioration in skills and strain families and communities. Finding jobs for the long-term unemployed is an important national priority, because we are stronger when America fields a full team. The Budget provides resources for new public-private partnerships to help the long-term unemployed transition back into good jobs that can support their families. To help more recently displaced workers, the Budget proposes a New Career Pathways program that will reach as many as one million workers a year with a set of core services, combining the best elements of two existing programs—

Trade Adjustment Assistance for Workers and Workforce Investment Act Dislocated Workers.

Investing in Health Professions Education to Improve Access to Health Care Providers and Services. The Budget invests in the health care workforce to improve access to health care services, including support for 15,000 providers in the National Health Service Corps that will serve areas across the United States experiencing a shortage of medical providers. In addition, the Budget creates new graduate medical education residency slots in primary care and other high-need specialties. Most of these new residents will be trained in community based settings, including rural and underserved areas.

EXPANDING OPPORTUNITY FOR MIDDLE CLASS SECURITY

Our economy is moving forward and businesses are creating jobs. But to build real, lasting economic security we need to create more opportunities for all working and middle class Americans to get ahead. The Budget includes a series of proposals to help ensure that if you work hard and play by the rules, you can find a good job, feel secure about your community, and support a family.

Raising the Minimum Wage to $10.10. Over the past 30 years, modest minimum wage increases have not kept pace with the higher costs of basic necessities for working families. No one who works full time should have to raise his or her family in poverty. The Administration supports raising the minimum wage so that hard-working Americans can earn wages that allow them to support their families and make ends meet. The President knows this is important for workers, and good for the economy. That is why the President is calling on the Congress to raise the Federal minimum wage in stages to $10.10 per hour and index it to inflation thereafter, while also raising the minimum wage for tipped workers for the first time in over 20 years. The President is leading by example by signing an Executive Order to raise the minimum wage to $10.10 for individuals working under new and replacement Federal service, construction, and concession contracts.

Extending Unemployment Insurance for 1.7 Million Americans Looking for Work. As a starting point in achieving economic opportunity and mobility, the Congress should act to extend unemployment insurance for the 1.7 million Americans who have lost this vital economic lifeline. At more than 35 percent, the percentage of unemployed workers who are long-term unemployed is much higher than the last time emergency unemployment benefits expired. Economists have estimated that extending unemployment insurance would provide significant returns, leading to 240,000 more jobs.

Partnering with Communities to Expand Opportunity. The Budget supports the Administration's Promise Zone initiative, which supports partnerships between the Federal Government, local communities, and businesses to create jobs, increase economic security, expand educational opportunities, increase access to quality, affordable housing, and improve public safety. Communities are chosen through a competitive process and put forward a plan on how they will partner with local business and community leaders to make investments that reward hard work and expand opportunity. In exchange, the Federal Government partners with these communities to help them secure the resources and flexibility they need to achieve their goals.

The President announced the first five Promise Zone communities earlier this year and will create an additional 15 Promise Zones in the year ahead. The Budget includes Promise Zone tax incentives to stimulate growth and investments in targeted communities, such as tax credits for hiring workers and incentives for capital investment within the Zone. Through a combination of the base budget and the additional resources provided in the Opportunity, Growth, and Security Initiative, the Budget will support the President's vision for Promise Zones by funding 40 new Promise Neighborhoods and 10-14 new Choice Neighborhoods.

Ensuring Workers Receive the Pay and Overtime They Earned. The Budget increases support for DOL's Wage and Hour Division to increase enforcement of the laws that ensure workers receive appropriate wages and overtime pay, as well as the right to take job-protected leave for family and medical purposes. The Wage and Hour Division will be able to hire 300 new investigators across the United States to help in this effort, and will use risk-based approaches to target the industries and employers most likely to break the law.

Ending Homelessness. The President has set ambitious goals to end homelessness across the Nation, and we have made significant progress, including reducing the total number of homeless veterans by almost 18,000 since 2009. By investing in homeless assistance and supportive services programs at both the Department of Housing and Urban Development (HUD) and VA, the Budget keeps us on a path to end veterans' homelessness in 2015 and end chronic homelessness in 2016. In addition, the Budget makes investments in rental assistance, which plays an important role in helping extremely low-income families avoid homelessness by providing stable and affordable housing. The Budget funds renewed assistance for 4.5 million low-income families through HUD's core rental assistance program, including providing 40,000 new housing vouchers for low-income families, including 10,000 for homeless veterans.

Expanding the EITC for Childless Workers. Few things help families with children pull themselves up through hard work like the Earned Income Tax Credit (EITC). However, the maximum EITC available to childless workers (including non-custodial parents) is only $500, and the credit is unavailable to workers under age 25, which means that it cannot shape work decisions during the crucial years at the beginning of a young person's career. The Budget will double the maximum credit (to $1,000), make the credit available to workers at slightly higher income levels (e.g., a full-time minimum wage worker at the current minimum wage), and lower the age limit from 25 to 21, as a way to support

and reward work. The proposal will also update the childless worker EITC upper age limit for increases in the Social Security Normal Retirement Age (raising it from 64 to 66). These changes will be paid for by closing tax loopholes that let some high-income professionals avoid income and payroll taxes.

Helping Workers with Disabilities Remain in the Workforce. In addition to the Administration's continued commitment to Vocational Rehabilitation programs, the Budget provides new authority and $400 million in new resources for the Social Security Administration (SSA), in partnership with other Federal agencies, to test innovative strategies to help people with disabilities remain in the workforce. Early-intervention measures, such as supportive employment services for individuals with mental impairments, targeted incentives for employers to help workers with disabilities remain on the job, and incentives and opportunities for States to better coordinate services, have the potential to achieve long-term gains in the employment and the quality of life of people with disabilities, and the proposed demonstration authority will help build the evidence base for future program improvements. The cost of the demonstrations could be offset by a proposal to automate coordination of disability benefit payments between the Office of Personnel Management and SSA, reducing overpayments, and other program integrity measures. The proposed childless worker EITC expansion will also benefit over one million workers with disabilities, encouraging and supporting them in maintaining employment.

Improving Retirement Security. Workers must have a place to invest their hard-earned savings that provides an appropriate balance of risk and return, and many private sector providers do not offer retirement savings options tailored to smaller balance savers. The retirement system should help these potential savers and encourage them to begin building their retirement security. The Budget builds on the President's announcement in the State of the Union to create a new simple, safe, and affordable "starter" retirement savings account—the MyRA—that will be available through employers and help millions of Americans save for retirement. The Budget also continues to propose automatic enrollment in Individual Retirement Accounts (IRAs)—or "auto-IRAs"—for employees without access to a workplace savings plan.

ENSURING OUR NATION'S SAFETY AND SECURITY

Economic growth and opportunity can only be achieved if America is safe, secure, and resilient, both at home and abroad. At home, the Budget supports efforts to help make communities safer by reducing gun violence and supporting emergency preparedness, and makes reforms to our criminal justice system to reduce recidivism and achieve better outcomes. Beyond our borders, the Budget provides resources to sustain ready, modern, and capable defense forces and support the effective operation and protection of our diplomats, both of which are critical to providing for the Nation's security and sustaining our global leadership role. These resources advance our strategic rebalancing toward the Asia-Pacific region, support key investments in Power Africa, and provide other resources critical to improving Global Health Security and combating global climate change. The Budget strengthens executive branch oversight of signals intelligence activities and positions the United States to address threats from terrorism and cyber attacks, enhances the protection of U.S. diplomatic facilities and personnel overseas, meets our peacekeeping commitments for the world's most challenging crises, funds humanitarian and diplomatic efforts in Syria, and supports transition and reform throughout the Middle East and North Africa. The Budget also ensures that even after we have ended two wars, we continue to meet our obligations to our servicemembers and veterans who have given so much to our Nation.

Making Communities Safer by Reducing Gun Violence. The Budget supports the President's "Now is the Time" initiative, a set of concrete policies to help reduce gun violence in our schools and communities in the wake of the Sandy Hook Elementary School tragedy. The Budget supports additional background checks, continued focus on inspections of federally-licensed firearms dealers, improved tracing and ballistics analysis, and efforts to keep guns out of the hands of dangerous criminals and other prohibited persons. To support those on the frontlines across the United States, the Budget provides training for State and local law enforcement to prevent and respond to active shooters and prevent mass casualties. The Budget also enhances our ability to identify mental health issues early and ensures individuals get referred to treatment before dangerous situations develop. To increase the safety of schools nationwide, the Budget will continue support for the Comprehensive School Safety Program, and other initiatives to enhance our schools' physical security and create safer and more nurturing school climates that help prevent violence.

Reforming the Criminal Justice System with the "Smart on Crime" Initiative. Last summer, the Attorney General introduced the Smart on Crime initiative, which is designed to promote fundamental reforms to the criminal justice system that will improve public safety, save money, and ensure the fair enforcement of Federal laws. The Budget supports the initiative's strategy of containing incarceration costs over the long-term by reducing recidivism rates and encouraging Federal prosecutors to seek sentences in certain low-level drug cases that maintain the highest degree of public safety and consider the long-term incarceration costs to the taxpayer.

Maintaining High Safety Standards in the Transportation Sector. As energy production in the United States continues to rapidly increase, the Budget seeks to maintain high safety standards. The Budget addresses risks through new investments in data-driven safety interventions, research and testing, additional safety personnel, emergency response training, community outreach, and other strategies. In addition, the Budget proposes a Pipeline Safety Reform initiative to both enhance and reform the Federal standards that help protect the Nation's safety.

Advancing National Security Priorities.
The Budget advances the Administration's national security objectives and provides the resources and capabilities to protect our security and interests around the world. The Budget reflects a focused effort to address our highest defense priorities—bringing the war in Afghanistan to a responsible end, working to disrupt and disable terrorist networks, combatting new threats like cyber attacks, and being ready to respond to provocations whenever and wherever necessary—within a constrained fiscal environment. Moreover, it addresses critical national security requirements, while protecting privacy and civil liberties and providing responsible management of taxpayer resources.

Investing in Long-Term Partnerships in Afghanistan. The Budget continues to support U.S. security, diplomatic, and development goals in Afghanistan while scaling down military operations and assistance. The Budget includes resources to maintain a strong, long-term partnership in the country by supporting military training and assistance as well as economic development, health, education, governance, security, and other civilian assistance programs necessary to reinforce development progress and promote stability.

Rebalancing American Engagement Toward the Asia-Pacific Region. The United States and its interests are inextricably linked with Asia's economies and security. The Budget makes strategic, coordinated, and Government-wide investments in a wide range of tools across the Asia-Pacific region, which will help create American jobs, empower American businesses, and maintain the security and stability necessary for economic growth. The Budget provides resources to help deepen U.S. trade and investment in the region, strengthen regional cooperation, and enhance regional and country-specific capabilities to address security, development, and economic challenges.

Powering Africa. The Administration is bringing to bear a wide range of U.S. Government tools and expertise to support investment in Africa's energy sector. The Budget supports infrastructure projects through the Millennium Challenge Corporation and our contribution to the African Development Bank, leverages private sector investment through the Export-Import Bank and Overseas Private Investment Corporation, and provides critical technical assistance to African partners through the Department of State, the U.S. Agency for International Development, and U.S. Trade and Development Agency. Both the investments in the power sector themselves and the resulting economic growth will expand the markets for U.S. goods in sub-Saharan Africa.

Enhancing the Protection of U.S. Diplomatic Facilities and Personnel Overseas. The Budget provides $4.6 billion for the Department of State security programs, including security staff, construction, and infrastructure upgrades. With a sustained level of investment in security upgrades, the Budget provides funding for the construction of new embassy and consulate compounds. These and other investments will ensure that the Administration continues to safeguard over 86,000 U.S. Government employees, from more than 30 agency components, in more secure overseas working environments. When combined with contributions from other agencies, the Budget provides $2.2 billion for capital security construction, as recommended by the Benghazi Accountability Review Board.

Addressing Cyber Threats. Cyber attacks targeting the financial industry, critical infrastructure, and the Federal Government demonstrate that no sector, network, or system is immune to infiltration by those seeking financial gain, perpetrating malicious and disruptive activity, or stealing commercial or Government secrets and property. Cyber threats are constantly evolving and require a coordinated, comprehensive, and resilient plan for protection and response. The Budget identifies and promotes cross-agency cybersecurity initiatives and priorities, including improving cybersecurity information sharing while protecting individual privacy and civil liberties and enhancing State and local capacity to respond to cyber incidents.

Assisting Countries in Transition and Promoting Reforms in Middle East and North Africa. Building on the Administration's significant and continuing response to the transformative events in the Middle East and North Africa region, the Budget includes $1.5 billion to respond to the crisis in Syria, including providing humanitarian assistance, and continues to support transitions and reforms in the region. This funding builds on several initiatives the United States is supporting to respond to regional developments since the beginning of the Arab Spring, including fiscal stabilization support, technical assistance, trade, and asset recovery initiatives.

Supporting Global Health by Investing in High Impact Interventions. The Administration is investing in proven interventions to continue progress toward the goals of achieving an AIDS-free generation and an end to preventable child and maternal deaths. The Budget continues the President's pledge to provide $1 for every $2 pledged by other donors to the Global Fund to Fight AIDS, Tuberculosis, and Malaria by providing $1.35 billion, which will increase our leverage and accelerate progress against these three diseases. The Opportunity, Growth, and Security Initiative includes an additional $300 million for the Global Fund to encourage even more ambitious pledges from other donors. The Budget supports continued expansion of evidence-based HIV/AIDS prevention and treatment services through the Department of State's bilateral President's Emergency Plan for AIDS Relief program.

Supporting the Nation's Servicemembers, Veterans, and Their Families. The Nation has a solemn obligation to take care of its servicemembers and veterans. To deliver on this commitment, the Budget provides significant resources to support veterans' medical care, help military families, assist servicemembers transitioning to civilian life, reduce veterans' homelessness, and improve the disability claims processing system.

REDUCING LONG-RUN DEFICITS AND PROMOTING SUSTAINABLE GROWTH

Budgets, particularly in times of divided Government, lay out what an Administration believes is the best path forward. Last year, President Obama detoured from that path by embedding in the Budget a potential compromise that had been the subject of discussions with the Congress the previous year. That approach was intended as a show of good faith to spark additional negotiations with congressional Republicans about our long-term debt and deficits, and to encourage all parties to come together to remove the damaging cuts caused by sequestration that have hurt our economy.

The compromise embedded in last year's Budget—which included policies like changing the measure of inflation used by the Federal Government to the chained Consumer Price Index ("Chained-CPI") that Republicans had asked for in previous fiscal negotiations—remains on the table. However, in light of congressional Republicans' unwillingness to negotiate on fundamental issues and agree to a balanced plan to deal with our long-term fiscal challenges, this year the Administration is returning to a more traditional Budget presentation that lays out the President's vision. This includes the proposals discussed above to invest in growth and opportunity and pay for those investments by reforming spending programs and closing tax loopholes.

With respect to the Nation's long-term fiscal challenges, this year's Budget focuses squarely on the primary drivers of long-term deficits and proposes further health and tax reforms to control the rate of health care cost growth and generate the revenue required to meet our obligations and make needed investments as our society ages. The President's plan includes specific reforms to Medicare, Medicaid, and other Federal health programs that would reduce deficits by $402 billion over the next 10 years while helping keep health care cost growth low and encouraging greater efficiencies and quality of care. The President's plan also includes tax reform measures that would make the tax code more efficient and fair, and would reduce the deficit by about $650 billion over the next decade. In addition, the President

is also committed to bipartisan comprehensive immigration reform. The Congressional Budget Office has found that immigration reform along the lines the President has proposed would increase growth while reducing the deficit by about $160 billion in the next decade, and by almost $1 trillion over the next 20 years.

Building on the progress already made, the Budget's deficit reduction measures are more than enough to achieve the key fiscal goal of stabilizing the debt as a share of GDP. If the Budget's proposed policies are implemented, deficits will stabilize at less than 2 percent of GDP, and the Budget will be in primary surplus starting in 2018, meaning that revenues are covering programmatic costs. Meanwhile, debt would peak at 74.6 percent of GDP in 2015 and then decline each year after that, falling to 69.0 percent of GDP in 2024.

Projected Debt Held by the Public as Percent of GDP

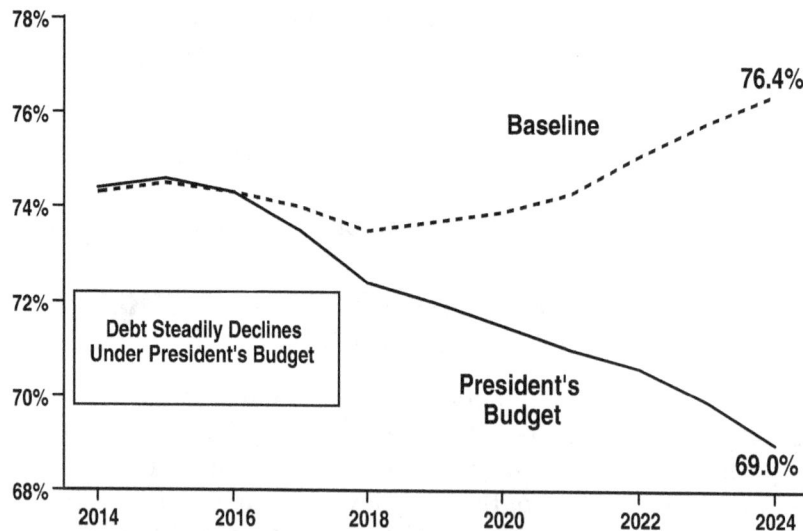

IMPLEMENTING ACA AND MAKING ADDITIONAL HEALTH REFORMS

The Affordable Care Act (ACA) has taken historic and significant steps toward putting the Nation back on a sustainable fiscal course while laying the foundation for a higher-quality, more secure health care system. Through premium tax credit and cost sharing assistance to make cov-

erage affordable and increased Federal support to States expanding Medicaid coverage for low-income adults, ACA ensures that every American can access high-quality, affordable coverage, providing health insurance to millions of Americans who would otherwise be uninsured.

With the full implementation of ACA beginning this year, millions of people have enrolled in either private insurance through the Health Insurance Marketplace or for coverage through Medicaid and the Children's Health Insurance Program (CHIP). In addition, more than three million young adults already have gained coverage under the health care law by staying on their parents' plans until their 26th birthday.

While there is much more work to be done, we now live in an era where no family will be denied coverage because of a pre-existing condition like high blood pressure or asthma. No American will have to worry that losing a job means you cannot get health coverage. Small businesses may be able to get financial help to pay for new affordable coverage options for their employees.

The challenges in our health care system were decades in the making and will not be solved overnight, but every day more Americans are signing up for insurance and getting the peace of mind of knowing that they can get the care they need without losing everything they have worked and saved for. Americans across the Nation started this year with new health plans that give them the security of knowing that if they want to change jobs or start their own business, they will have access to affordable health insurance for their family.

Supporting Implementation of the Affordable Care Act. Efficiently and effectively implementing ACA is one of the Administration's highest priorities. The Budget fully funds the ongoing implementation of ACA, which is already providing coverage for millions of Americans that previously did not have access to affordable health care. The Budget continues to support implementation of ACA's health insurance coverage improvements through the operation of Health Insurance Marketplaces and the delivery of premium tax credits and cost sharing assistance to help make coverage affordable, drive down long-term health care costs, and improve care for millions of citizens.

Implementing Additional Health Care Reforms. In addition, the Budget strengthens Medicare, Medicaid, and other Federal health programs through payment innovations and other reforms that encourage high-quality and efficient care and continue the progress of reducing cost growth. In total, these reforms would reduce deficits by $402 billion in the next decade, and about $1 trillion over the following decade.

Encouraging High-Quality, Efficient Care among Medicare Providers. The Budget continues a set of proposals that build on initiatives included in ACA to help extend Medicare's solvency while encouraging provider efficiencies and improved patient care. This includes proposals to encourage efficient post-acute care by adjusting payment updates for certain post-acute care providers and to incentivize the use of appropriate services through bundled payment and other approaches. The Budget also proposes to better align payments to rural providers with the cost of care and reduce Medicare bad debt payments in a way that more closely matches private sector standards. Additional proposals to promote efficiency in the Medicare program include: improving payment accuracy for Medicare Advantage; constraining Medicare cost growth; better aligning payments to teaching hospitals with patient care costs; modifying payment updates for certain clinical laboratory services; creating appropriate incentives for physicians' self-referral of specified services; addressing excess payments for Medicare Part B drugs to hospitals and physicians; and expanding the availability of Medicare data for performance improvement, fraud prevention, and other purposes. Also, the Budget builds on ACA initiatives that promote quality in the Medicare program by linking payment to the quality of care in additional provider settings. Together, these proposals would save approximately $229 billion over 10 years.

Encouraging Beneficiaries to Seek High-Value Services. The Budget includes structural changes that will encourage Medicare beneficiaries to seek high-value health care services. To help improve the financial stability of the Medicare program, the Budget reduces the Federal subsidy of Medicare costs for those beneficiaries who need that subsidy the least. The Budget includes several modifications for new beneficiaries starting in 2018, such as a modified Part B deductible and a modest copayment for certain home health episodes. Research indicates that beneficiaries with Medigap plans that provide first- or near-first dollar coverage have less incentive to consider the costs of health care services, thus raising Medicare costs and Part B premiums for all beneficiaries. The Budget applies a premium surcharge for new beneficiaries beginning in 2018 if they choose such Medigap coverage. In addition, the Budget modifies incentives in the Medicare prescription drug program to encourage utilization of generic drugs by low-income beneficiaries. Together, these proposals would save approximately $68 billion over 10 years.

Improving Quality and Lowering Drug Costs for Federal Health Programs. The Budget includes proposals that lower drug costs, while improving quality and reducing waste in the Medicare Part D program. The Budget proposes to close the coverage gap for brand drugs in the Part D benefit by 2016, four years earlier than under current law, by increasing the discounts offered by the pharmaceutical industry. The Budget also proposes to align Medicare payments for drugs with Medicaid policies for low-income beneficiaries. In addition, the Budget would improve drug plans through bonuses for the highest quality Part D plans and by providing the Secretary of Health and Human Services the authority to suspend coverage and payment for questionable Part D prescriptions. Together, these proposals will save Medicare $125 billion over 10 years. In addition, the Budget includes two proposals designed to increase access to generic drugs and biologics by stopping companies from entering into anti-competitive deals intended to block consumer access to safe and effective generics, by awarding brand biologic

manufacturers seven years of exclusivity, rather than 12 years under current law, and by prohibiting additional periods of exclusivity for brand biologics due to minor changes in product formulations. These two proposals will save the Federal Government $15 billion over 10 years, including savings in Medicare and Medicaid.

Lowering Medicaid Drug Costs for States and the Federal Government. The Budget includes targeted policies to lower drug costs in Medicaid. First, the Budget improves the Medicaid drug rebate program by clarifying the definition of brand drugs, collecting an additional rebate for generic drugs whose prices grow faster than inflation, clarifying the inclusion of certain prenatal vitamins and fluorides in the rebate program, and taking actions to promote the integrity of the rebate program. The Budget also corrects a technical error to the ACA alternative rebate for new drug formulations, limits to 12 quarters the timeframe for which manufacturers can dispute drug rebate amounts, and excludes authorized generic drugs from average manufacturer price calculations for determining manufacturer rebate obligations for brand drugs. In addition, the Budget improves Medicaid drug pricing by calculating Medicaid Federal upper limits based only on generic drug prices. These proposals are projected to save the Federal Government $9 billion over 10 years.

Cutting Waste, Fraud, and Abuse in Medicare and Medicaid. The Administration has made targeting waste, fraud, and abuse in Medicare, Medicaid, and the Children's Health Insurance Program a priority and is aggressively implementing new tools for fraud prevention included in ACA, including the fraud prevention system, a predictive analytic model similar to those used by private sector experts. In addition, the Budget proposes a series of policies to build on these efforts that will save nearly $1.1 billion over the next 10 years. Specifically, the Budget proposes to implement new initiatives to reduce improper payments in Medicare; require prior authorization for power mobility devices and advanced imaging, which could be expanded to other items and services at high risk of fraud and abuse; direct States to track high prescribers and utilizers of prescription drugs in Medicaid to identify aberrant billing and prescribing patterns; support efforts to investigate and prosecute allegations of abuse or neglect of Medicaid beneficiaries in additional health care settings and in the territories; and strengthen the Federal Government's ability to identify and act on fraud, waste, and abuse through Medicaid Integrity Program improvements. In addition, the Budget would alleviate State program integrity reporting requirements by consolidating redundant error rate measurement programs to create a streamlined audit program with meaningful outcomes, while maintaining the Federal and State government's ability to identify and address improper Medicaid payments.

Making Targeted and Sensible Reforms to the Medicaid Program. The Budget proposes to preserve the existing partnership between States and the Federal Government while making Medicaid more efficient and sustainable. Under current law, States have experienced challenges in preventing overpayments for durable medical equipment (DME). Starting in 2015, the Budget would limit Federal reimbursement for a State's

Medicaid spending on certain DME services to what Medicare would have paid in the same State for the same services. The Budget also better aligns Medicaid Disproportionate Share Hospital payments with expected levels of uncompensated care. These proposals are projected to save approximately $6 billion over 10 years.

Improving Care Delivery for Low-Income Medicare-Medicaid Beneficiaries. The Budget proposes a budget-neutral pilot in a limited number of States to provide qualifying low-income adults under age 55 benefits under the Program for All-Inclusive Care for the Elderly (PACE). Under current law, PACE provides comprehensive long-term services to qualifying individuals age 55 and older. Pilots will test whether PACE programs can effectively serve a younger population without increasing costs. The Budget also proposes to implement a streamlined, single beneficiary appeals process for managed care plans that integrate Medicare and Medicaid payment and services and serve Medicare-Medicaid enrollees to address the sometimes conflicting requirements in each program. In addition, the Budget proposes to permanently authorize a demonstration that provides retroactive drug coverage for certain low-income Medicare beneficiaries through a single plan, establishing a single point of contact for beneficiaries seeking reimbursement for claims.

MAKING THE TAX CODE MORE SIMPLE AND FAIR

By slowing health care cost growth, ACA and the Budget's additional health reforms will tackle one of the two key drivers of long run deficits. But over the coming decades, an aging population will also put increasing pressure on the budget. For example, by the end of the 10-year budget window in 2024, the ratio of retirees to workers will be almost 50 percent higher than it was at the beginning of the 2000s, when we last balanced the Federal budget, and it will increase further over the subsequent decade. Even with reforms to Medicare and other entitlements and tough

choices that will bring discretionary spending to historically low levels as a share of GDP, we will need additional revenue to maintain our commitments to seniors while also making the investments that are needed to grow our economy and expand opportunity.

The President believes that we can obtain that needed revenue by doing what leaders of both parties have called for—reforming our tax code to reduce inefficient, unfair tax breaks. Tax reform holds the potential to improve economic growth by reducing complexity for individuals and small businesses, curbing inefficient tax subsidies that distort individual and business decision-making, and reducing the deficit. As a first step toward balanced deficit reduction and tax reform, the President proposes that the Congress immediately enact two measures that would raise $650 billion in revenue by broadening the tax base and reducing tax benefits for those who need them the least—without increasing marginal tax rates.

Reducing the Value of Itemized Deductions and Other Tax Preferences to 28 Percent for the Wealthiest Americans. Currently, a millionaire who contributes to charity or deducts a dollar of mortgage interest enjoys a deduction that is more than twice as generous as that for a middle class family. The Budget would limit the tax rate at which high income taxpayers can reduce their tax liability to a maximum of 28 percent, a limitation that would affect only the top three percent of families in 2014. This limit would apply to all itemized deductions, as well

as other tax benefits such as tax-exempt interest and tax exclusions for retirement contributions and employer sponsored health insurance. The proposed limitation would restore the deduction rate to the level it was at the end of the Reagan Administration.

Observing the Buffett Rule. The Budget also puts forward a specific proposal to comply with the Buffett Rule, requiring that wealthy millionaires pay no less than 30 percent of income—after charitable contributions—in taxes. This proposal will prevent high-income households from using tax preferences, including low tax rates on capital gains and dividends, to reduce their total tax bills to less than what many middle class families pay.

Beyond these measures, the President is committed to working with the Congress to further reform the tax code to make it fairer, promote economic growth and job creation, and improve competitiveness.

FIXING OUR BROKEN IMMIGRATION SYSTEM

The President believes that we must fix our broken immigration system by continuing to strengthen our border security, cracking down on employers who hire undocumented workers, modernizing our legal immigration system, and providing a pathway to earned citizenship for hardworking men and women who pay a penalty and taxes, learn English, pass a background check, and go to the back of the line.

In addition to contributing to a safer and more just society, common sense immigration reform will also boost economic growth, reduce deficits, and strengthen Social Security. Common sense immigration reform will contribute to growth by strengthening the workforce by attracting and retaining the best and brightest students who we train at U.S. universities, increasing capital investment and overall productivity, and increasing the number of entrepreneurs starting companies in the United States. Moreover, by adding

younger workers to the labor force, reforming our broken legal immigration system will help balance an aging population and improve the economic and budget outlook as the baby boom generation retires.

The Congressional Budget Office has estimated that the immigration bill that passed with bipartisan support in the Senate last year would reduce the deficit by about $160 billion in the first decade and by about $850 billion over 20 years. Meanwhile, the Social Security Actuaries have found that the Senate bill would reduce the Social Security shortfall by $300 billion over the first 10 years and would close eight percent of the 75-year Social Security shortfall.

The Administration supports the bipartisan Senate approach, and calls on the House of Representatives to act on comprehensive immigration reform this year.

* * *

The Budget provides a roadmap for creating jobs, growing the economy, and expanding opportunity for all Americans.

The Budget invests in manufacturing, research, clean energy, infrastructure, education, and security, building a foundation for long-term economic growth. The Budget promotes economic opportunity and mobility by rewarding hard work with fair wages, putting a secure retirement within reach, and ensuring health care is affordable and reliable. The Budget includes enhanced efforts to deliver a 21st Century Government that is more effective, efficient, and supportive of economic growth. The Budget responsibly pays for new investments, reduces the deficit as a share of the economy to below two percent by 2023, and puts debt as a share of the economy on a downward path after 2015. The Budget also addresses the Nation's long-term fiscal challenges by building on the savings and reforms in the Affordable Care Act, reforming other mandatory programs, and ending wasteful tax breaks that benefit the wealthiest.

It is a Budget that shows how we can build on the progress that has been made over the last five years and ensure that our Nation remains strong and prosperous, both now and in the future.

CREATING A 21ST CENTURY GOVERNMENT

Under the President's direction, the Administration is working to deliver a 21st Century Government that is more effective, efficient, and supportive of economic growth. The President is committed to creating a Government that will make a significant, tangible, and positive difference in the lives of the American people and the economy, and to driving lasting change in how Government works.

The Budget supports the President's Management Agenda, a comprehensive and forward-looking plan to deliver better, faster, and smarter services to citizens and businesses; increase quality and value in the Government's core administrative functions and continue efforts to enhance productivity and achieve cost savings across the Government; open Government-funded data and research to the public to spur innovation and economic growth; and unlock the full potential of today's Federal workforce and build the workforce we need for tomorrow. The Agenda reflects the Administration's commitment to building a Government that focuses on results and draws on evidence-based practices to ensure that every taxpayer dollar is used wisely and to the maximum effect.

EFFECTIVENESS: DELIVER A WORLD-CLASS CUSTOMER SERVICE EXPERIENCE FOR CITIZENS AND BUSINESSES

Government must build, buy, and deliver services that meet the expectations of a 21st Century society, taking into account the rapid pace of innovation and user experience to which American citizens and businesses are accustomed. With more than half of U.S. adults now using smart phones, citizens expect digital services that are simple, accessible, and easy to use. As part of the Budget, the Administration will launch new efforts to deliver a world-class customer service experience to citizens and businesses.

Improving Key Citizen- and Business-Facing Transactions. By making it faster and easier for individuals and businesses to complete transactions with the Government, online or offline, the Government can deliver the world-class service that citizens expect. The Budget builds on work already underway to improve key transactions that are large in scale, meaningful, and have the potential to significantly reduce the cost per transaction. The Budget includes initiatives designed to create user-friendly experiences for common services in areas such as veterans' pension and disability applications, Social Security, and taxpayer assistance. For example, the Budget provides $100 million for the Social Security Administration (SSA) for a new customer service modernization initiative to significantly improve internet and in-person services at SSA. The Opportunity, Growth, and Security Initiative includes $150 million in additional funding to further reduce wait times and enhance services at SSA. The Administration will also invest in building an eBenefits web portal at the Department of Veterans Affairs, which will allow veterans to manage their own benefits, while providing faster, more accurate benefits claim processing. For businesses, the Budget proposes funds for the Small Business Administration's (SBA) SBA ONE, a single application for SBA loans that reduces time and cost for lenders to process loans, as well as for SelectUSA, which offers a single point of Federal contact for foreign companies that want to do business with and invest in the United States.

Delivering Smarter Information Technology (IT). During the first term, the Administration made progress improving the delivery of IT. By establishing new mechanisms such as PortfolioStat, a data-driven review of agency IT portfolios that has resulted in nearly $1.6 billion in savings since March 2012, and promoting new technologies such as cloud computing that give agencies the ability to purchase IT services in a utility-based model where they pay only for the services they consume, the Administration stopped the out of control Federal IT spending, which had been growing at seven percent per year the decade before the President took office.

However, as it became clear from the problems surrounding the initial rollout of *HealthCare. gov* in 2013, there is still much more to do. The Administration is committed to delivering smarter IT services, shifting the focus of Government IT projects from compliance to delivering on intended impact and meeting user needs. The Administration will begin implementing these efforts this year, and push further in 2015. To do this, we need the best talent working inside Government, the best companies working with Government, and the best processes in place to ensure accountability for delivering results for the American people. For example, the Budget funds technology-enabled solutions to create more visibility into contracting opportunities for small, innovative companies. The Budget also funds BusinessUSA, a centralized, one-stop online platform to make it easier for businesses to access services such as loan programs and training to help them grow and hire.

EFFICIENCY: INCREASE QUALITY AND VALUE IN CORE OPERATIONS AND ENHANCE PRODUCTIVITY TO ACHIEVE COST SAVINGS

To achieve cost savings and maximize the value of Government investments, the Administration will pursue initiatives to streamline the way Government delivers services internally, with a particular focus on the core administrative functions that are common across the Federal Government. The Administration will also continue ongoing efforts to enhance efficiency and identify savings.

Increasing Quality and Value in Core Operations. The Budget will maximize the value of every taxpayer dollar while increasing productivity and the quality of services through:

Expanding the Use of Strategic Sourcing Solutions. The Administration's efforts to better leverage the Government's buying power through the use of strategic sourcing has saved over $300 million since 2010 on commonly purchased goods such as office supplies and services such as package delivery. Creation of central vehicles that can be used by all Federal agencies has reduced

contract duplication and reduced prices for some common office supplies by over 65 percent. Such efforts save taxpayer dollars directly through reduced prices and duplication that allows agencies to focus scarce human capital resources on more complex, mission-critical efforts.

Expanding the Use of High-Quality, High-Value Shared Services. Today, many agencies are spending too much time and money on administrative and operating functions that are not central to their core mission and shared by other agencies. These functions could be handled by Federal Shared Service Providers (SSPs), reducing duplication and costs while increasing quality of services through concentrated expertise. In some administrative areas, the Government has already coalesced around a small number of SSPs. For example, payroll services are provided for all Federal agencies by service centers at the Departments of Agriculture, the Interior, Defense (DOD), State, and the General Services Administration. In the largest financial management shared service arrangement established to date, the Department of Housing and Urban Development has signed an interagency agreement with the Department of the Treasury (Treasury) to transition all of its core financial management functions to Treasury beginning in 2015. The Administration will continue to drive efficiencies and cost savings by increasing the performance and capacity of the SSPs.

Establishing Cost and Quality Benchmarks for Core Administrative Operations. Federal agencies often do not have the tools to measure their performance in key administrative areas such as human resources, finance, acquisition, IT, and real property. Beginning in 2014 and continuing in 2015, the Administration will leverage the Executive Councils, which represent the chief administrative and operating officials at Federal agencies, to establish cost and quality benchmarks in each of these key areas.

Enhancing Productivity to Achieve Cost Savings. The Administration will continue efforts to enhance productivity, reorganize or consolidate Federal programs to reduce duplication, and identify cost savings to allow the Government to invest more in productive activities. The President is again asking the Congress to revive an authority that Presidents had for almost the entire period from 1932 through 1984—the ability to submit proposals to reorganize the Executive Branch through a fast-track procedure. In effect, the President is asking to have the same authority that any business owner has to reorganize or streamline operations to meet changing circumstances and customer demand.

Examples of continuing efforts to enhance productivity include:

Consolidating Business and Trade Promotion Into a Single Department. As the President indicated in 2012, if given Presidential reorganization authority, the first proposal would be to consolidate a number of agencies and programs into a new Department with a focused mission to foster economic growth and spur job creation. By bringing together the core tools to expand trade and investment, grow small businesses, and support innovation, this reorganization would help American businesses compete in the global economy, expand exports, and create more jobs at home.

Cutting Improper Payments. The Administration has made reducing improper payments—payments made to the wrong entity, in the wrong amount, or for the wrong reason—a priority. When the President took office in 2009, the improper payment rate was 5.42 percent and rising. Since then, the Administration, working with the Congress, significantly reduced improper payments through yearly reviews by agency inspectors general and expanded audits for high priority programs. This strengthened accountability and transparency in payments resulted in the improper payment rate declining to 3.53 percent in 2013 when factoring in DOD commercial payments. Furthermore, agencies recovered more than $22 billion in overpayments through payment recapture audits and other methods in 2013.

The Administration set a cross-agency priority goal to reach a Government-wide improper payment rate of three percent or less by the end of 2016. To support that goal, the Administration is advancing data analytics and improved technology to prevent improper payments before they happen. The Office of Management and Budget (OMB) has begun conducting a comprehensive analysis of agency-specific corrective actions to identify programs with the highest return-on-investment or potential for substantially reducing improper payments. This analysis will help shape future guidance on improper payments.

Saving on Real Estate Costs. The Federal Government is the largest property owner in the United States. There are opportunities for savings by using Federal space more efficiently and disposing of unneeded space, and the President has made it a priority to shrink and reduce the cost of operating the Federal real estate inventory. Laying the groundwork for the Administration's long-term strategy on real property, in 2012 the Administration issued a Freeze the Footprint policy and directed agencies to freeze the growth in their real estate inventory. In early calendar year 2014, the Administration will begin publicly tracking the Government's adherence to a fixed baseline—730.2 million square feet—composed of office and warehouse space, and agencies will continue to pursue mobile workforce strategies and tighter internal controls on space acquisitions.

Through the Freeze the Footprint policy, the Administration continues its work, in collaboration with the Federal Real Property Council, to improve the quality of data on the real estate inventory and to develop key performance metrics. In addition, the Budget includes $57 million to start up the Civilian Property Realignment Act (CPRA). CPRA would create an independent board of private and public sector real estate experts that would make recommendations to the Congress on properties that should be sold, consolidated, co-located, or reconfigured. Legislation to create CPRA would help to streamline the disposal process, generate $2 billion in savings through the disposal of excess properties, and provide funds for real property reinvestment. Further, modernization would support the consolidation of the Federal real estate inventory and help reduce the Government's operating costs.

Reforming Military Acquisition. DOD must procure weapon systems and critical goods and services needed by the Armed Forces to execute its national security mission. The military services and defense agencies have a portfolio of 81 ongoing major weapon system acquisition programs, and DOD contracts account for approximately 70 percent of all Federal procurement. The Budget continues to invest in DOD's Better Buying Power (BBP) reform, charting a path to greater productivity in the military acquisi-

tion system. New BBP initiatives enforce affordability caps, measure cost performance, and align contractor profitability with acquisition goals. DOD-instituted best practices for procurement include applying lessons learned, expanding strategic sourcing, establishing acquisition professional reviews, and instituting peer reviews to ensure effective competition. These actions help further the Administration's ongoing Government-wide goal to ensure smarter and more fiscally responsible buying across Government.

Reducing Administrative Overhead. In November 2011, the President signed an Executive Order to promote efficient spending that called for agencies to make a 20 percent reduction in their 2013 spending on administrative areas. These included travel, advisory contracts, printing, extraneous promotional items, and transportation. In May 2012, the Administration outlined a series of actions for further spending reductions and increasing both transparency and oversight of Federal conference and travel activity. As a result, agencies have reduced travel and conference spending alone by more than $3 billion. Overall, agencies have saved over $16 billion on administrative activities. The Administration is continuing these efforts through the strategic sourcing, shared services, and administrative benchmarking efforts outlined above. Specific examples include a 20 percent reduction in operating budgets for DOD's headquarters staff through consolidating duplicative efforts and strengthening management functions.

Reforming TVA. Since its creation in the 1930s during the Great Depression, the federally owned and operated Tennessee Valley Authority (TVA) has been producing electricity and managing natural resources for a large portion of the Southeastern United States. TVA's power service territory includes most of Tennessee and parts of Alabama, Georgia, Kentucky, Mississippi, North Carolina, and Virginia, covering 80,000 square miles and serving more than nine million people. TVA is a self-financing Government corporation, funding operations through electricity sales and bond financing. The 2014 President's Budget announced the Administration's intentions to undertake a strategic review of options for addressing TVA's financial situation, including the possible divestiture of TVA. Since then, TVA has undergone a major internal review and taken significant steps to improve its future operating and financial performance. In addition, TVA has committed to resolve its capital financing constraints. The Administration supports TVA's ongoing operating and financial initiatives and intends to closely monitor TVA's performance. The Administration continues to believe that reducing or eliminating the Federal Government's role in programs such as TVA, which have achieved their original objectives, can help mitigate risk to taxpayers. The Administration recognizes the important role TVA serves in the Tennessee Valley and stands ready to work with the Congress and TVA's stakeholders to explore options to end Federal ties to TVA, including alternatives such as a transfer of ownership to State or local stakeholders.

Continuing PortfolioStat. In March 2012, OMB initiated the PortfolioStat process, designed as a data-driven effort with agencies to examine IT portfolios and identify common areas of spending to decrease duplication and drive down costs. As a result of PortfolioStat, agencies reported nearly $1.6 billion in savings and identified more than $2.5 billion in savings that could be achieved over the 2013–2015 period. The Administration is committed to continuing the PortfolioStat process to drive further management improvements, save billions of dollars across the Federal Government, and

improve services to Americans through the effective use of technology.

Expanding Federal Cloud Computing. The Budget includes investments to transform the Government IT portfolio through cloud computing, giving agencies the ability to purchase IT services in a utility-based model, paying for only the services consumed. As a result of the Administration's Cloud First policy, Federal agencies adopting cloud-based IT systems are increasing operational efficiencies, resource utilization, and innovation across the Government. To accelerate the pace of cloud adoption, the Administration established the Federal Risk Authorization Management Program, a Government-wide program standardizing how we secure cloud solutions. To further grow the use of cloud-based services, the Government is working to establish a credential exchange system that allows citizens and businesses to securely access online services at different agencies without the need for multiple digital identities and passwords.

Consolidating Data Centers. Under the President's Federal Data Center Consolidation Initiative, the Administration is working to consolidate unnecessary Federal data centers across the Nation. Since agencies began executing their data center consolidation plans in 2011, more than 600 data centers have been closed (a complete listing of these can be found on *Data.gov*), leading to a net reduction in data centers for the first time in over a decade. Closing these facilities increases agency IT efficiencies, strengthens our cybersecurity posture and decreases the Government's energy and real estate footprint.

ECONOMIC GROWTH: OPEN GOVERNMENT ASSETS AS A PLATFORM FOR INNOVATION AND JOB CREATION

By opening up Government-generated assets including data and the fruits of federally funded research and development (R&D)—such as intellectual property and scientific publications—to the public, Government can empower individuals and businesses to significantly increase the public's return on investment in terms of innovation, job creation, and economic prosperity.

PortfolioStat-Related Savings, 2013-2015

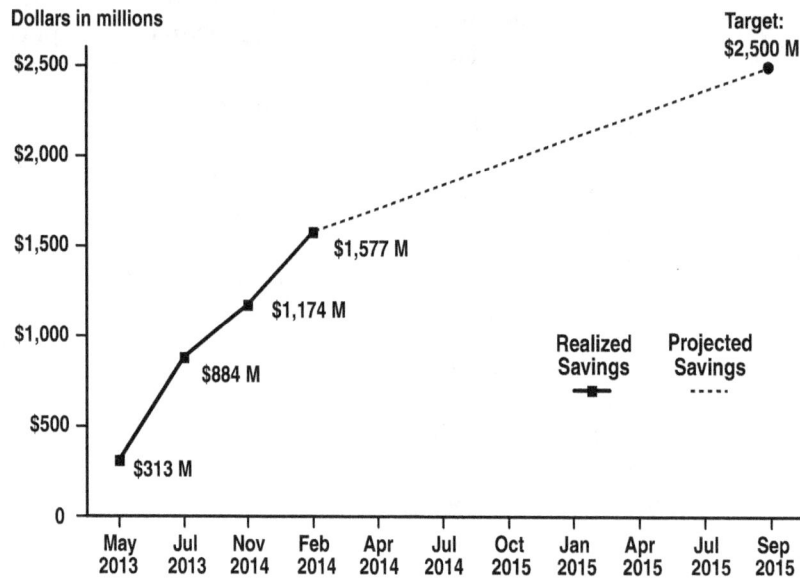

Dollars in millions

Target: $2,500 M

$2,500 –

$2,000 –

$1,500 – $1,577 M

$1,000 – $1,174 M

                                            Realized   Projected
                                            Savings   Savings
               $884 M   ■━   ·····

$500 –

        $313 M

0 –
        May   Jul   Nov   Feb   Apr   Jul   Oct   Jan   Apr   Jul   Sep
        2013   2013   2014   2014   2014   2014   2015   2015   2015   2015   2015

Opening Data to Spark Innovation. The Administration has placed a high priority on transparency and, in particular, on opening Government data as fuel for private sector innovation and public use. Since 2009, the Administration has released tens of thousands of data sets to the public while protecting individual privacy, on everything from credit card complaints, to weather and climate measurements, to what different hospitals charge for different procedures. The use of this data has resulted in new start-up companies and ventures, creating jobs and driving innovation. Private companies have used Government data sets to bring transparency to retirement plans, help consumers find deceptive, erroneous, and fraudulent charges on their credit and debit card bills, and increase crop yields and address climate change by enabling rapid adaptations in crop selection and management. By continuing investments in open data, the Administration supports efforts to unlock Federal data sets with a high potential for economic impact, including in the areas of health care, energy, education, public safety, tourism, and agriculture.

Accelerating and Institutionalizing Lab-to-Market Practices. The Federal Government's investment in R&D yields extraordinary long-term economic impact through the creation of new knowledge, new jobs, and ultimately new industries. The Federal R&D enterprise must continue to support fundamental research that is motivated primarily by an interest in expanding the frontiers of human knowledge and diffusing this knowledge through open data and publications. At the same time, economic growth can be accelerated through more effective transition of R&D results from the laboratory to the marketplace, based on close collaboration with industry.

The Budget reflects the Administration's commitment to accelerating the transfer of the results of federally funded research to the commercial marketplace by proposing increased funding for technology transfer from Federal labs in the National Institute of Standards and Technology, and for the National Science Foundation's public-private Innovation Corps program to bring discoveries ripe for innovation out of the university lab.

PEOPLE AND CULTURE: UNLOCK THE POTENTIAL OF THE FEDERAL WORKFORCE AND BUILD THE WORKFORCE WE NEED FOR TOMORROW

To fully capitalize on the talents in today's workforce at all levels, and recruit and develop the capabilities needed for the future, the Administration is committed to undertaking executive actions that will attract and retain the best talent in the Federal workforce and foster a culture of excellence.

Creating a Culture of Excellence and Engagement to Enable Higher Performance. Data-driven approaches to enhancing management, performance, and innovation across the Federal workforce are critical to fostering a culture of excellence. In 2015, the Administration will support the development of Government-wide enterprise training and resource exchanges across agencies to share best practices and increase leadership development opportunities within Government.

Building a World-Class Federal Management Team Starting with the Senior Executive Service (SES). To ensure the Government sustains a first-class Federal workforce, the Administration will continue to invest in civil service leadership. The Administration will take administrative actions to produce a Federal executive corps with a broader, stronger experience base. For example, the Budget includes funding for the Office of Personnel Management to build a stronger onboarding program for new SES, and leadership and engagement training opportunities for current SES that emphasize diversity and the changing needs of a 21st Century workforce.

Enabling Agencies to Hire the Best Talent from All Segments of Society. The Administration is committed to working with labor groups to improve hiring outcomes by exploring flexible approaches to recruit and retain individuals with high-demand talents and skills. Beginning in 2015, the Administration will launch demonstration projects to identify promising practices in recruiting, hiring, onboarding, and deploying talent across agencies. The goal of these projects is to increase diversity, reduce skills gaps, and improve organizational outcomes.

IMPROVE RESULTS: SETTING GOALS AND TRACKING PERFORMANCE

As the Administration works to deliver on this Agenda, it is committed to driving effective performance management within the Government by using the framework developed with the Congress in the Government Performance and Results Act (GPRA) and the GPRA Modernization Act. To improve outcomes, the Administration will drive progress in three ways: through a discrete set of Cross Agency Priority Goals, where multiple agencies come together around a central goal; through Agency Priority Goals where leaders are focused on improved implementation; and through agency strategic plans covering the broad range of outcomes within an agency's mission. All three sets of goals can be found on *Performance.gov.*

These goals and strategic plans reflect key Administration priorities and were chosen by agencies to achieve maximum impact. Each publicly identified goal will have Goal Leaders, an action plan, and performance indicators. OMB and Goal Leaders will regularly review progress and take corrective action as needed to keep implementation on track. Agencies will provide regular updates on their progress through *Performance.gov.*

DEPARTMENT OF AGRICULTURE

Funding Highlights:

- Provides $23.7 billion in discretionary resources for the Department of Agriculture to invest in rural communities; nutrition assistance for vulnerable populations; renewable energy and energy improvements to cut carbon pollution and make America more energy independent; and agricultural research in key areas such as climate resilience and improved crop production techniques. This includes:

  o Doubling funding for broadband access to rural communities in need;

  o Launching three new multidisciplinary agricultural research institutes dedicated to crop science and pollinator health, advanced biobased manufacturing and anti-microbial resistance research;

  o Providing the Special Supplemental Nutrition Program for Women, Infants, and Children (WIC) the resources it needs to support estimated participation, which will improve birth outcomes and support child development; and

  o Strengthening bee and other pollinator habitats, a key component of strong U.S. food production.

Opportunity, Growth, and Security Initiative:

- Through the Opportunity, Growth, and Security Initiative, supports:

  o Construction of a new biosafety research laboratory;

  o Reforms to encourage a shift toward competitively awarded research funding;

  o Forest Service construction and renovation projects, as part of the National Parks Centennial Initiative and the President's America's Great Outdoors Initiative; and

  o Activities to increase the resiliency of the Nation's natural resources including landscape and watershed restoration, hazardous fuels reduction, and community forest enhancement and protection.

Reforms:

• Brings about a fundamental shift in wildfire funding to safeguard communities and ecosystems, investing in programs to improve the resilience of the Nation's forests and rangelands and providing a stable funding source for wildfire suppression.

• Reforms crop insurance subsidies to companies and farmers to make the program less costly to the taxpayer while still maintaining a quality safety net for farmers.

The U.S. Department of Agriculture (USDA) provides leadership on issues related to food, agriculture, economic development in rural communities and natural resources, including energy, based on sound public policy, the best available science, and efficient management. USDA works to expand economic opportunity through the development of innovative practices and research and provides financing needed to help expand job prospects and improve housing, utilities, and community infrastructure in rural America. The Department also works to promote sustainable agricultural production to protect the long-term availability of food. USDA programs safeguard and protect America's food supply by reducing the incidence of food-borne hazards from farm to table. The Department's programs also improve nutrition and health through food assistance and nutrition education. USDA supports agricultural and economic development in developing countries through research and technical assistance to combat chronic hunger and achieve global food security. In addition, USDA manages and protects America's public and private lands by working cooperatively with other levels of government and the private sector to preserve and conserve the Nation's natural resources through restored forests, improved watersheds, and healthy private working lands.

The recently enacted Agricultural Act of 2014 extends numerous authorities for five years and establishes stability for important agriculture, rural development, renewable energy, and nutrition programs. Building on this achievement, the Budget provides $23.7 billion in discretionary resources to support this important mission, a decrease of roughly $938 million from the 2014 enacted level. While investments are made in renewable energy, rural development, and key research areas, the Budget makes tough choices to meet tight discretionary caps. The Opportunity, Growth, and Security Initiative provides additional support for key priorities.

Supports Communities in Rural America

Encourages Job Creation in Rural Communities. The Budget provides $58 million for a new economic development grant program designed to target small and emerging private businesses and cooperatives in rural areas. The program will utilize performance targets and evidence of what works best to create jobs and foster economic growth, strengthening the agency's grant allocation and evaluation process. It is anticipated that this new program will aid in creating or saving nearly 14,000 jobs and assisting over 10,000 businesses.

Promotes Innovation and Job Growth

Encourages Development of Rural Renewable Energy. The Budget provides $5 billion in loans to rural electric cooperatives and utilities that will support the transition to clean-energy generation and increased energy efficiency. Specifically, this funding will be targeted to cut carbon pollution and promote renewable and clean energy as well as energy efficiency improvements at electric generation, transmission, and distribution sites in rural communities. In addition, the Budget proposes a program level of $52 million for the Rural Energy for America Program to assist agricultural producers and rural small businesses in developing renewable energy systems, energy efficiency improvements, and renewable energy development.

Stimulates Broadband Deployment in Rural Areas. Roughly 25 percent of rural households lack access to high speed internet. The Budget proposes to double the current funding for broadband grants that serve the neediest, most rural communities, which are least likely to have access to high-speed broadband infrastructure. This level of funding is anticipated to support 16 rural communities.

Spurs American Innovation by Advancing Priority Research. USDA research plays a key role in fostering innovation and advancing technologies that increase the efficiency, sustainability, and profitability of American agriculture. At the same time, the Administration recognizes that continued fiscal constraint requires trade-offs to focus resources on the most important national priorities. As such, the Budget supports research in key areas important to American agriculture such as climate resilience and advanced genetics. The Budget also includes $325 million for the Agriculture and Food Research Initiative competitive research program. In addition, the Budget includes $75 million to support three multidisciplinary institutes, with one dedicated to advanced biobased manufacturing, another to focus on anti-microbial resistance research, and the third on crop science and pollinator health. These institutes, recommended by the President's Council of Advisors on Science and Technology, will leverage the best research within the public and private sectors to create opportunities for new business ventures funded by the private sector.

Above the base level of funding in the Budget for agricultural and forestry research, the Opportunity, Growth, and Security Initiative provides an additional $295 million to support high priority in-house research; enhance funding for competitive research, including an additional $20 million to encourage competitively awarded grants through land grant formula programs; and build a new biosafety research laboratory in Athens, GA. This modern facility is USDA's highest research construction priority and would result in the consolidation of two outdated facilities.

Prevents Hunger and Supports Healthy Eating

Prevents Hunger. The Administration strongly supports the Supplemental Nutrition Assistance Program (SNAP) and other programs that reduce hunger and help families meet their nutritional needs. SNAP is the cornerstone of the Nation's nutrition assistance safety net, touching the lives of 47 million Americans, the majority of whom are children, the elderly, or people with disabilities. In addition to supporting SNAP, the Budget also invests $30 million to support summer electronic benefit pilots, which are proving successful in reducing childhood hunger and improving nutrition in the months when school meals are unavailable.

Supports Healthy Eating. The Budget supports the ongoing implementation of the Healthy, Hunger-Free Kids Act of 2010 with an increased investment of $35 million in school equipment grants to aid in the provision of healthy meals and continued support for other school-based resources. The Budget also provides $6.8 billion to support the 8.7 million individuals expected to participate in the Special Supplemental Nutrition Program for Women, Infants, and Children (WIC), which is critical to the health of pregnant women, new mothers, infants, and young children. The Budget also supports changes to the WIC food package that will improve consumption of nutritious foods that are important to healthy child development. In addition, the Budget invests $13 million in a newly authorized Healthy Food Financing Initiative, which will provide funding to improve access to affordable, healthy foods in underserved areas.

Protects Natural Resources

Strengthens Critical Habitats for Bees and Other Pollinators. In recent years, honey bee colony collapse disorder and other pollinator declines have led to rising concerns among both the scientific and agricultural communities regarding the health of these insect populations, the risks posed to pollinator services and the implications for agriculture. To help combat this multi-faceted problem, the Budget provides $50 million across multiple agencies within USDA to enhance research through public-private grants, strengthen pollinator habitat in core areas, double the number of acres in the Conservation Reserve Program that are dedicated to pollinator health, and increase funding for surveys to determine the impacts on pollinator losses. Agricultural productivity is directly dependent on pollinators, especially bees, for producing more than one-third of food products.

Conserves Landscapes. The Budget proposes full funding for Land and Water Conservation Fund (LWCF) programs in the Department of the Interior (DOI) and USDA. 2015 marks the 50th anniversary of the landmark Land and Water Conservation Act that enables vital support to sustain the outdoor recreation and conservation areas the public values. Similar to last year's proposal, the Budget includes a mix of discretionary and mandatory funding in order to transition to all mandatory funding beginning in 2016. These funds will assist in conserving lands for national parks, refuges, and forests, as well as State and local recreation and conservation areas. Funding will also enable collaborative projects for DOI and the U.S. Forest Service to jointly and strategically conserve the most critical landscapes while improving management efficiency. These projects will support the President's America's Great Outdoors Initiative to promote job creation and economic growth by strengthening the natural infrastructure for outdoor recreation and enjoyment.

Continues Interagency Collaboration to Improve Water Quality. Over the past two years, USDA, the Environmental Protection Agency, and State water quality agencies have collaborated to select more than 150 priority watersheds, where voluntary conservation programs could help reduce water impairments from nonpoint source pollution. The Budget builds upon this collaboration by having agencies work with key Federal partners, agricultural producer organizations, conservation districts, States, Tribes, non-governmental organizations, and other local leaders to implement a monitoring framework and begin collecting baseline performance data to demonstrate that this focused and coordinated approach can achieve significant improvements in water quality.

Implements Targeted Reforms

Safeguards Communities and Ecosystems from Wildfire Damage. Fire is a natural occurrence that can be highly beneficial to landscapes when managed properly; however, population growth near forests and rangelands, past management practices, and a changing climate have dramatically increased wildfire risk and resulting costs. The Budget calls for a fundamental change in how wildfire suppression is funded in order to help reduce fire risk, manage landscapes more holistically, and increase the resiliency of the Nation's forests and rangelands and the communities that border them. The Budget supports congressional proposals to fund suppression of the most severe fire activity—including large fires that require emergency response, are near urban areas, or for abnormally active fire seasons—as extraordinary costs that are outside the discretionary caps. Importantly, because this funding would not allow the total funding available under existing cap adjustments to grow, it would not increase overall discretionary spending.

This new approach for funding suppression of catastrophic fires better safeguards non-suppression programs from transfers that have diminished their effectiveness in addressing threats to communities and landscapes. This allows for enhanced capabilities in programs such as the Forest Service Integrated Resource Restoration Program, the Collaborative Forest Landscape Restoration Program, and the Hazardous Fuels Program, as well as the Fuels Management and Resilient Landscapes programs in DOI. Since improving community resilience to wildland fires is the responsibility of Federal, State, local, and tribal governments and homeowners, the Budget also targets funding for fuels management and certain State programs to communities that implement programs to reduce fire risk on non-Federal lands, including improved building standards for fire resiliency and defensible spaces.

Restructures Crop Insurance Subsidies. With the recent passage of the newly enacted Agricultural Act of 2014, many of the Administration's previously proposed reforms have been realized. However, these reforms did not include any of the Administration's proposals for improvements and efficiencies for the crop insurance program, which continues to be highly subsidized and costs the Government on average $9 billion a year to run: $3 billion per year for the private insurance companies to administer and underwrite the program and $6 billion per year in premium subsidies to the farmers. The Budget includes proposals to reduce subsidies to farmers, as well as crop insurance companies, to more reasonable levels. These proposals will modify the structure of the crop insurance program so that it is less costly to the taxpayer yet still provides a quality safety net for farmers. Collectively these proposals are expected to save $14 billion over 10 years.

DEPARTMENT OF COMMERCE

Funding Highlights:

- Provides $8.8 billion in base discretionary funding for the Department of Commerce to create the conditions for economic growth by promoting trade and investment, spurring innovation, gathering and acting on environmental intelligence, and fueling a data-driven economy. This includes:

  o Funding for the National Institute of Standards and Technology laboratories to accelerate advances ranging from cybersecurity to advanced manufacturing, and to further expand lab-to-market transfers of manufacturing and other technologies;

  o Supporting key trade enforcement and promotion activities that will grow the economy, invest in underserved markets and regional economic development, and encourage greater investment in the United States;

  o Expanding SelectUSA, an initiative to attract, retain, and expand business investment in the United States in order to create jobs, spur economic growth, and promote U.S. competitiveness;

  o Continuing the Administration's strong support for the National Oceanic and Atmospheric Administration's critical weather, research, and oceans programs, including fully funding its next generation of weather satellites to maintain launch dates and provide critical, time-sensitive information to decision-makers throughout the Government and private sector; and

  o Providing $753 million to support key research and testing of innovative design methods necessary to achieve an effective 2020 decennial census at the lowest cost possible.

Opportunity, Growth, and Security Initiative:

- Through the Opportunity, Growth, and Security Initiative, supports:

  o A National Network for Manufacturing Innovation with up to 45 manufacturing innovation institutes across the Nation, building on the four institutes already launched and the five institutes that the Administration has committed to funding, led by the Departments of Energy, Defense, and Agriculture;

o   National Institute of Standards and Technology efforts to accelerate advances in top research priorities including advanced manufacturing, forensics, cybersecurity and disaster resilience, and improve scientific facilities;

o   National Oceanic and Atmospheric Administration (NOAA) research, including weather and ocean research, and modernization of its observation and data gathering capabilities by replacing a NOAA research vessel;

o   Catalytic investments in communities and regional economies to increase their ability to accelerate production of value-added goods and services, including their capacity for advanced manufacturing;

o   Development of data and tools that businesses can use to help market and sell goods abroad; and

o   A Nation that is better prepared for the impacts of climate change by improving coastal resilience to severe weather events, climate hazards, and changing ocean conditions, including through research grants to improve severe weather prediction and the understanding of climate change impacts on various sectors, including fisheries.

Reforms:

•   Invests in regional economic competitiveness by providing $210 million to the Economic Development Administration to support community and regional economic development, commercialization of research and development, and catalytic capital projects—while making reforms to ensure that these funds have the greatest impact for distressed communities.

•   Closes one ocean science laboratory and consolidates another to improve efficiency and reduce costs.

The Department of Commerce (Commerce) plays a critical role in promoting U.S. economic growth and providing vital scientific and environmental information. The Budget provides Commerce with $8.8 billion to support mission areas across its diverse bureaus. Key investments are made in areas such as export promotion, investment promotion, and enforcement activities, development of weather satellites, wireless and broadband access, and research and development to support long-term economic growth. At the same time, efficiency gains, such as from streamlining operations in the Census Bureau, and reductions in lower-priority activities enable Commerce to achieve administrative and programmatic savings.

Invests in America's Long-Term Growth and Competitiveness

Strengthens U.S. Manufacturing and Innovation. The Budget provides $141 million, a $13 million increase over the 2014 enacted level for the Hollings Manufacturing Extension Partnership, with the increase focused on expanding technology and supply chain capabilities to support technology adoption by smaller manufacturers to improve their competitiveness. The Budget also includes $15 million for the Advanced Manufacturing Technology Consortia, a public-private partnership that will support industry consortia to develop technology road maps to address common manufacturing challenges faced by American businesses.

The Budget maintains the President's commitment to increase funding for key basic research agencies, including $680 million for National Institute of Standards and Technology (NIST) laboratories. This funding will accelerate advances in a variety of important areas, ranging from cybersecurity and forensic science to advanced communications and disaster resilience. In response to the President's 2011 Memorandum on Accelerating Technology Transfer and Commercialization, the Budget provides $6 million for NIST efforts to accelerate and expand technology transfer across the Federal Government, which will enhance the competitiveness of U.S. industry by sharing innovations and knowledge from Federal laboratories.

Promotes American Exports and Investment in the United States. To promote exports and foreign investment in the United States, the Budget includes $497 million for the renamed International Trade and Investment Administration (ITIA), an eight percent increase over the 2014 enacted level. Funding for ITIA includes $15 million to accelerate operations of the Interagency Trade Enforcement Center, an interagency effort to address unfair trade practices and barriers to boost U.S. exports, and $20 million to expand SelectUSA, which promotes "onshoring" and actively brings job-creating investment to the United States from around the world. The Budget will expand SelectUSA, supporting the first-ever, fully coordinated U.S. Government effort to recruit businesses to invest and create new jobs in the United States. Other funds support increased export promotion activities in underserved markets around the world and ITIA's role in the Administration's BusinessUSA initiative, a one-stop shop to connect businesses with Federal Government resources more effectively and efficiently.

Enhances Export Control Enforcement. The Budget includes $111 million for the Bureau of Industry and Security to sustain export licensing and enforcement activities, as well as to support the bureau's ongoing work under the Administration's Export Control Reform (ECR) initiative. The $9 million increase from the 2014 enacted level will support the bureau's expanded export licensing and export enforcement operations that will improve service to U.S. exporters as controlled items shift from the State Department to the Commerce Department's jurisdiction. The Administration's continued efforts to implement the ECR initiative will advance national security and economic competitiveness by better focusing U.S. controls on transactions to destinations or end users of concern, while facilitating secure trade for controlled items with U.S. allies and close partners.

Promotes Regional Economic Development. The Budget includes $210 million for the Economic Development Administration (EDA) to support innovative economic development planning, regional capacity building, and catalytic capital projects. The Budget includes $25 million for the Regional Innovation Strategies Program to promote economic development planning and projects that spur entrepreneurship and innovation at the regional level. The Budget also proposes reforms to the economic development grants to ensure grantees demonstrate measurable progress in achieving economic development goals, and provides EDA the flexibility to award catalytic grants tailored to address communities' specific economic needs, delivering the greatest impact for distressed regions.

Continues Strong Support for Weather Satellites and Weather Forecasting. The Budget provides $2 billion to continue the development of NOAA's polar-orbiting and geostationary weather satellite systems, as well as satellite-borne measurements of sea level and potentially damaging solar storms. These satellites are critical to NOAA's ability to provide accurate forecasts and warnings that help to protect lives and property. The Budget also fully supports the National Weather Service, including funding for research, modeling, and supercomputing capacity to accelerate advancements in forecasting. Further, the Budget provides funding for centralized hydrological forecasting and studies that will inform ongoing efforts to enhance the National Weather Service's decision-support capabilities, and build a Weather Ready Nation that is more resilient to extreme weather events.

Strengthens Research and Ocean and Coastal Stewardship. The Budget includes significant investments in NOAA's ocean and coastal research and observing programs, while increasing support for habitat and species conservation activities that are essential to restoring and maintaining healthy, sustainable oceans. Increased funding for NOAA's research and development activities will enhance the agency's ability to detect, understand, and forecast global and ecosystem-scale changes and provide sound, science-based information to support decision-making and help communities prepare for the consequences of a changing climate. The Budget also supports investments such as coastal zone management grants, which promote well-coordinated ocean and coastal science and management activities. The Budget includes a proposal to close one ocean science laboratory and consolidate another, which will allow for more efficient operations through reduced fixed costs.

Prioritizes Critical Telecommunications Investments, Innovation, and Policy Coordination. The Budget demonstrates the Administration's continued commitment to broadband telecommunications as a driver of economic development, job creation, technological innovation, and enhanced public safety. The President's dual broadband vision—supported by the Budget— of freeing up 500 MHz of Federal spectrum and connecting over 99 percent of schools to high-speed broadband connections through the ConnectED initiative will create thousands of quality jobs and ensure that students have access to the best educational tools available. The Budget supports implementation of telecommunications provisions enacted in the Middle Class Tax Relief and Job Creation Act of 2012, which will reduce the deficit by nearly $20 billion over the next 10 years through spectrum auctions. These auctions will increase commercial access to wireless broadband spectrum while investing $7 billion to realize the vision of a fully-interoperable public safety and first responder broadband network. The Budget also provides $7.5 million for the National Telecommunications and Information Administration's new Internet Policy Center to enhance the Department's coordination and policy-making across broadband stakeholders, as well as additional investments of over $20 million for the Federal Communications Commission to make critical reforms to its Universal Service Fund program, make information technology upgrades, and provide robust program support for high priority 2015 spectrum auctions.

Protects Innovators and Ensures a World-Class Patent System. Through implementation of the America Invents Act, the U.S. Patent and Trademark Office continues to make it easier for American entrepreneurs and businesses to bring their inventions to the marketplace sooner, converting ideas into new products and new jobs. The Budget proposes several legislative reforms designed to improve the transparency and efficiency of the American patent system, complementing a series of administrative actions the Administration announced in June 2013, which will help to protect innovators from frivolous litigation and ensure the highest-quality patents in the system.

Invests in an Efficient and Effective 2020 Decennial Census. The Budget provides $753 million, an increase of $281 million over the 2014 enacted level, to support key research and testing of innovative design methods necessary to achieve an effective 2020 decennial census at the lowest cost possible. This research and testing phase must be complete by the end of 2015 to make important 2020 operational decisions. Without this additional funding for key testing, much of the cost containment efforts leading up to the 2020 Census will face increasing operational risk and decreasing accuracy.

Supports Evidence-Based Decision-Making

Improves and Expands Federal Statistical Measures. The Budget includes $16 million to invest in the development of three Commerce statistical measures that will improve evidence-based decision-making across the Federal Government and the private sector. In the Census Bureau, $5 million is provided to improve the supplemental poverty measure to allow for more fair and accurate indexing and analysis of poverty programs. An additional $5 million is provided to the Census Bureau to increase access to critical business datasets and to create a new field of research into the conditions and outcomes of business investments in research, development, and innovation by expanding existing data projects.

In the Bureau of Economic Analysis (BEA), an investment of $4 million will improve the measurement and understanding of U.S. foreign direct investment as part of "Build it Here, Sell it Everywhere," supporting the SelectUSA initiative and its foreign and domestic stakeholders. An additional investment of $2 million in BEA will initiate "Big Data for Small Business," a new data program that will collect a new Small Business Gross Domestic Product measure to support decision-making by business owners and investors as well as small business analyses.

DEPARTMENT OF DEFENSE

Funding Highlights:

- Provides $495.6 billion in discretionary funding for the base budget of the Department of Defense to carry out our national defense strategy and protect national security. This includes:

    o Ending the war in Afghanistan and, pending the signing of a Bilateral Security Agreement, maintaining a small force of Americans and international partners to train and assist Afghan forces and carry out limited counterterrorism operations in pursuit of any remnants of al Qaeda;

    o Supporting Government-wide efforts to rebalance diplomatic, economic, and military resources to the Asia-Pacific region while also upholding responsibilities elsewhere;

    o Protecting the homeland and ensuring a safe, secure, and effective nuclear deterrent;

    o Sustaining our ability to project power and win decisively against both state adversaries and terrorist threats;

    o Making progress toward restoring balance to the Joint Force by gradually raising readiness levels negatively impacted by sequestration while supporting the transition to a smaller military that is more agile and technologically superior;

    o Providing funds to recruit and retain the best-trained All-Volunteer Force; support military families; care for wounded, ill, and injured servicemembers; make further, measurable progress toward eliminating sexual assault in the military; and help servicemembers effectively transition to civilian life; and

    o Sustaining investments in science and technology programs, which drive innovation in military capabilities as well as in the civilian economy.

Opportunity, Growth, and Security Initiative:

- Through the Opportunity, Growth, and Security Initiative, supports:

    o Accelerated modernization of key weapons systems, faster progress toward restoring readiness lost under sequestration, and improvements to the Department's facilities.

Reforms:

- Takes steps to slow the growth in military compensation and benefit costs to free up funds for training and modernization while ensuring we continue to honor and support our men and women in uniform.

- Retires aging aircraft and adjusts the planned acquisition and refurbishment of select naval assets, allowing for critical investments in new weapons systems and platforms.

- Aligns infrastructure with current needs and includes institutional reform efforts, such as a 20 percent cut in operating budgets for headquarters staff, which will consolidate duplicative efforts and streamline Department-wide management functions.

The Department of Defense (DOD) provides military forces and capabilities to deter war and protect the security of the United States and its interests around the world. The Budget provides $495.6 billion for DOD's base budget in 2015, which adheres to the levels agreed to in the Bipartisan Budget Act of 2013 (BBA). This funding level will allow the military to protect U.S. interests and fulfill the updated defense strategy—but with somewhat increased levels of risk. The Department can manage these risks under the President's 2015 Budget plan, but risks would grow significantly if sequester-level cuts return in 2016, if proposed reforms are not accepted, and if uncertainty over budget levels continues.

As the war in Afghanistan nears an end, DOD is making a strategic rebalance to the Asia-Pacific region while maintaining a military presence and engagement with allies and partners in the greater Middle East and elsewhere to protect our Nation's interests. The Budget supports this adjustment and makes strategic investments in the priorities identified in the 2012 Defense Strategic Guidance and the 2014 Quadrennial Defense Review, such as increasing our ability to effectively address the security challenges and opportunities of cyberspace, continuing to invest in research and development to feed innovation in both the military and civilian sectors, and combatting terrorism around the world. The Budget also maintains our commitment to providing servicemembers with the right mix of equipment,

infrastructure, and training to keep our forces ready for a wide range of contingencies and missions. The Budget supports DOD's efforts to improve the defense acquisition system and, for the first time in its history, to achieve auditable financial statements. The Budget sustains our commitment to the All-Volunteer Force—the backbone of our modern military—and strives to better support our servicemembers and their families, including those who are making the transition from military to civilian life.

Responsibly Ends the War in Afghanistan

Thirteen years after it began, the war in Afghanistan will end in December 2014, when Afghan forces assume full responsibility for their country's security. Pending the signing of a Bilateral Security Agreement, American and coalition forces will continue to train and sustain the Afghan National Security Forces (ANSF) after 2014, and the United States will work collaboratively with the ANSF to target al Qaeda and other entities that threaten the safety and security of the United States and our allies. While most U.S. troops will depart, those who remain will train key Afghan units, oversee military assistance programs, and support ongoing counterterrorism efforts. To support these activities, the Budget will provide the resources necessary to maintain our commitment to sustain the ANSF, provide logistical support to coalition partners in Afghanistan, return U.S. forces to their home stations, and repair or replace lost or damaged equipment.

The President continues to assess the size of the residual force needed in Afghanistan to carry out these activities and other ongoing responsibilities. As a result, the Budget includes a placeholder for DOD's 2015 Overseas Contingency Operations (OCO) funding equivalent to the amount provided in the President's 2014 Budget. The Administration continues to propose a multi-year cap that limits Government-wide OCO funding to $450 billion over the 2013-to-2021 period. The Administration plans to submit details of the DOD OCO request as a Budget amendment after making a determination on enduring force levels in Afghanistan.

Supports Strategic Rebalancing Toward Asia

DOD and other agencies are devoting increased time and resources to strengthening and transforming U.S. alliances and economic ties across the Asia-Pacific region. DOD's overarching objective in the region is to sustain a stable security environment and a regional order rooted in economic openness, peaceful resolution of territorial and maritime disputes, free flow of commerce, democratic principles of governance, and political freedom. Toward that end, the Budget supports an integrated "whole-of-government" approach involving many Federal agencies, including DOD funding for continued rotational forces, military-to-military cooperation, capacity-building activities, joint training events, and essential force modernization. The benefits of these types of investments were made clear in November 2013, when the United States, the Philippines, and other nations were able to respond quickly and effectively to Typhoon Haiyan. The combination of U.S. leadership and capable allies and partners will help provide for a peaceful and prosperous Asia-Pacific region supported by international norms, rule of law, and effective institutions.

The Budget provides for a U.S. force posture that is geographically distributed, operationally resilient, and politically sustainable, giving our leaders increased options as they plan for military-to-military engagements, conduct joint and multinational training exercises, and prepare to respond to unforeseen contingencies. By the close of the decade, the majority of U.S. naval forces, including its most capable platforms and systems, will be deployed to the Asia-Pacific region. As an example of investments in this area, the Budget provides $128 million for military infrastructure; in Guam to bolster its position as a strategic hub in the western Pacific, of which $51 million will support important steps toward establishing fully capable Marine Air-Ground Task Forces throughout the region.

Protects Readiness and Modernization Priorities

Training and readiness are the foundation of ensuring a capable military that provides the Nation with a range of options to deter or defeat aggression or intimidation against the United States and its allies, friends, and interests. However, sequestration degraded the ability of the force to accomplish its full range of assigned missions to expected timelines and standards. The Budget provides $198.7 billion in operation and maintenance funding, in addition to other resources, to continue the Department's efforts to restore readiness and avoid a hollow force.

The Budget also protects investments in critical and emerging military capabilities, aiming to ensure that the United States maintains a decisive edge in areas such as power projection; global strike; nuclear weapons and delivery systems; space and cyberspace; special operations; undersea warfare; and intelligence, surveillance, and reconnaissance. For example, the Budget invests $11.5 billion in basic and applied research and advanced technology development, including $2.9 billion for the Defense Advanced Research Projects Agency, which conducts high-risk, high-reward scientific research that has fed cutting-edge technological innovation in the United States for over 50 years.

Makes Hard Choices in an Era of Constrained Resources

The discretionary caps originally put in place by the Budget Control Act of 2011 required all Federal agencies to make difficult choices to prioritize key missions and programs, streamline infrastructure and overhead, and find ways to operate more efficiently. In 2013, sequestration required further sharp cuts, and the BBA provides modest relief in 2014 and 2015. To continue to support the Nation's defense strategy in this context, DOD has made strategic choices to reduce end strength and force structure, revise some weapons' investment plans, and control rising compensation and benefits costs. The Department also seeks to rightsize its infrastructure in order to allocate scarce resources to the highest priorities.

Builds a Smaller and More Agile Force. As DOD makes the transition out of a decade of war, it is reducing military end strength and force structure to build a smaller force that is more agile and technologically superior. End strength in the Army and Marine Corps will gradually fall over the next few years. Once implemented, these changes will generate substantial annual savings, which will help the Department fund readiness and training more fully. The 2013 National Defense Authorization Act requires comparable reductions in DOD's civilian and contractor workforces.

Modernizes DOD's Compensation and Benefits System. Since 2001, military pay and benefits have grown 40 percent more than in the private sector. The Budget proposes reforms to slow this cost growth, including changes to TRICARE, lower commissary subsidies phased in over time, and modestly slower growth in the Basic Allowance for Housing, while still providing a robust compensation and benefits system that honors the service of our men and women in uniform and their families. For calendar year 2015, the Budget provides a 1.0 percent increase to basic pay, a 1.5 percent increase in the Basic

Allowance for Housing, and a 3.4 percent increase in the Basic Allowance for Subsistence. All of these changes have been recommended by the uniformed military leadership and are necessary to slow the growth in compensation and benefit costs in a responsible way and preserve funding needed for investments in platforms and readiness.

Retires Unneeded Weapons Systems. In concert with reductions in ground forces personnel, the Budget includes significant changes to many of DOD's weapons programs. For example, the Army plans to retire its aging Kiowa Warrior helicopters and instead use upgraded Apaches teamed with unmanned aerial vehicles to meet the Kiowas' armed reconnaissance mission. The Navy plans to temporarily decommission selected cruisers and return them to service after significant modernization overhauls. The Air Force plans to retire all of its single-mission A-10 Warthog aircraft and reduce the size of the C-130 fleet. These decisions position DOD to better support its highest priority missions.

Aligns Infrastructure with Current Needs. In order to align DOD's infrastructure with its mission and force structure, the Budget requests authorization for a new round of Base Realignment and Closure (BRAC) in 2017. Without a new round of BRAC, DOD will be forced to maintain unnecessary infrastructure with resources that it could otherwise use to field needed military capabilities. Further, the Office of the Secretary of Defense has directed DOD components to reduce headquarters operating budgets by 20 percent over the next five years, and it will also reorganize itself consistent with that goal.

Generates More Value Out of Every Defense Dollar. Generating more value out of each defense dollar is a critical goal of DOD's ongoing efforts to improve the defense acquisition system, operate with greater energy efficiency, and achieve audit readiness. In the area of acquisition reform, the Department has expanded its Better Buying Power initiative to achieve affordable programs, promote effective competition, control costs throughout the product lifecycle, and create incentives to drive productivity and innovation in both industry and Government. The Budget also continues to invest in energy efficiency initiatives at DOD, which consumes almost three-quarters of all the energy used by the Federal Government. These include improving the fuel efficiency of existing equipment, developing and fielding innovative energy technologies, expanding renewable energy sources, and improving the energy efficiency of buildings. Importantly, DOD is executing nearly $1.2 billion in third-party-financed contracts for enhanced energy conservation performance in response to the President's $2 billion goal. DOD continues to make progress in improving the quality of its financial information. The Marine Corps recently achieved the first ever clean audit opinion on a military Service budget statement, and each Service is making great efforts to build on that momentum.

Strengthens the All-Volunteer Force

People are at the heart of our military power, and the Budget provides the resources necessary to sustain the All-Volunteer Force, including investments in family programs, health and wellness, and veteran transition programs.

Supports Military Families. Supporting military families continues to be a top Administration priority. The Budget provides robust funding to ensure consistent and effective family services are available, including mental health and counseling services, deployment and relocation assistance, child care and youth programs, military spouse employment programs, and others. In addition, the Budget invests in expanding strategies for program delivery to address the fact that most servicemembers and their families no longer live on DOD installations. For example, the Department continues to leverage the Military OneSource platform to provide confidential, no-cost counseling and information on the full range of issues and challenges military families face, anywhere in the world.

Cares for Wounded, Ill, and Injured Servicemembers. To provide quality health care for the Nation's 9.6 million eligible military beneficiaries, the Budget provides $47.4 billion for the DOD Unified Medical Budget to support the DOD Military Health System. The Budget sustains strong programs that support wounded, ill, and injured servicemembers and their families and help servicemembers transition into civilian life and the workforce. In particular, DOD is improving its support for servicemember mental and emotional health by increasing collaboration among its suicide prevention programs and working to eliminate the stigma associated with accessing mental health services.

Addresses Sexual Assault in the Military. Sexual assault remains a significant problem in the military, just as in the civilian world. DOD will undertake 16 distinct initiatives aimed at eliminating sexual assault from the military, including major efforts to ensure an appropriate command climate for every member, accountability for perpetrators and commanders, and proper care and services for victims—including dedicated legal representation throughout the reformed military justice process. In addition, the President has directed DOD to complete a full-scale review of its progress in preventing and responding to sexual assault in the military by December 1, 2014. This review will include benchmarks and metrics to assess the effectiveness of DOD's efforts, as well as an examination of options for reforming the military justice system to enhance victim reporting, protect victims' rights, and hold offenders appropriately accountable. The Budget provides the funds needed to implement these initiatives and to continue making improvements to DOD's sexual assault prevention and response programs.

Helps Servicemembers Transition to Civilian Life. The Administration continues to build on last year's work to support service men and women as they make the transition from military to civilian life. DOD has partnered with other Federal agencies to ensure that all servicemembers participate in effective pre-separation programs that help them plan and prepare for this major transition, including Transition GPS (Goals, Plans, Success), which reflects the first major redesign of the interagency Transition Assistance Program in over 20 years. The Budget supports initiatives to ensure separating servicemembers have the skills needed to pursue employment after military service, providing pre-separation counseling and employment workshops and mandating compliance with a Career Readiness Standard before transition. In addition, the Budget provides targeted resources for Wounded Warriors in order to reduce disability evaluation processing time, ensuring that recovering servicemembers have active recovery plans and that those who transition to veteran status will have timely access to the benefits they deserve.

Proposes Additional Investments in Defense

The Budget's Opportunity, Growth, and Security Initiative provides $26.4 billion for DOD to accelerate modernization of key weapons systems, make faster progress toward restoring readiness lost under sequestration, and improve its facilities.

Accelerates Modernization of Key Weapons Systems. Consistent with the reductions in discretionary spending required by the Budget Control Act and the BBA, DOD has reduced or slowed down planned purchases of a variety of weapons systems and equipment over the last three Budgets. The Opportunity, Growth, and Security Initiative would allow DOD to accelerate the schedules for developing and buying new or upgraded systems in order to ensure that the United States maintains technological superiority over potential adversaries. For example, it provides enhanced resources for procurement of manned and unmanned aircraft, helicopters, ground vehicles, and communication systems. It also expands the research and development efforts that underpin all defense modernization programs.

Makes Faster Progress Toward Restoring Readiness Lost Under Sequestration. In 2013, significant reductions in funding degraded readiness throughout the Joint Force by requiring sharp cuts to training, maintenance, and support. For example, the Air Force had to ground 33 squadrons and reduce an additional seven squadrons to basic "takeoff and land" training for several months. Although the base budget provides the resources needed to continue gradually restoring readiness and balance, the Opportunity, Growth, and Security Initiative provides the resources to expedite progress by supporting increased activity at depot maintenance facilities around the country; greater training support; and increased funding for fuel, spare parts, and transportation costs.

Improves DOD Facilities. Sequestration required significant funding cuts for DOD facilities, forcing the Department to defer some sustainment, restoration, and modernization (SRM) costs, as well as some military construction projects. The base budget provides the funds necessary to keep DOD bases, housing, and other facilities safe, secure, and operational, but not enough to avoid long-term deterioration. The Opportunity, Growth, and Security Initiative provides additional resources for SRM and construction at hundreds of DOD installations that will generate jobs and reduce future costs to replace buildings, roads, runways, and other facilities.

NATIONAL INTELLIGENCE PROGRAM

Funding Highlights:

- Provides $45.6 billion in base discretionary funding for the National Intelligence Program to support national security goals and reflect a deliberative process to focus funding on the most critical capabilities. This includes:

  o Funding to continue integrating intelligence across the Government to help policy officials make decisions informed by the latest and most accurate intelligence available;

  o Countering the proliferation of weapons of mass destruction by strengthening collection capabilities;

  o Supporting military operations around the world by addressing both current and future needs;

  o Adapting to evolving cyberspace capabilities to help protect Federal networks, critical infrastructure, and America's economy, while improving the security of intelligence networks against intrusion and counterintelligence threats; and

  o Enhancing information sharing through expanded use of the IT cloud to facilitate greater efficiency and improved data security across the intelligence information environment.

Reforms:

- Supports the new presidential policy directive that governs signals intelligence collection and strengthens Executive Branch oversight of signals intelligence activities.

- Continues efforts to rightsize the workforce and to preserve critical current and future mission capabilities in the current fiscal environment.

- Reduces lower priority programs to enable investments in the most critical National Intelligence Program capabilities.

The National Intelligence Program (NIP) funds Intelligence Community (IC) activities in six Federal Departments, the Central Intelligence Agency, and the Office of the Director of National Intelligence. The IC provides intelligence collection, the analysis of that intelligence, and the responsive dissemination of intelligence to those who need it—including the President, the heads of Executive Departments, military forces, and law enforcement agencies. The IC's efforts play a critical role in protecting American citizens, safeguarding the U.S. economy, and fostering continued economic growth. The Budget advances the Administration's national security objectives and the National Intelligence Strategy, while protecting privacy and civil liberties and providing responsible management of taxpayer resources. The Budget represents a focused effort to address the most critical national security requirements while accepting and managing risk within a constrained fiscal environment. Savings are achieved by reducing personnel, eliminating legacy capabilities, scaling back operations on lower priority missions, and implementing new solutions for the delivery of information technology services. Reflecting the Administration's commitment to transparency and open government, the Budget continues the practice begun in the 2012 Budget of disclosing the President's aggregate funding request for the NIP. However, the details regarding the NIP budget remain classified, so the Budget highlights key NIP-funded activities but does not publicly disclose detailed funding requests for intelligence activities.

Advances National Security Goals

Integrates Intelligence. The Budget continues to support efforts to improve intelligence integration to more efficiently and effectively harness the strengths and capabilities across the IC. Through National Intelligence Managers and their associated Unifying Intelligence Strategies, the Director of National Intelligence has brought together the expertise to fulfill the goals of the National Security Strategy and the National Intelligence Strategy, as guided by the National Intelligence Priorities Framework. The IC is working to ensure that integrated intelligence information flows anywhere and anytime it is required by any authorized user, from the President to U.S. troops on the ground.

Continues Key Capabilities to Counter Weapons of Mass Destruction and Disrupt Terrorism. The IC enhances collection capabilities to prevent the proliferation of weapons of mass destruction. The IC continues to lead operations to defeat al Qaeda and other violent extremists, penetrate and analyze targets of interest, identify and disrupt counterintelligence threats, and provide strategic warning to policymakers on issues of geopolitical and economic concern. The Administration also remains committed to measuring performance to evaluate progress, ensure key intelligence gaps are closed, and create accountability for results across the entire NIP.

Supports the Military Services. The Budget supports the ability of the IC to play a key role in informing military strategy and decision-making. The IC provides situational awareness for military leaders, particularly as needed for force protection, targeting support, and other timely and actionable intelligence. Planners look to the IC for adversary plans, intentions, and capabilities. The Budget balances its focus between current, immediate needs for U.S. military forces engaged in operations with enduring intelligence requirements for potential future military and security needs.

Adapts to Evolving Cyberspace Operations. Cyber threats are constantly evolving and require a coordinated and comprehensive way of thinking about cyberspace activities. No U.S. sector, network, or system is immune from penetration by those who seek to make financial gain, to perpetrate malicious and disruptive activity, or to steal commercial or government secrets and property. The IC's goal is for relevant pieces of information to be available—to those with appropriate access—in order to connect the dots in identifying cybersecurity threats while protecting individual privacy and civil liberties.

Enhances Information Sharing While Safeguarding Intelligence Networks. The IC depends on robust information technology capabilities to support operations and information sharing and collaboration with authorized users. The Budget expands the use of common, secure, shared IT capabilities and services through the integrated cloud hosting environment, continues support for the protection of the critical networks that facilitate information sharing and operational requirements, and accelerates various information protection and access control mechanisms. The IC supports the Senior Information Sharing and Safeguarding Steering Committee, which the President established by Executive Order in 2011, to guide and prioritize Government-wide investments in classified networks and to support the Administration's National Strategy for Information Sharing and Safeguarding.

Makes Difficult Cuts and Reforms

Enhances Transparency and Reforms Signals Intelligence Programs. After a comprehensive review of signals intelligence programs, and in light of new and changing technologies, the President announced how the IC will use its signals intelligence capabilities in a way that protects national security while supporting foreign policy, respecting privacy and civil liberties, maintaining the public trust, and reducing the risk of unauthorized disclosures.

In addition, the President has issued a new policy directive for signals intelligence activities at home and abroad. This directive lays out new principles that govern how the IC conducts signals intelligence collection and strengthens Executive Branch oversight of signals intelligence activities. The Budget fully supports this new directive.

Rightsizes the Workforce. Recognizing the challenges of this fiscal environment, the IC continues to review its operational, investment, and infrastructure programs to identify efficiencies. The Budget reduces Government personnel levels, as supported by the Congress, with a continued aim to rightsize the workforce while focusing on sustaining the skills in the current IC workforce that have been developed over the past decade.

Achieves Savings Through Reducing Lower Priority Programs. The NIP budget reflects a deliberative process to ensure that the IC focuses on those programs that have the most significant return on investment and terminates or reduces those considered lower priority or underperforming. For example, the Budget continues the IC's migration to more efficient information technology and collection architectures that posture the IC for future capabilities.

DEPARTMENT OF EDUCATION

Funding Highlights:

- Provides $68.6 billion in discretionary funding for the Department of Education to build upon investments in preschool access, ongoing K-12 reforms, and efforts to make college an affordable and valuable investment for all Americans. Activities supported at the Department include:

  o Establishing a landmark Preschool for All initiative, to ensure that America's four-year-olds have access to a high-quality early education;

  o Introducing a new Race to the Top Equity and Opportunity competition centered on increasing the academic performance of high-need students and closing the achievement gap;

  o Supporting the ConnectED initiative that will connect 99 percent of American students to the digital age, by providing teachers the professional development and support they need to take full advantage of next-generation broadband and high-speed wireless networks in schools and libraries and provide high-quality instruction that prepares students for college and careers;

  o Investing in high school redesign, to create more innovative schools that personalize teaching and learning for students, prepare students early to succeed in college and careers, and expose them to the demands of our high-tech economy;

  o Making our schools safer through the President's Now Is the Time initiative to reduce gun violence and prevent future tragedies;

  o Maintaining investments in formula programs that support low-income and high-need students, including Title I Grants to Local Educational Agencies and Special Education Grants to States;

  o Investing in programs that are driving change on the ground for school-aged children such as Promise Neighborhoods, the Teacher Incentive Fund, Investing in Innovation, and School Improvement Grants;

  o Implementing the President's plan to make college more affordable and improve outcomes by supporting the development of a new college ratings system, spurring performance-based reforms at the State level, rewarding institutions that produce strong outcomes for Pell Grant recipients, and helping borrowers manage their student loan debt; and o   Supporting and testing innovative strategies and practices that improve college completion rates and make college more affordable, particularly for low-income students, through the First in the World fund, to help meet the goal of having the highest proportion of college graduates in the world by 2020.

Opportunity, Growth, and Security Initiative:

- Through the Opportunity, Growth, and Security Initiative, supports:

  o   Additional Preschool Development Grants to reach two-thirds of States by 2015, laying a stronger foundation for Preschool for All; and

  o   Additional funds to expand access to professional development to a total of 100,000 teachers in 500 districts to take greater advantage of the universal broadband provided through the ConnectED initiative; supporting 35 additional Promise Neighborhoods; and investing more intensively in high school redesign and closing the achievement gap through Race to the Top.

Reforms:

- Improves the impact of the Federal investment in science, technology, engineering, and mathematics (STEM) education by creating a fresh framework for delivering STEM education, supporting what works, and reducing fragmentation.

- Targets campus-based student aid programs so that funding goes to institutions that are effective in enrolling and graduating Pell Grant-eligible students and keeping their costs low.

Americans must be prepared with the skills and knowledge necessary to compete in the 21st Century economy. Expanding educational opportunities is critical to equipping all children with these skills and positioning them to succeed as adults. Under the leadership of the Department of Education (ED), the Administration has increased access to preschool, spurred sweeping reforms in K-12 education that are showing results, and made going to college an accessible dream for more Americans. For example, high school graduation rates have reached the highest level on record, and students are making gains in reading and math, especially in States that have undertaken reforms to raise standards, improve teacher effectiveness, and turn around low-performing schools. Pell Grants are larger than when the President took office and are currently helping nearly nine million students afford a college education. The Budget continues an emphasis on early education and on making college more affordable—investments that lead to a brighter future. In addition, the Budget builds on ongoing K-12 reforms with a new Race to the Top Equity and Opportunity competition that will help ensure all children have access to a high-quality education that helps them meet high academic standards. The Budget also includes new investments to help school districts prepare teachers for the digital age, and to redesign America's high schools to prepare students early for success in college and in high-demand careers.

Enhances Access to High-Quality Early Childhood Education

The President believes that all children should have access to a high-quality preschool education. Research has shown that supporting children at this stage of life leads to significant benefits in school and beyond. This is particularly true for low-income children, who often start kindergarten academically behind their peers by many months. Providing high-quality early childhood education to all children will enable them to start school ready to learn and realize their full potential. The Budget maintains support for the landmark 2014 Preschool for All proposal to ensure four-year-olds across the Nation have access to high-quality preschool programs. The proposal, financed through an increase in the tobacco tax, establishes a Federal-State partnership to provide all low- and moderate-income four-year-old children with high-quality preschool, while providing States with incentives to expand these programs to reach additional children from middle class families and put in place full-day kindergarten policies. To support this effort, the Budget also proposes to double the Department's current discretionary investment in preschool by funding Preschool Development Grants at $500 million in 2015. An additional $250 million would be provided through the Opportunity, Growth, and Security Initiative, for a total discretionary investment of $750 million. This would be sufficient funding to reach two-thirds of States by 2015, laying a stronger foundation for Preschool for All. These grants will ensure that States and localities willing to commit to expanding preschool access are able to make the critical investments necessary to support high-quality programs. The preschool initiative is coupled with companion investments in the Department of Health and Human Services (HHS) in voluntary home visiting and high-quality early care and education for infants and toddlers.

Targets the Achievement Gap Through a New Race to the Top Competition

As the 2013 report by the Equity and Excellence Commission made clear, the problem of inequitable opportunities for students in the Nation's highest poverty schools denies those students the quality education needed to compete successfully in the global economy and imposes a substantial economic cost on the Nation. The Budget acts on the findings in this report by proposing a new $300 million Race to the Top (RTT) Equity and Opportunity competition centered on closing the achievement gap. Additional resources would be provided through the Opportunity, Growth, and Security Initiative. The RTT initiative will link together State and local fiscal, student achievement, and human resource data systems, allowing them to work in concert to provide underserved students access to high-quality teachers and leaders, coursework, and other evidence-based supports. RTT Equity and Opportunity grants will reward tracking resources at the school level and using data, including return on investment metrics, to target intensive interventions to schools that most need the extra help. The initiative will also leverage resources from other Federal programs, such as Title I Grants and State Longitudinal Data Systems, which the Budget proposes to double in funding to $70 million. The Budget maintains significant investments in Title I Grants and Individuals with Disabilities Education Act (IDEA) Grants to States to ensure communities receive a critical base of support for their low-income and high-need students.

Supports Teachers and Helps Prepare Them for the Digital Age

The President has called on the Federal Communications Commission to take steps to connect 99 percent of American students to the digital age through next-generation broadband and high-speed wireless networks in their schools and libraries. The Budget proposes $200 million for a ConnectEDucators initiative to ensure that students receive the full benefit of this connectivity by providing professional development opportunities and high-quality digital instructional resources to teachers to help them make effective use of these new resources. The Opportunity, Growth, and Security Initiative would add $300 million to this initiative to provide a total of 100,000 teachers in 500 school districts across the United States with access to professional development in this area. In addition, the Budget proposes $5 billion in mandatory funds for RESPECT (Recognizing Educational Success, Professional Excellence, and Collaborative Teaching) grants to support teachers by improving preparation and early career assistance; helping teachers as they lead the transition to college- and career-ready standards; and ensuring that teachers have a supportive work environment.

Redesigns High Schools to Teach Real-World Skills

The President has called for a comprehensive effort to rethink the high school experience, challenging schools to scale up innovative models that personalize teaching and learning for students, so that they receive the rigorous and relevant education needed to graduate and transition into postsecondary learning and adulthood. The Budget provides $150 million for a new program to redesign high schools to focus on providing students with challenging, relevant learning experiences, and reward schools that build new partnerships with colleges, employers, and other partners to enhance instruction and to help develop the knowledge and skills students need for success in today's economy. Additional resources would be provided through the Opportunity, Growth, and Security Initiative.

Builds on High-Priority School Safety and STEM Initiatives

The Budget invests in the President's plan to reduce gun violence and increase school safety, building on efforts underway in 2014. The Budget provides $80 million to help schools create safer and more nurturing school climates through evidence-based behavioral intervention practices, provide support and services to children exposed to pervasive violence, collect data on school safety and climate, and disseminate best practices. This investment will continue the collaboration with the Department of Justice and HHS to support comprehensive school safety strategies and to increase access to mental health services.

The Budget proposes a fresh Government-wide reorganization of STEM education programs designed to enable more strategic investment in STEM education and more critical evaluation of outcomes. This proposal reduces fragmentation of STEM education programs across Government, and focuses efforts around the five key areas identified by the Federal STEM Education 5-Year Strategic Plan: P-12 instruction; undergraduate education; graduate education; broadening participation in STEM to women and minorities

traditionally underrepresented in these fields; and education activities that typically take place outside of the classroom. In line with the reorganization, the Budget provides $170 million to ED to lead a cohesive and robust initiative around transforming STEM teaching and learning and working toward the President's goal of recruiting, preparing, and retaining 100,000 effective STEM teachers over the next decade.

Advances K-12 Reforms Through Programs Showing Results

The Department of Education has focused its reforms on building evidence and improving outcomes. ED's most mature reforms are its signature K-12 initiatives—RTT, Investing in Innovation (i3), School Improvement Grants (SIG), Teacher Incentive Fund (TIF), and Promise Neighborhoods—which have contributed to a sea change in how schools across the Nation deliver education. The Budget continues to invest in these priority programs, the successes of which are now becoming apparent:

- States have made major reforms in their teacher and principal evaluation policies, supported by investments in TIF and RTT that will help identify, reward, and support effective teachers and principals;

- The i3 program is helping to uncover what works in education through rigorous evaluations of projects focused on supporting our educators in delivering effective instruction; ensuring successful implementation of high-quality standards and assessments; and improving our low-performing schools;

- By next year, nearly 40 percent of the Nation's 5,000 lowest achieving schools will be implementing turn-around strategies; early data indicate significant achievement gains in many of the SIG schools that outpace the national average;

- Forty-six States are implementing rigorous college- and career-ready academic standards and nearly all will field test performance-based assessments tied to those standards this spring, a movement fueled by previous RTT grants. The eight States that implemented college- and career-ready standards (as part of RTT) in time for the latest National Assessment of Educational Progress exams showed improvement from 2009 to 2013 in either reading or math scores, and large cities made even greater gains; and

- The President named the first five Promise Zones in January 2014, and 15 other communities will be created in the year ahead. In support of the goals of this initiative, the Budget requests $100 million to support current Promise Neighborhoods and create up to five more and the Opportunity, Growth, and Security Initiative adds $200 million to support another 35 awards.

Makes a High-Quality College Education More Affordable

The President has placed a high priority on making college affordable and helping Americans obtain a meaningful college degree. Beginning in 2009, the Administration has increased the maximum Pell Grant by $1,000, to $5,730 in school year 2014-15, and provided additional tax benefits to help families pay for college. The Administration ended the inefficient guaranteed student loan program, using those savings to fund the Pell Grant program, and has expanded the income-driven repayment options available to borrowers so they can manage their student loan debt. In addition, in 2013, ED introduced the College Scorecard to assist prospective students and their families when searching for and selecting a college, and the President announced the development of a college ratings system to identify schools providing the best value and encourage all institutions to improve student access, affordability, and outcomes. The Budget builds on this progress and charts a path forward on the President's plan to make college more affordable and provide a better bargain for the middle class.

Supports a New College Ratings System, Bonuses, and Pell Grant Reforms to Improve Performance and Outcomes in Higher Education. In August, the President directed ED to develop and publish a new college ratings system that will identify colleges that provide the best value to students and encourage all colleges to improve. The Budget supports the development and refinement of the ratings system through funding for data initiatives or other necessary projects. The Budget provides new College Opportunity and Graduation Bonuses to reward colleges for improving educational outcomes for low- and moderate-income students. In addition, the Administration will provide Pell Grant eligibility to students who are co-enrolled in adult and postsecondary education as part of a career pathway program to allow adults without a high school diploma to gain the knowledge and skills they need to secure a good job. The Administration will also strengthen academic progress requirements in the Pell Grant program to encourage students to complete their studies on time.

Promotes Innovation and Competition in Higher Education. There are many promising reforms at both the State and institutional levels that the Administration seeks to encourage. In particular, there is the potential for breakthroughs on cost and quality through State reforms—such as performance-based funding and strong alignment between the K-12, postsecondary, and workforce systems—and institutional innovations, such as accelerated degrees and competency-based education. The Federal Government can act as a catalyst for innovation by investing in promising policies and practices and challenging States and higher education institutions to offer students a greater range of affordable, high-quality options. The Budget increases investment in the First in the World fund to $100 million, which will support and test promising institutional innovations and practices that improve educational outcomes and make college more affordable for students and families.

The Budget also provides $75 million for College Success Grants to support sustainable strategies to reduce costs and improve student outcomes at Minority Serving Institutions. In addition, the Budget funds pilot and demonstration programs to test various approaches that improve student outcomes, supports post-secondary evaluation, and provides for more frequent data collection through the National Postsecondary Student Aid Survey. In adult education, the Administration is spurring innovation through the creation of model public-private partnerships to increase access to high-quality programs and improve participant outcomes. In addition, the Budget proposes a $4 billion mandatory fund to support States that are committed to investing in higher education and improving performance and outcomes at their public higher education institutions.

Ensures that Student Debt Remains Affordable. The Administration is helping student borrowers with existing debt manage their obligations through income-driven repayment plans such as Pay-As-You-Earn (PAYE) that cap student loan payments at 10 percent of discretionary income. ED has contacted struggling borrowers to make sure they are aware of these new options, and ensure that they have the information they need to choose the best plan for them. The Budget proposes to extend PAYE to all student borrowers and reform the PAYE terms to ensure that the program is well-targeted and provides a safeguard against rising tuition at high-cost institutions.

DEPARTMENT OF ENERGY

Funding Highlights:

- Provides $27.9 billion in discretionary funds for the Department of Energy that will: position the United States to compete as a world leader in clean energy and advanced manufacturing; enhance U.S. energy security; cut carbon pollution and respond to and prepare for the threat of climate change; and modernize the nuclear weapons stockpile and infrastructure. This includes:

    o Advancing the Administration's "all-of-the-above" energy strategy by investing $4.2 billion in the Department's discretionary applied energy programs to drive energy sector innovation;

    o Investing in energy productivity, manufacturing technologies, and advanced transportation to strengthen U.S. competitiveness and cut carbon pollution;

    o Maintaining the President's commitment to increase funding for key basic research agencies by providing more than $5 billion for the Office of Science to conduct basic research and invest in research infrastructure in areas such as foundational science for clean energy and fundamental physics;

    o Providing $2.3 billion for the Office of Energy Efficiency and Renewable Energy to build on the Administration's success in reducing U.S. dependence on fossil fuels, promoting energy efficiency, and doubling U.S. renewable electricity generation; and

    o Maintaining a safe, secure, and effective nuclear arsenal to deter adversaries and protect the Nation, while working to enhance national security through partnerships to detect, secure, and eliminate unnecessary nuclear and radiological material worldwide.

Opportunity, Growth, and Security Initiative:

- Through the Opportunity, Growth, and Security Initiative, supports:

    o Additional investments in clean energy to accelerate both research and the development and deployment of new technologies, including innovative new materials, processes, and system designs for sustainable vehicles and fuels, advanced manufacturing, solar and wind energy, and more efficient buildings;

    o A Race to the Top for Energy Efficiency and Grid Modernization that will provide incentives for States to modernize their electricity grids and reduce energy waste;

o Strengthened national resilience to the effects of climate change, including investments specifically for identifying and analyzing critical infrastructure vulnerabilities as well as funds for grants to support State and local level resilience planning; and

o Accelerated national security investments within the National Nuclear Security Administration, including facilities construction, deferred maintenance projects, and research and development to keep nuclear weapons safe, reliable, and effective.

Reforms:

- Achieves savings and efficiencies by eliminating $4 billion annually in fossil fuel subsidies, cutting low priority and low performing programs, and increasing utilization of existing facilities and infrastructure.

- Supports ongoing efforts to improve management and performance through the reorganization of the management structure and by supporting a more robust policy analysis process.

The Department of Energy (DOE) is charged with advancing the energy, environmental, and nuclear security of the United States, promoting scientific and technological innovation in support of those missions, and ensuring the environmental cleanup of the national nuclear weapons complex. It facilitates many of the President's highest priorities, including cutting carbon pollution, increasing climate preparedness, and supporting clean energy and innovation, which are critical to job creation, long-term economic growth, and national security. In total, the Budget provides $27.9 billion in discretionary funds for DOE to support its mission, a 2.6 percent increase over the 2014 enacted level. The Budget includes $11.7 billion for nuclear security, a four percent increase over the 2014 enacted level. In light of the current discretionary caps, these increases in funding are significant and a testament to the importance of clean energy and innovation to the Nation's economic future, and to the importance of nuclear security to the Nation's safety. While funding has increased in these critical areas, the Administration has identified areas for savings and efficiency, such as eliminating $4 billion annually in fossil fuel subsidies, cutting low priority and low performing programs, and increasing utilization of existing facilities and infrastructure.

Invests in Clean Energy, Innovation, and Jobs of the Future

Promotes Energy Innovation to Keep America Competitive, Respond to the Threat of Climate Change, and Empower Energy and Manufacturing Industries of Tomorrow. The Budget provides $2.3 billion for the Office of Energy Efficiency and Renewable Energy (EERE) to accelerate research and development (R&D), build on ongoing successes, increase the use of critical clean energy technologies, and reduce costs further. Within EERE, the Budget increases funding by 15 percent above 2014 enacted levels for sustainable vehicle and fuel technologies, by 39 percent for energy efficiency and advanced manufacturing activities, and by 16 percent for innovative renewable power projects such as those in the SunShot Initiative to make solar power directly price-competitive with other forms of electricity by 2020. The Budget provides funding within EERE to help State and local decision-makers develop policies and regulations that encourage greater deployment of renewable energy, energy efficiency technologies, and alternative fuel vehicles. The Budget also supports technical assistance to States and local communities to help ensure shale gas is developed in a safe, responsible way that helps build diverse and resilient regional economies that can withstand boom-and-bust cycles and can be leaders in building and deploying clean energy technologies. Within the Office of Electricity Delivery and Energy Reliability, the Budget also invests $180 million in R&D and other activities that will facilitate the transition from the current electricity delivery infrastructure to a Smart Grid. The Budget also provides $863 million for the Office of Nuclear Energy, which includes funding for R&D on advanced small modular reactors. The Budget provides $476 million for the Fossil Energy Research and Development program primarily dedicated to further lowering the costs of carbon capture and storage and advanced power systems, which are key elements of achieving the President's climate goals and the all-of-the-above energy strategy. In addition, the Budget requests $325 million for the Advanced Research Projects Agency–Energy, a program that seeks to fund transformative energy research, and over $900 million for basic clean energy research in the Office of Science.

The Opportunity, Growth, and Security Initiative accelerates research and the development and deployment of new, high impact clean energy technologies by providing an additional $484 million for activities leading to innovative materials, processes, and system designs; validation of new technologies; and increased Federal energy cost savings.

Invests in Energy Productivity and Advanced Transportation to Reduce Costs and Strengthen Domestic Manufacturing. The Budget supports progress toward the President's goal of cutting energy wasted by homes and businesses—doubling energy productivity by 2030. The Budget provides $227 million for the Weatherization Assistance Program to help tens of thousands of low-income families save hundreds of dollars a year on their energy bills by making their homes more energy efficient. DOE's Federal Energy Management Program will continue to assist agencies to improve the energy efficiency of Federal buildings by investing in both efficiency and new renewable

energy. The Budget invests in a national effort to develop and commercialize emerging energy-efficient and cross-cutting manufacturing technologies. As an integral part of this initiative, the Budget provides DOE with $305 million to expand efforts on innovative manufacturing processes, including Clean Energy Manufacturing Innovation Institutes as part of a larger national network of manufacturing innovation institutes. In addition, the Budget helps States and localities improve the integration and utilization of natural gas in manufacturing and transportation. Building on previous investments supporting U.S. electric and alternative-fuel vehicle development and manufacturing, the Budget provides $359 million in discretionary funding for DOE vehicle technology activities. These activities include the EV Everywhere initiative, a targeted effort to make electric-powered vehicles as affordable and convenient as gasoline-powered vehicles for the average American family within a decade, and support, through the Clean Cities program, to promote the adoption of alternative fuel vehicles. The Budget also promotes fuel supply diversification by providing $253 million at DOE to develop and demonstrate conversion technologies to produce advanced biofuels, such as "drop-in" replacements for gasoline, diesel, and jet fuel. In addition, the Budget invests $2 billion over the next 10 years from Federal oil and gas development revenue in a new Energy Security Trust that would provide a reliable stream of mandatory funding for R&D on cost-effective transportation alternatives utilizing cleaner fuels such as electricity, homegrown biofuels, renewable hydrogen, and domestically produced natural gas that reduce U.S. dependence on oil.

To further increase U.S. energy productivity, the Opportunity, Growth, and Security Initiative includes one-time funding for Race to the Top performance-based awards to support State governments that implement effective policies to cut energy waste and modernize the grid, and additional funds to strengthen national resilience to the effects of climate change, including investments for grants to support State and local level resilience planning.

Invests in Basic Research and Research Infrastructure to Keep America Competitive. To continue the cutting-edge R&D that is essential to U.S. innovation and economic competitiveness, the Budget provides over $5 billion to the Office of Science, which funds research grants and unique scientific facilities in multiple areas of science, including physics, biology, climate and environmental sciences, fusion, computational science, materials science, and chemistry.

Cuts Wasteful Spending and Improves Efficiency

Eliminates Unnecessary Fossil Fuel Subsidies. As the Nation continues to pursue clean energy technologies that will support future economic growth, it should not devote scarce resources to subsidizing the use of fossil fuels produced by some of the largest, most profitable companies in the world. That is why the Budget proposes to eliminate unnecessary fossil fuel subsidies that impede investment in clean energy sources and undermine efforts to address the threat of climate change. In total, the Budget would repeal over $4 billion per year in tax subsidies to oil, gas, and other fossil fuel producers.

Protects Americans from Nuclear Threats

Ensures a Safe, Secure, and Effective Nuclear Deterrent. The Budget proposes $8.3 billion for Weapons Activities, an increase of $533 million, or 6.9 percent above the 2014 enacted level, to maintain a safe, secure, and effective nuclear deterrent as described in the Administration's Nuclear Posture Review (NPR) of 2010. Building on last year's jointly conducted cooperative analysis and planning process, the National Nuclear Security Administration (NNSA) and the Department of Defense (DOD) agreed on a prioritized plan and associated budget to meet the key NPR goals within the fiscal constraints of the Bipartisan Budget Act. Key nuclear stockpile programs, like the W76 and B61 life extensions, are sustained.

The Budget continues to make investments in improving or replacing aging facilities; adding funds for tritium production and plutonium manufacturing and experimentation; and sustaining the existing stockpile by maintaining the underlying science, surveillance, and other support programs. These foundational capabilities provide the bedrock that supports a safe, secure, and effective nuclear deterrent, and enables the United States to continue its nuclear testing moratorium in place since 1992. The Budget reflects a concerted effort to reduce the impact of the current fiscal environment on these capabilities. The Uranium Processing Facility, which has experienced cost growth in the design, will apply lessons learned from the analysis of the Chemistry and Metallurgy Research Replacement-Nuclear Facility.

To accelerate modernization and maintenance of nuclear facilities, the Opportunity, Growth, and Security Initiative accelerates funding for infrastructure planning and improvements found in the Readiness in Technical Base and Facilities and the Site Stewardship programs. The Budget also includes funds to increase nuclear science and engineering research and development found in the Campaigns. The Budget also proposes $1.4 billion to fund naval reactors. This funding continues operational support to nuclear powered submarines and aircraft carriers, and development of the reactor for the replacement to the OHIO class ballistic missile submarine, and recapitalization of the program's 55-year old nuclear fuel infrastructure.

Reflecting a close partnership and shared commitment between NNSA and DOD to the Nation's defense, a portion of future funding for NNSA will continue to be included in DOD's outyear budget, providing allocations to NNSA in each budget year.

Prevents the Proliferation of Nuclear Material, Technologies, Facilities, and Expertise. The Budget proposes $1.6 billion to prevent the proliferation of nuclear materials, technologies, and expertise that can support the spread of nuclear weapons and nuclear terrorism.

This funding supports Administration priorities by securing and eliminating unnecessary proliferation-attractive nuclear and radiological material, developing and fielding technologies to deter or detect nuclear proliferation, and implementing international nonproliferation regulatory controls and working to strengthen international nuclear safeguards and security regimes.

The Opportunity, Growth, and Security Initiative would accelerate nonproliferation research and development and expand international scientific engagement.

Following a year-long review of the plutonium disposition program, the Budget provides funding to place the Mixed Oxide (MOX) Fuel Fabrication Facility in South Carolina into cold-standby. NNSA is evaluating alternative plutonium disposition technologies to MOX that will achieve a safe and secure solution more quickly and cost effectively. The Administration remains committed to the U.S.-Russia Plutonium Management and Disposition Agreement, and will work with its Russian partners to achieve the goals of the agreement in a mutually beneficial manner.

Protects the Public from Harmful Exposure to Radioactive Waste and Nuclear Materials at DOE Sites. The Budget includes $5.6 billion for the Environmental Management program to ensure that nuclear waste from the production of weapons during the Cold War is safely processed, secured, and disposed of in a timely manner. The program's cleanup actions include removing radioactive waste from underground storage tanks, decontaminating and decommissioning old production facilities, and remediating soil and groundwater.

Securing the Long-Term Disposal of Nuclear Waste

Supports the Administration's New Strategy for the Management and Disposal of Spent Nuclear Fuel and High-Level Radioactive Waste. The Administration released its *Strategy for the Management and Disposal of Used Nuclear Fuel and High Level Radioactive Waste* in January 2013 after determining that Yucca Mountain was not a workable solution for disposing of the Nation's spent nuclear fuel and high-level radioactive waste. Fundamentals of the Strategy include the creation of a well-defined consent-based facility siting process, implementation of interim storage in the near term, development of geologic disposal as a permanent solution, establishment of a new body to run the program, and an approach to make funds collected to support nuclear waste management more directly available for that purpose. The Strategy provides a framework for an integrated program for nuclear waste management and the Budget continues to lay the groundwork for full implementation, including sustainable funding mechanisms. The Budget provides $79 million for R&D and process development activities in the areas of transportation, storage, disposal, and consent-based siting.

DEPARTMENT OF HEALTH AND HUMAN SERVICES

Funding Highlights:

- Provides $77.1 billion in base discretionary resources for the Department of Health and Human Services to help make coverage affordable, drive down long-term health care costs, and improve care for millions of Americans, as well as to train new health care providers, address public health priorities, assist vulnerable populations, and support medical research. Activities supported at the Department include:

  o Supporting the Affordable Care Act's health insurance coverage improvements that are already providing coverage for millions of Americans through the operation of Health Insurance Marketplace and the delivery of subsidies to make coverage affordable;

  o Investing in a new initiative to improve access to high-quality health care providers and services;

  o Promoting innovative medical research by providing $30.2 billion for the National Institutes of Health, including increased resources for Alzheimer's disease research and its contribution to the BRAIN initiative;

  o Improving and expanding mental health services for youth and families through the President's Now is the Time initiative and targeted investments in the Medicaid program;

  o Strengthening national preparedness for naturally occurring and terrorist threats to public health through the development and acquisition of next generation medical countermeasures;

  o Investing in high-quality services for the Nation's youngest children, with increased funding for Early Head Start-Child Care Partnerships and additional funds to expand evidence-based, voluntary home visiting; and

  o Assisting vulnerable populations by investing in improving outcomes for children in foster care and supporting services for the victims of domestic violence and human trafficking.

Opportunity, Growth, and Security Initiative:

- Through the Opportunity, Growth, and Security Initiative, supports:

  o Preparing our children to succeed in life, by providing high-quality early learning opportunities to a total of more than 100,000 children through Early Head Start-Child Care

Partnerships, and supporting Head Start grantees who are expanding program duration and investing in teacher quality;

o Long-term public health improvements, including additional funding to increase biomedical research at the National Institutes of Health to improve the health of Americans and to promote economic growth through innovation, and accelerate the Department's advanced development of a universal flu vaccine; and

o Construction of two new Indian Health Service healthcare facilities to improve the health of American Indians and Alaska natives.

Reforms:

• Implements payment innovations and other reforms in Medicare and Medicaid and other Federal health programs that encourage high-quality and efficient delivery of health care, improve program integrity, and preserve the fundamental compact with seniors, individuals with disabilities, and low-income Americans. These improvements will save approximately $402 billion over the next decade.

The Department of Health and Human Services (HHS) is the principal Federal agency charged with protecting the health of all Americans and providing essential human services. The Budget includes $77.1 billion in discretionary funding to support HHS's mission, $0.8 billion below the 2014 enacted level. The Budget prioritizes core services and programs and makes targeted investments in training and support of health care providers, innovative biomedical research, food and drug safety, mental health services, health care for American Indians and Alaska natives, early childhood programs, and services for other vulnerable populations.

Improves Health Care Access, Research, and Quality of Services

Ensures Quality, Affordable Health Care by Implementing the Affordable Care Act. The Affordable Care Act ensures that every American has access to high-quality, affordable coverage, providing health insurance to millions of Americans who would otherwise be uninsured. The Health Insurance Marketplace provides millions of Americans and small businesses with "one stop shopping" for affordable, private coverage. The Affordable Care Act also provides premium tax credit and cost sharing assistance to make coverage affordable and increases Federal support to States expanding Medicaid coverage for newly eligible low-income adults. Efficiently and effectively implementing these coverage improvements is one of the Administration's highest priorities. The Budget provides resources to continue to support these efforts, including the operations of the Marketplace to help individuals enroll in the best health insurance coverage option available for themselves and their families.

The Affordable Care Act is also contributing significantly to putting the Nation back on a sustainable fiscal course, while laying the foundation for a higher-quality, more efficient health care system. The Congressional Budget Office has estimated that the Affordable Care Act will reduce the deficit by about $100 billion over the first decade and by more than $1 trillion in the second decade. At the same time, the Affordable Care Act is already delivering better care at lower cost. To help ensure the prudent use of Federal funds, the Budget includes $25 million over two years to monitor and prevent fraud, waste, and abuse in the Health Insurance Marketplace.

Trains New Health Care Providers and Improves Access to High-Quality Health Care Providers and Services. The Budget invests approximately $14.6 billion over 10 years to implement innovative policies to train new health care providers and ensure that the future health care workforce is prepared to deliver high-quality and efficient health care services. To encourage and enhance training of primary care practitioners, and other physicians in high-need specialties, the Budget proposes $5.23 billion over 10 years to support 13,000 new residents through a new competitive graduate medical education program that incentivizes high-quality physician training. In 2015, this new program includes $100 million in mandatory funding to support pediatric training in children's hospitals. To continue encouraging provider participation in Medicaid, the Budget extends increased payments for primary care services delivered by certain physicians by one year, through 2015, with modifications to expand provider eligibility to additional primary care providers and better target primary care services. The Budget also invests more than $3.9 billion over the next six years in the National Health Services Corps to place 15,000 health care providers in the areas of the Nation that need them most. Across the United States, 1,200 health centers operate nearly 9,200 primary care sites that serve as high-quality, dependable sources of primary care services in communities. In addition to the investments in provider training, the Budget invests $4.6 billion in the Health Centers program in 2015 and $8.1 billion in new resources over the following three years to support services for an estimated 31 million patients.

Improves and Expands Access to Mental Health Services. The Budget includes $164 million to support the President's Now is the Time initiative, to expand mental health treatment and prevention services across the Substance Abuse and Mental Health Services Administration and the Centers for Disease Control and Prevention (CDC). The Now is the Time initiative includes $55 million for Project AWARE (Advancing Wellness and Resilience in Education) to help

States and communities implement plans to keep schools safe and refer students with behavioral health challenges to the services they need, as well as to provide Mental Health First Aid training in schools and communities to equip adults who work with youth to detect signs of mental illness; $50 million to train 5,000 new mental health professionals to serve students and young adults; $20 million for Healthy Transitions to help support transitioning youth (ages 16-25) and their families in accessing and navigating behavioral health treatment systems; and $5 million to change the attitudes of Americans about behavioral health workforce needs.

The Budget also makes targeted improvements to the Medicaid program to increase access to mental health services, particularly for youth. The Budget establishes a new Medicaid demonstration project in partnership with the Administration for Children and Families to encourage States to provide evidence-based psychosocial interventions to children and youth in foster care. The goal is to reduce reliance on psychotropic medications, which are disproportionately prescribed to foster children, and improve outcomes for these young people. The Budget works to ensure Medicaid enrollees receive the most appropriate care, by improving access to mental health services in the community for youth in psychiatric residential treatment facilities and providing a pathway for certain individuals in eligible mental health facilities to receive home and community-based care services.

Improves Access to Health Care for American Indians and Alaska Natives (AI/AN). The Budget includes $4.6 billion for the Indian Health Service (IHS) to strengthen Federal, tribal, and urban programs that serve over two million AI/AN at over 650 facilities in 35 States. The Budget provides increased resources to purchase health care services outside of the Indian health system when services are not available at IHS-funded facilities. To increase access to health care services and improve the Indian health system, the Budget also funds construction of, and staffing at, new and replacement health clinics. The Budget fully funds tribal contract support costs. In addition, the Opportunity, Growth, and Security Initiative includes an additional $200 million for the construction of IHS healthcare facilities, which on average are 25 years older than other health care facilities.

Supports Biomedical Research at the National Institutes of Health (NIH). Biomedical research contributes to improving the health of the American people. The Budget includes $30.2 billion for NIH to support research at institutions across the United States, continuing the Administration's commitment to investment in Alzheimer's research and NIH's contribution to the multiagency BRAIN (Brain Research through Advancing Innovative Neurotechnologies) initiative. The Budget increases funding for innovative, high-risk high-reward research to help spur development of new therapeutics to treat diseases and disorders that affect millions of Americans, such as cancer and Alzheimer's disease. The Budget includes funding for a new advanced research program modeled after the cutting-edge Defense Advanced Research Projects Agency (DARPA) program at the Department of Defense. NIH will also implement new policies to improve transparency and reduce administrative costs. The Opportunity, Growth, and Security Initiative includes an additional $970 million for NIH, which would support about 650 additional new grants and further increase funding for the BRAIN and DARPA-inspired initiatives, and invest in other critical priorities.

Strengthens National Preparedness for All-Hazards, Including Naturally Occurring Threats and Intentional Attacks. The Budget includes $462 million to enhance the advanced development of next generation medical countermeasures against chemical, biological, radiological, and nuclear threats, including resources for the NIH Concept Acceleration Program, and the Food and Drug Administration's (FDA's) medical countermeasures regulatory science initiatives. The Budget also provides $415 million for the Project BioShield Special Reserve Fund, continuing the Government's long-term commitment to the acquisition of new medical countermeasures

against chemical, biological, nuclear and radiological threats. The Budget provides an additional $170 million to continue support for high-priority pandemic influenza activities. In addition, the Opportunity, Growth, and Security Initiative supports $50 million to enhance progress on pandemic influenza preparedness, including supporting clinical trials for promising universal flu vaccine candidates.

Expands Capacity to Detect, Prevent, and Respond to Infectious Diseases. The goal of the Global Health Security (GHS) Agenda is to reduce risks posed to the United States and global interests by emerging infectious diseases. The Budget increases CDC's GHS activities by $45 million to train epidemiologists and expand public health emergency management capacity and Global Disease Detection Centers in up to 10 countries. The Budget also invests $30 million for the Advanced Molecular Detection Initiative to identify the sources of emerging infectious diseases faster, determine whether microbes are resistant to antibiotics, and study how microbes are moving through a population. The Budget more than doubles CDC funding to combat antibiotic resistance.

Expands Access to HIV/AIDS Treatment, Care, and Prevention. The Budget expands access to HIV/AIDS prevention and treatment activities and supports the goals of the National HIV/AIDS Strategy and HIV Care Continuum Initiative to reduce HIV incidence, increase access to care and improve health outcomes for people living with HIV, and reduce HIV-related health disparities. The Budget invests $2.3 billion for the Ryan White HIV/AIDS Program and $1.1 billion for CDC HIV/AIDS, sexually transmitted diseases, tuberculosis, and hepatitis activities. The Budget also focuses HIV resources on implementing effective, scalable, and sustainable prevention strategies for persons living with HIV and populations at highest risk for HIV.

Strengthens the Safety of U.S. Food and Medicines. The Budget includes $2.6 billion in budget authority and $4.7 billion in total resources for the FDA. Within this total, the Budget invests $24 million in new resources to support food safety, and with new clarity provided by the Drug Quality and Security Act, $25 million to strengthen oversight of compounding pharmacies. These resources will support inspectors and the food industry by enhancing FDA's capacity with regard to produce commodities and processing operations. In addition, FDA will conduct routine and follow-up inspections of high-risk compounding pharmacies.

Improves Conditions for Vulnerable Populations

Continues Strong Support for High-Quality Early Childhood Programs. The Budget supports initiatives that will help every child reach his or her potential and strengthen the Nation's competitiveness. This includes $650 million in the base Budget and $800 million in the Opportunity, Growth, and Security Initiative for Early Head Start-Child Care Partnerships to provide access to high-quality infant and toddler care for more than 100,000 children, and additional resources in the Opportunity, Growth, and Security Initiative to support Head Start grantees who are expanding program duration and investing in teacher quality. Further, the Budget provides discretionary and mandatory resources for States to support higher-quality child care, and dedicates $200 million in discretionary funds to improve the quality of child care. In addition, the Budget invests $15 billion in mandatory funds over the next 10 years to extend and expand evidence-based, voluntary home visiting programs, which enable nurses, social workers, and other professionals to connect families to services and educational supports that improve a child's health, development, and ability to learn.

Promotes Responsible Fatherhood and Prevents Teen Pregnancy. The Budget proposes to modernize the Child Support Enforcement Program, which touches the lives of one-quarter of the Nation's children and helps secure contributions toward their financial and emotional well-being from non-custodial parents.

The Budget proposes to change current law to encourage non-custodial parents to take greater responsibility for their children while maintaining rigorous enforcement efforts. The Budget also continues funding for evidence-based models that prevent teenage pregnancy to build on the dramatic progress that has been made in this area.

Supports Victims of Domestic Violence and Human Trafficking. The Budget provides $140 million for shelters, supportive services, and a hotline for victims of domestic violence. The Budget also includes $10 million for an HHS initiative to prevent and address domestic human trafficking in addition to anti-trafficking efforts by the Departments of Justice and Homeland Security. This initiative will provide direct services to domestic victims of trafficking, train service providers, and invest in data collection, research, and evaluation.

Supports Work Opportunities for Low-Income Parents. The Budget proposes to redirect $602 million in annual Temporary Assistance for Needy Families funding to a Pathways to Jobs initiative, which will support State partnerships with employers to provide subsidized job opportunities for low-income individuals. This proved in recent years to be an effective strategy for getting disadvantaged adults back into the workforce, and the Budget proposes to build on that success.

Provides Targeted Energy Assistance to Low-Income Families. The Budget provides $2.8 billion for the Low Income Home Energy Assistance Program to help families with residential heating and cooling costs, including $200 million in contingency funds to address extreme weather conditions or short-term spikes in energy prices and $50 million for competitive grants to reduce energy burdens. The requested funding level represents a difficult decision in a challenging budget environment. The Administration will continue to invest in weatherization and energy efficiency to help cut costs for low-income households.

Improves the Way Federal Dollars are Spent and Strengthens Long-Term Viability of Current Programs

Improves Medicare's Sustainability by Encouraging High-Quality, Efficient Care. The Budget proposes a robust set of initiatives to strengthen Medicare by implementing payment innovations that encourage high-quality and efficient care, with enhancements to proposals addressing payments to skilled nursing facilities, Medicare Advantage plans, and program integrity. Structural changes that will encourage Medicare beneficiaries to seek high-value health care services are also included from last year's Budget. The Budget also retains a modified version of last year's proposal for income-related premiums. The revised proposal simplifies the prior proposal, but still improves the fiscal stability of the program by reducing the Federal subsidy of Medicare costs for those who need that subsidy the least. The Budget also includes new proposals that would build a stronger foundation for Medicare's future by expanding value-based purchasing, strengthening quality incentives and reducing the risk of prescription drug abuse in the Medicare Part D program. These Medicare proposals would extend the solvency of the Hospital Insurance trust fund by approximately five years.

Supports Permanent, Fiscally Responsible Reform to Medicare's Payments to Physicians. Medicare payments to physicians are determined under a formula, commonly referred to as the "sustainable growth rate" (SGR). This formula has called for reductions in physician payment rates since 2002, which the Congress has consistently overridden for over 10 years. Under the SGR, physician payment rates would be reduced by about 24 percent in April 2014. The Administration applauds the bipartisan reform efforts in the Congress and is committed to working with the Congress to continue progress toward reforming Medicare physician payments to provide predictable payments that incentivize quality and efficiency in a fiscally responsible way. As part of these ongoing reform efforts, the Administration supports a period of payment stability lasting several years to allow time for the continued development of scalable alternative payment models. After such a period of payment stability, the Administration supports incentives for providers to join such models, with a streamlined value-based purchasing program for providers who do not join. Such models should encourage integrated care where networks of providers work together to coordinate care and are rewarded for providing high-quality, efficient care. Successful care delivery models should engage seniors and individuals with disabilities in achieving this goal. Input from physicians and other professionals is important in designing these models as well. To complement these changes, the Administration also supports reforms to improve the accuracy of Medicare's current physician payment system.

Provides Tools to States to Improve Medicaid and the Children's Health Insurance Program (CHIP). Medicaid is critically important to providing health care coverage to the neediest Americans, and the Administration strongly supports State efforts to expand Medicaid with the increased Federal funding provided in the Affordable Care Act. The Budget strengthens Medicaid and CHIP by providing tools to States, territories, and the Federal Government to fight fraud, waste, and abuse, and make it easier for eligible children to get and maintain coverage. The Budget also includes other program improvements aimed at improving efficiency and effectiveness as States expand Medicaid. The Administration remains committed to providing affordable, comprehensive coverage for children covered by CHIP, and the Budget proposes to extend the CHIP performance bonus fund in anticipation of work with the Congress to ensure their coverage.

Cuts and Reforms the Community Services Block Grant (CSBG). CSBG provides funding for the important work of community action agencies, but the program's current structure does little to hold these agencies accountable for outcomes. The Budget provides $350 million for CSBG and proposes to competitively award funds to high-performing agencies that are most successful at meeting community needs.

Eliminates Duplicative Programs. The Budget makes room for new investments through a series of eliminations and reductions among programs, such as the Preventive Health and Health Services Block Grant (PHHSBG). The PHHSBG is duplicative with existing activities that could be more effectively implemented through targeted programs within CDC. In addition, the Budget proposes small, targeted reductions in select HHS direct health care programs (e.g., immunizations and cancer screenings) because these services are now financed and provided through expanded insurance coverage for those gaining new coverage.

DEPARTMENT OF HOMELAND SECURITY

Funding Highlights:

- Provides $38.2 billion in non-disaster, net discretionary budget authority for the Department of Homeland Security to protect the Nation from terrorist attacks, address critical capital needs, and carry out core homeland security functions such as transportation security, cybersecurity, disaster preparedness, and border security. This includes:

  o Funding for major asset acquisitions, such as completing construction of the National Bio- and Agro-Defense Facility, and resources to procure the Coast Guard's eighth National Security Cutter;

  o Supporting the EINSTEIN intrusion detection and prevention system and continuous diagnostics and mitigation, key Administration cybersecurity initiatives to address threats and vulnerabilities against Federal computer systems and networks;

  o Funding for programs that lead to job growth and expansion of the U.S. economy, including a historic 25,775 Customs and Border Protection officers resulting in faster processing and inspecting of passengers and cargo at U.S. ports of entry, as well as more seizures of illegal items, such as drugs, guns, and counterfeit goods;

  o Focusing resources for immigration detention of mandatory and priority individuals, such as violent criminals and those who pose a threat to national security, while expanding less costly alternatives to detention programs; and

  o Providing $6.8 billion for disaster relief, of which $6.4 billion is requested as a discretionary cap adjustment pursuant to the Budget Control Act.

Opportunity, Growth, and Security Initiative:

- Through the Opportunity, Growth, and Security Initiative, supports:

  o State and local investments in homeland security and emergency preparedness through a reformed National Preparedness Grant Program; and

  o Efforts to strengthen national resilience to the effects of climate change, including investments specifically for identifying and analyzing critical infrastructure vulnerabilities as well as funds for grants to support State and local level resilience planning and climate adaptation projects.

Reforms:

- Supports risk-based security initiatives at the Transportation Security Administration that enhance the efficiency of passenger screening operations, while improving the customer experience for the traveling public.

- Eliminates duplicative, stand-alone Federal Emergency Management Agency grant programs, consolidating them into a new homeland security grant program to better develop, sustain, and leverage core capabilities across the United States to support national preparedness.

The Department of Homeland Security's (DHS) mission is to ensure that America is safe, secure, and resilient against terrorism and other hazards. DHS has responsibility for leading all levels of government and working with the private sector to prepare for and respond to natural disasters and other threats, and for facilitating information sharing and collaborative planning between Federal, State, local, and tribal partners. DHS interacts with millions of people each day, from processing one million international arrivals at U.S. ports of entry, to screening approximately 1.8 million air passengers and their luggage, patrolling 3.4 million square miles of U.S. waterways, and naturalizing almost 3,100 new citizens. The Budget supports these priorities by including $38.2 billion for the Department and $6.8 billion for disaster relief.

Protects the Homeland

Continues Strong Support for Cybersecurity Initiatives. The Budget includes $549 million to support the EINSTEIN intrusion detection and prevention system and continuous diagnostics and mitigation, key Administration cybersecurity initiatives that work to identify and address threats and vulnerabilities against Federal computer systems and networks. These initiatives are conducted through the National Protection and Programs Directorate (NPPD), which protects Federal computer systems and networks from cyber attack, disruptions, and exploitations, strengthens State and local governments' cybersecurity capacity, and supports private sector efforts to protect critical infrastructures. The Budget also supports the design of a Federal Cyber Campus to co-locate key civilian cybersecurity agencies to promote a whole of government approach to cybersecurity incident response.

Sustains Essential Fire and Emergency Response Coverage. The Budget provides $1 billion in assistance to States and local governments for the retention, rehiring, and hiring of firefighters and emergency management personnel in 2015.

Sustains and Expands CBP Staffing Levels. The Budget proposes an historic level of 25,775 Customs and Border Protection (CBP) officers, including the 2,000 new CBP officers funded through 2014 appropriations as well as 2,000 additional officers through proposed increases to user fees. These officers will help CBP process increased travel and trade that flows through our air, land, and sea ports of entry. This investment is projected to add nearly 66,000 new jobs and $4 billion to the Gross Domestic Product, while helping to reduce wait times, and expediting the flow of trade and tourism. In addition, these officers will conduct 46,000 more seizures of illegal items, including potentially over $5.5 million in counterfeit and fraudulent goods, further protecting U.S. businesses.

Supports "Now Is the Time" by Strengthening Training and Public Awareness to Enforce Gun Safety Measures. To better protect American communities from gun related violence, the Budget includes $10 million in targeted investments at DHS. These funds will be used to train local law enforcement to respond to mass shooting events and for the DHS "If You See Something, Say Something" public awareness program, which helps individuals understand the need for community involvement in efforts to prevent gun violence.

Promotes Secure Long-Term Growth

Supports Individuals on the Path to Citizenship. The Budget includes $10 million to assist individuals on the pathway to naturalization and increases support for local programs that develop innovative techniques to improve citizenship education and naturalization preparation. Also, the Budget proposes directing $3 million in application fees toward establishing the United States Citizenship Foundation, a new public-private partnership to support citizenship and the integration into American communities.

Invests in Research and Development in Homeland Security. To continue progress in enhancing homeland security technology and developing state-of-the-art solutions for first responders, the Budget proposes $514 million for research and development activities. This funding will target opportunities in cybersecurity, explosives detection, nuclear detection, and chemical and biological detection. In addition, the Budget includes $300 million—the amount needed to leverage existing resources to initiate construction in 2015 of the National Bio- and Agro-Defense Facility—to study large animal zoonotic diseases and develop countermeasures to protect our citizens and agricultural economy from future threats.

Makes Smart Choices to Balance Priorities

Reinvests Savings from TSA Risk-Based Security. The Transportation Security Administration (TSA) Risk-Based Security initiatives, such as TSA Pre-Check, use information, intelligence, and technology to focus agency resources on high-risk passengers while streamlining security procedures for low-risk passengers. Currently over 35 percent of the traveling public enjoy expedited screening through TSA Pre-Check lanes or other Risk-Based Security programs. By moving away from a "one-size-fits-all" approach to passenger screening, TSA will improve the customer experience while enhancing the efficiency and effectiveness of its screening operations. In 2015, Risk-Based Security will yield over $100 million in staffing efficiencies for TSA. The Budget reinvests a portion of this savings to fund the tools and technology needed to support and expand these programs.

Streamlines and Restructures FEMA Grant Programs. First responders are at the forefront of addressing natural disasters and other threats. The Budget provides $2.2 billion for State, local, and tribal governments to hire, equip, and train first responders and build preparedness capabilities. To better target these funds, the Budget proposes eliminating duplicative, stand-alone grant programs, and consolidating them into the National Preparedness Grant Program. This initiative is designed to build, sustain, and leverage core capabilities as established in the National Preparedness Goal. The National Preparedness Grant Program will apply a comprehensive process that identifies and prioritizes deployable capabilities, ensures grantees put funding to work more quickly, and requires grantees to regularly report progress in the acquisition and development of these capabilities.

Aligns Immigration Detention and Alternatives to Detention Capabilities with Risk. To ensure the most cost effective use of Federal dollars, the Budget aligns Immigration and Customs Enforcement (ICE) capabilities with immigration enforcement priorities and policies so that mandatory and priority individuals, including violent criminals and those who pose a threat to national security, are kept in detention, while low-risk non-mandatory detainees are allowed to enroll in alternatives to detention programs, including electronic monitoring and supervision. As ICE continues to focus on mandatory and priority cases, it will work to reduce the time that removable aliens spend in detention custody. To achieve this goal, ICE will continue to work with the Department of Justice to expedite removal of convicted criminal aliens, reducing costly stays in immigration detention prior to deportation.

Keeps Capital Investment on Track. The Budget provides approximately $3 billion for major asset acquisitions planned in 2015. In addition to funding Coast Guard recapitalization priorities, including the eighth National Security Cutter, the Budget continues to procure new border surveillance technology and aircraft for CBP to improve the security of U. S. borders.

Enhances the Administration's Employment Eligibility Verification System, E-Verify. While repairing the Nation's broken immigration system will require congressional action, the Budget continues investments to streamline the current system while looking forward to comprehensive reform. To assist U.S. employers with maintaining a legal workforce, the Budget provides $124 million to support, expand, and enhance E-Verify. The Budget also funds an expanded administrative review process in E-Verify that will further empower employment-authorized individuals to ensure their government records are correct. Proposed funding bolsters the system's fraud prevention and detection capabilities, provides for additional customer service enhancements, and supports E-Verify's continued expansion. Over half a million employers are currently enrolled in E-Verify and the program continues to grow by approximately 1,500 new employers each week.

DEPARTMENT OF HOUSING AND URBAN DEVELOPMENT

Funding Highlights:

- Provides $46.7 billion for Department of Housing and Urban Development (HUD) programs, including funding to expand the number of rental assistance vouchers and increase homeless assistance for vulnerable families, as well as for targeted neighborhood investments to help revitalize high-poverty neighborhoods. This includes:

  o Funding rental housing assistance to support 4.5 million low-income families, including Housing Choice Vouchers for 2.2 million very low-income families;

  o Investing $2.4 billion for Homeless Assistance Grants to continue progress toward the Administration's goals of ending chronic homelessness and homelessness among veterans and families;

  o Expanding affordable housing for the elderly and persons with disabilities by providing $45 million to assist over 5,000 new households;

  o Investing $120 million to transform neighborhoods with distressed HUD-assisted housing and concentrated poverty into opportunity-rich, mixed-income neighborhoods through the Choice Neighborhoods program;

  o Investing $15 billion in the Project Rebuild program to help hardest hit communities reduce blight from foreclosed and abandoned homes and turn the corner to recovery;

  o Providing $1 billion to capitalize the Housing Trust Fund to expand the supply of housing targeted to extremely low-income families; and

  o Providing $650 million to address the housing needs of Native American Tribes and $332 million for the Housing Opportunities for Persons with AIDS program.

Opportunity, Growth, and Security Initiative:

- Through the Opportunity, Growth, and Security Initiative, supports:

  o An additional 7 to 10 Choice Neighborhood grants to revitalize distressed areas; and

  o Increased job training and financial incentives for a total of 50,000 households in public housing through Jobs-Plus, an evidence-based program that has been shown to boost annual incomes by $1,300 on average.

Reforms:

- Proposes a series of reforms to the Community Development Block Grant and HOME Investment Partnerships programs to improve administrative efficiency, drive regional coordination, and ultimately strengthen the long-term viability of the programs.

The Department of Housing and Urban Development's (HUD) mission is to create strong, sustainable, inclusive communities and help all Americans who need quality, affordable housing. To achieve this mission, HUD supports home ownership, access to affordable housing free from discrimination, and community development. HUD's work is critical to the Administration's efforts to strengthen communities, bolster the economy, and improve the quality of life for the American people. The Budget provides $46.7 billion for HUD programs to support these efforts, $1.2 billion above the 2014 enacted level. Funding is prioritized to protect vulnerable families and to revitalize neighborhoods with distressed HUD-assisted housing and concentrated poverty. At the same time, the Budget includes tough choices required by the constrained fiscal environment, including funding reductions to project-based rental assistance and community development, and some curtailment of the expansion of new construction of affordable housing.

Provides Housing Assistance to Vulnerable Families

Supports Affordable Rental Housing for 4.5 million Families. The Budget includes $20 billion for the Housing Choice Voucher program, $0.9 billion more than the 2014 enacted level, to help more than 2.2 million very low-income families afford decent housing in neighborhoods of their choice. This funding level not only supports all existing vouchers, but restores reductions in assisted housing units that resulted from the 2013 sequestration funding cut and provides an additional 40,000 new vouchers, including 10,000 for homeless veterans as discussed below. The Budget also includes $9.7 billion for the Project-Based Rental Assistance program to

maintain affordable rental housing for 1.2 million families. This amount is $0.2 billion below the 2014 enacted level, but sufficient to continue assistance to the same number of units currently subsidized. Further, the Budget provides $6.5 billion in operating and capital subsidies to preserve affordable public housing for 1.1 million families, an increase of $0.3 billion over the 2014 enacted level. An additional $10 million for the Rental Assistance Demonstration (RAD) will be targeted to public housing properties in high-poverty neighborhoods, including designated Promise Zones, where the Administration is also supporting comprehensive revitalization efforts. RAD leverages private financing to reduce backlogs of capital repairs and the Budget proposes to eliminate the cap on the number of units eligible for this demonstration.

Makes Progress on the Federal Strategic Plan to Prevent and End Homelessness. The Budget provides $2.4 billion for Homeless Assistance Grants, $0.3 billion above the 2014 enacted level. This funding supports new permanent supportive housing units and maintains over 330,000 HUD-funded beds that assist the homeless nationwide. In addition, under the Housing Choice Voucher program, the Budget proposes $75 million to expand assistance under the HUD-Veterans Affairs Supportive Housing (HUD-VASH) program to 10,000 homeless veterans. Supported by the collection of robust data and using best practices from across the Nation, this evidence-based investment will continue to make progress toward the President's homelessness goals, including providing the resources needed to end veterans homelessness by 2015 and to end chronic homelessness by 2016. Between 2010 and 2013, homelessness among veterans declined by 24 percent, and the total number of individuals experiencing chronic homelessness on a single night declined by 15.7 percent.

Invests in High-Poverty Communities

Transforms Distressed HUD-Assisted Housing and High-Poverty Neighborhoods. The Budget provides $120 million for Choice Neighborhoods to change neighborhoods of concentrated poverty into opportunity-rich, mixed-income neighborhoods. This funding level, $30 million above the 2014 enacted level, will be used to revitalize HUD-assisted housing and surrounding neighborhoods through partnerships between local governments, housing authorities, nonprofits, and for-profit developers. Preference for these funds will go to designated Promise Zones—high-poverty communities where the Federal Government is working with local leadership to invest and engage more intensely to create jobs, leverage private investment, increase economic activity, reduce violence, and expand educational opportunities. To further support Promise Zones, the Budget includes companion investments of $100 million in the Department of Education's Promise Neighborhoods program and $29.5 million in the Department of Justice's Byrne Criminal Justice Innovation Grants program, as well as tax incentives to promote investment, jobs, and economic growth. To help public housing residents increase their employment and earnings, the Budget also provides $25 million for the evidence-based Jobs-Plus program, a $10 million increase over the 2014 enacted level. Through Jobs-Plus, public housing residents receive on-site employment and training services, financial incentives that encourage work and "neighbor-to-neighbor" information-sharing about job openings, training, and other employment-related opportunities. Rigorous evaluations have found that this program improves employment outcomes for public housing residents who participate.

The Opportunity, Growth, and Security Initiative includes $125 million more for Jobs-Plus to increase employment opportunities for a total of 50,000 public housing residents. It also includes an additional $280 million for Choice Neighborhoods and $75 million for Integrated Planning and Investment Grants. These investments will help fully realize the President's vision for Promise Zones, and assist communities in developing comprehensive housing and transportation plans that help expand economic opportunity.

Helps Hardest Hit Communities Turn the Corner to Recovery

The Budget provides $15 billion for the Project Rebuild program. This funding builds on the proven success of the Neighborhood Stabilization Program by helping hardest hit communities address blight and rehabilitate homes in struggling neighborhoods. In addition to partnering with local governments, Project Rebuild funding will support new and existing community land banks, incentivize private investments in hardest hit communities, and fund job training programs to strengthen local workforce capacity. Collectively, these programs will stabilize neighborhoods and help the worst-affected communities turn the corner to recovery.

Supports the Housing Sector with Household Counseling

The Budget provides $60 million for the HUD Housing Counseling program, a $15 million increase over the 2014 enacted level. This funding increase recognizes the program's improved performance, including grant administration that is timelier and less burdensome on applicants. The Budget also includes $50 million for the National Foreclosure Mitigation Counseling program, which is administered by the Neighborhood Reinvestment Corporation, a federally-chartered non-profit organization.

The Budget includes a demonstration project for the Homeowners Armed With Knowledge project (HAWK) program. This program will test designs and incentives for combining Federal Housing Administration-insured mortgages with housing counseling to improve the availability and sustainability of homeownership for first-time homebuyers.

Makes Tough Choices, but Strengthens the Long-Term Viability of Block Grant Programs

The Budget provides $2.8 billion for the Community Development Block Grant program and $950 million for the HOME Investment Partnerships Program. These funding levels represent a total decrease of $280 million below the 2014 enacted level for these two programs. However, the Budget also proposes a series of reforms to improve the programs' performance by eliminating small grantees, thereby improving efficiency, driving regional coordination, and supporting grantees in making strategic, high-impact investments that address local community goals. To support affordable housing priorities, the Budget also proposes an investment of $1 billion in mandatory funding for the Housing Trust Fund to create approximately 16,000 affordable units for extremely low- and very low-income households.

DEPARTMENT OF THE INTERIOR

Funding Highlights:

- Provides $12 billion in discretionary funding for the Department of the Interior, reflecting ongoing commitments to protect critical national landscapes, responsibly manage energy development on Federal lands and waters, and support Federal trust responsibilities to Native American Tribes and communities. This includes:

  o Launching an historic effort to revitalize the Nation's parks for the next century in commemoration of the National Park Service Centennial;

  o Proposing a dedicated source of long-term funding—reaching $900 million in 2015—for Land and Water Conservation Fund programs to support land conservation and resource protection, in collaboration with Federal, State, and local partners;

  o Investing in the safety, reliability, and efficiency of America's water infrastructure and in conservation, reuse, and applied science to address the Nation's water supply challenges;

  o Supporting tribal priorities in Indian Country, including full funding for contract support costs and a new initiative to address high rates of poverty, substance abuse, and homelessness; and

  o Investing in science to support decision-making in managing natural resources and carrying out tribal trust responsibilities, including $889 million for research and development.

Opportunity, Growth, and Security Initiative:

- Through the Opportunity, Growth, and Security Initiative, supports:

  o Full support for the National Parks Centennial Initiative, which will create thousands of jobs over three years and make America an even more attractive destination for travel and tourism;

  o Additional resources for the Department, especially the U.S. Geological Survey, to conduct scientific monitoring, research, and analysis that advances priorities such as energy development, ecological restoration, and climate resilience;

  o Enhancements in the climate resilience of landscapes, water resources, and other infrastructure; and o   Economic development and educational investments in Indian Country to support tribal self-determination and nation-building.

Reforms:

- Supports a fundamental shift in wildfire funding to safeguard communities and ecosystems, improve the resilience of our Nation's forests and rangelands, and provide stable funding for wildfire suppression.

- Continues efforts to manage and promote the ecological sustainability and resilience of ecosystems on a landscape and watershed scale, such as the California Bay-Delta, the Everglades, the Great Lakes, Chesapeake Bay, and the Gulf Coast.

- Proposes oil and gas management reforms to generate $2.5 billion in savings over 10 years, building on the Administration's efforts to encourage diligent development of Federal energy resources while improving the return to taxpayers from royalty reforms.

- Reforms oversight of mining on Federal lands and reduces the environmental impacts of coal and hardrock mining by dedicating and prioritizing funds to reclaim abandoned mines.

The Department of the Interior's (DOI's) mission is to protect America's natural resources and cultural heritage, manage development of energy and mineral resources on Federal lands and waters, provide scientific and other information about the Nation's natural resources, manage and develop water infrastructure, and honor trust responsibilities to American Indians and Alaska Natives and commitments to Insular areas. In support of this mission, the Budget provides $12 billion for DOI, a three percent increase over the 2014 enacted level. The Budget continues the Administration's historic commitment to America's natural heritage by proposing mandatory funds for Land and Water Conservation Fund programs. This funding will provide the stability needed for agencies and States to make strategic, long-term investments in the Nation's natural infrastructure and outdoor economy to support jobs, preserve natural and cultural resources, bolster outdoor recreation opportunities, and protect wildlife. The Budget also includes legislative proposals that will save taxpayers more than $2.7 billion over the next 10 years, including reforms to fees, royalties, and other payments related to oil, gas, coal, and other mineral development on Federal lands and waters.

Promotes Economic Growth by Investing in Natural, Cultural, and Energy Resources

Creates Jobs Through Conservation and Recreation. The America's Great Outdoors (AGO) initiative supports Federal, State, local, and tribal conservation efforts, while reconnecting Americans, particularly young people, to the outdoors. Investments for AGO programs support conservation and outdoor recreation activities nationwide that create and maintain millions of jobs, generate hundreds of millions of dollars in tax revenue, and spur billions in total national economic activity. 2015 marks the 50th anniversary of the landmark Land and Water Conservation Fund (LWCF) Act, which authorizes the use of receipts from oil, gas, and other non-renewable resources to reinvest in conserving public lands. The Budget proposes full funding for LWCF programs in DOI and the Department of Agriculture (USDA). Starting in 2015, the Budget proposes to invest $900 million annually, equal to the amount of receipts deposited in the LWCF each year. In 2015, $575 million is proposed to conserve lands in or near national parks, refuges, forests, and other public lands, including collaborative LWCF funds for DOI and the USDA's Forest Service to jointly and strategically conserve the most critical landscapes. Other AGO programs include $325 million in grant programs that assist States, Tribes, local governments, landowners, private groups, and sportsmen in preserving wildlife habitat, wetlands, historic battlefields, regional parks, and the countless other sites that form the mosaic of the Nation's cultural and natural legacy.

Launches Historic Effort to Revitalize National Parks for the Next Century. For nearly 100 years, National Park Service (NPS) parks and historic sites have preserved and shared America's cultural and historical identity. These places represent America's unique history and draw tourists from across the United States and around the world. To help achieve the President's America's Great Outdoors goals, the Budget proposes to invest in an historic effort to upgrade and restore national parks, while engaging thousands of youth, veterans, and others and leveraging private donations to build a legacy for the second century of NPS. In particular, the Budget—including mandatory, discretionary, and Opportunity, Growth, and Security Initiative resources—will allow NPS to ensure that 1,700 (or 20 percent) of the highest priority park assets are restored to good condition. The effort creates thousands of jobs over three years, provides over 10,000 work and training opportunities to young people, and engages more than 265,000 volunteers in support of public lands.

Safeguards Communities and Ecosystems from Wildfire Damage. Fire is a natural occurrence that can be highly beneficial to landscapes when managed properly; however, population growth near forests and rangelands, past management practices, and a changing climate have increased wildfire risk and resulting costs. The Budget calls for a fundamental change in how wildfire suppression is funded to help reduce fire risk, manage landscapes more comprehensively and increase the resilience of the Nation's forests and rangelands and the communities that border them. The Budget supports congressional proposals to fund suppression of the most severe fire activity—including large fires that require emergency response, are near urban areas, or for abnormally active fire seasons—as extraordinary costs that are outside the discretionary spending caps. Importantly, because this funding would not allow the total amounts available under existing cap adjustments to grow, it would not increase overall discretionary spending.

This new approach for funding suppression of catastrophic fires better safeguards non-suppression programs from transfers that have diminished their effectiveness in proactively addressing threats to communities and landscapes. This proposal allows for enhanced capabilities in programs such as the Forest Service's Integrated Resource Restoration Program, the Collaborative Forest Landscape Restoration Program, and the Hazardous Fuels Program, as well as the Fuels Management and Resilient Landscapes programs in DOI. Since responsibility for improving community resilience to wildland rests with Federal, State, local, and tribal governments and homeowners, the Budget also targets funding for fuels management and certain State programs to communities that implement programs to reduce fire risk on non-Federal lands, including improved building standards for fire resiliency and defensible spaces.

Protects and Restores Water Resources and Infrastructure. The Budget invests in the safety, reliability, efficiency, and ecological sustainability of our water infrastructure, to ensure the continued delivery to millions of customers of water and power, which serves as a foundation for a healthy economy, especially in the arid Western United States. The Budget invests in implementation of Indian water rights settlements in support of Federal trust responsibilities to Tribes and in the protection and restoration of fragile aquatic ecosystems, such as California's Bay-Delta and the San Joaquin River, to ensure that such environmental treasures are available for future generations. These investments are made possible by limiting the study of new projects and construction of ongoing projects and emphasizing water reuse, recycling, and conservation programs, in partnership with States and others, over new construction.

Makes Public Lands Available for Clean Energy Infrastructure Projects. To enhance energy security and create green jobs in new industries, the Budget invests in core DOI renewable energy development programs, providing roughly $95 million to review and permit new renewable energy projects on Federal lands and waters. These funds will allow DOI to continue progress toward its goal of permitting 20 gigawatts of renewable energy capacity and related transmission infrastructure by 2020 as part of the President's Climate Action Plan.

Continues Support for Responsible Development of the Nation's Oil and Gas Resources. The Budget proposes $170 million and $205 million, respectively, to fund the Bureau of Ocean Energy Management and the Bureau of Safety and Environmental Enforcement, which share responsibility for overseeing development of oil and gas resources on the Outer Continental Shelf (OCS). The current OCS five-year leasing program will make more than 75 percent of estimated undiscovered technically recoverable oil and gas resources on the OCS available for development. Funding supports continued reforms to strengthen oversight of industry operations following the 2010 Deepwater Horizon oil spill, with an additional emphasis on ensuring the safe and responsible development of Arctic OCS resources.

The Budget also provides support for onshore energy permitting and oversight on Federal lands, with an 18 percent increase in discretionary and fee-based funding for the oil and gas program of the Bureau of Land Management (BLM), relative to the 2014 enacted level. Combined with an extended and reformed permitting pilot office authority and ongoing administrative efforts, these resources will facilitate improved responsiveness to permit requests while strengthening oversight and enforcement of industry operations. BLM's costs would be partially offset through new inspection fees totaling $48 million in 2015, requiring the onshore industry to bear a greater share of the cost of managing the program from which it benefits, just as the offshore industry currently does.

Strengthens Tribal Nations. The Administration strongly supports the principle of tribal self-determination and improved outcomes across Indian Country with a $34 million increase over the 2014 enacted level for the Bureau of Indian Affairs (BIA), and through implementation of the Executive Order establishing the White House Council on Native American Affairs. BIA fully funds contract support costs that Tribes incur from managing Federal programs. Recognizing the need to address high rates of poverty, substance abuse, and homelessness in Indian Country, the Administration proposes to implement a new initiative called the "Tiwahe" or Family Initiative. The Tiwahe Initiative would support an integrated approach to providing culturally-appropriate human services, with the goal of empowering Native American families through social programs, family stability, and strong tribal communities.

Fulfills Commitments to Insular Communities. The Administration supports fulfillment of the commitments made through the Compact of Free Association with the Government of the Republic of Palau, as agreed to in September 2010. The Budget proposes mandatory funding, as negotiated in the Compact of Free Association, to fund U.S. financial commitments, promote economic development and stability for Palau, ensure U.S. strategic security in the Pacific, and demonstrate U.S. resolve in honoring U.S. agreements to Insular communities.

Improves Oversight and Use of Federal Dollars

Reforms Federal Oil and Gas Management. The United States Treasury received over $13 billion in 2013 from fees, royalties, and other payments related to oil and gas development on Federal lands and waters. A number of recent studies by the Government Accountability Office and DOI's Inspector General have found that taxpayers could earn a better return through policy changes and more rigorous oversight. The Budget proposes a package of legislative reforms to bolster administrative actions to reform the management of DOI's onshore and offshore oil and gas programs, with a key focus on improving the return to taxpayers from the sale of these Federal resources and on improving transparency and oversight. Proposed statutory and administrative changes focus on advancing royalty reforms, encouraging diligent development of oil and gas leases, and improving revenue collection processes. Collectively, these reforms will generate roughly $2.5 billion in net revenue to the Treasury over 10 years. Many States will also benefit from higher Federal revenue sharing payments as a result of these reforms.

Reforms Mining Operations and Reduces the Environmental Impacts of Mining. In order to increase safety and minimize environmental impacts, the Budget proposes an abandoned mine lands (AML) fee on hardrock mining, with receipts used by States, Tribes, and Federal agencies to restore the most hazardous hardrock AML sites on both public and private lands. For non-Federal lands, each State and Tribe would select its own priority projects according to national criteria, similar to how coal AML funds are allocated.

Eliminates Wasteful Spending and Provides a Fair Return to Taxpayers from Mineral Development. The Budget proposes a number of other actions that eliminate wasteful spending and ensure taxpayers receive a fair return from mining on Federal lands. This includes charging a royalty on select hardrock minerals—such as silver, gold, and copper—and terminating unwarranted payments to coal producing States and Tribes that no longer need funds to clean up abandoned coal mines.

Increases Investments in Science to Support Decision-Making. The Budget provides strong support for basic and applied science, including $889 million for research and development, which is a seven percent increase over the 2014 enacted level. This funding supports scientific monitoring, research, and analysis to assist decision-making in natural resource and land management and in fulfilling the special trust responsibilities of DOI and other federally mandated programs. Specific activities include science needed to conduct energy permitting, ecosystem restoration and management, Earth observations—such as water and wildlife monitoring—and tribal natural resource management.

DEPARTMENT OF JUSTICE

Funding Highlights:

- Provides $27.4 billion in discretionary funding for the Department of Justice to fund core law enforcement needs, safe and secure prisons, and other Federal, State, and local programs. This includes:

  o Providing new resources in support of the Now is the Time initiative to ensure that those who are not eligible to purchase or possess guns are prevented from doing so;

  o Funding to enhance criminal history records information, improve required inspections of licensed firearms dealers, and continue the Comprehensive School Safety Program;

  o Continuing strong support for law enforcement components focused on national security, cyber security, and counter terrorism efforts and reducing illegal trafficking and violent and financial crimes;

  o Reducing the time it takes for the Department to respond to legal assistance requests from foreign partners and to help develop legally sufficient requests, thereby improving the Department's ability to support foreign partners in investigating and prosecuting criminals;

  o Investing in efforts to combat and respond to violent crimes against women; and

  o Improving reentry initiatives by expanding Second Chance Act programs and working to reduce recidivism rates by providing drug treatment, increasing alternatives to incarceration, and strengthening family and parental ties.

Opportunity, Growth, and Security Initiative:

- Through the Opportunity, Growth, and Security Initiative, supports:

  o Targeted investments in State and local justice assistance grants, including additional resources for the Comprehensive School Safety Program and a new youth investment initiative;

  o Additional resources for infrastructure and personnel at Federal prisons to speed-up the process of bringing on-line newly completed or acquired prisons; and

○ Additional funding for investigating and prosecuting the full spectrum of financial fraud, helping to protect investors, consumers, and taxpayers.

Reforms:

• Supports the Administration's Smart on Crime initiative by providing dedicated funding to the United States Attorneys for Prevention and Reentry Coordinators, while improving reentry initiatives by expanding Second Chance Act programs and reducing recidivism rates by expanding drug treatment.

• Ensures that Federal funds flow to evidence-based activities by making additional resources available for alternatives to incarceration, gun safety initiatives, police hiring, and other initiatives to improve the targeting and effectiveness of grant assistance.

The Department of Justice (DOJ) is responsible for enforcing laws and defending the interests of the United States, protecting the public against foreign and domestic threats, providing Federal leadership in preventing and controlling crime, punishing those guilty of unlawful behavior, and ensuring the fair and impartial administration of justice for all Americans. The Budget supports these commitments and continues the progress that has been made in key areas.

The Budget provides $27.4 billion for DOJ in 2015, $122 million above the 2014 enacted level. In addition, the Opportunity, Growth, and Security Initiative includes funding for targeted investments for State and local justice assistance grants, including the Comprehensive School Safety Program, the Community Oriented Policing Services (COPS) Hiring Program, and a new youth investment initiative that will encourage State efforts to increase the availability of alternatives to incarceration, re-enroll youth into school after confinement, and reduce ethnic and racial disparities in the juvenile justice system. The Opportunity, Growth, and Security Initiative also provides additional resources for the Bureau of Prisons for infrastructure and personnel to continue the process of bringing on-line newly completed or acquired prisons, thereby reducing prison overcrowding, and for improved capacity for financial fraud enforcement at the Department, including hiring additional criminal prosecutors, civil litigators, investigators, and forensic accountants.

Enforces Laws and Protects U.S. Interests

Supports Now is the Time by Improving Law Enforcement's Ability to Implement and Enforce Gun Safety Measures. To protect American communities from gun-related violence and mass shootings, $182 million is provided to DOJ to help Federal, State, and local law enforcement continue to combat gun violence. These funds will support additional background checks, allow for continued focus on inspections of federally-licensed firearms dealers, improve tracing and ballistics analysis, and keep guns out of the hands of dangerous criminals and other prohibited persons. Of this amount, $13 million is provided to the FBI for investment in the National Instant Criminal Background Check System.

Promotes Cybersecurity Initiatives. Cyber threats are constantly evolving and require a coordinated and comprehensive plan for protection and response. The Budget identifies and promotes cross-agency cybersecurity initiatives and priorities, including improving cybersecurity information sharing while protecting individual privacy and civil liberties and enhancing State and local capacity to respond to cyber incidents. The Budget also supports the design of a Federal Cyber Campus to co-locate key civilian cybersecurity agencies to promote a whole-of-Government approach to cybersecurity incident response.

Preserves the Integrity of Digital Communications and Accelerates Legal Assistance. In order to better assist foreign government partners with investigating and prosecuting criminals, the Budget provides an additional $24 million to implement a strategy to reduce the current backlog of Mutual Legal Assistance Treaty requests, cut overall response times in half by the end of 2015, and process requests in a matter of weeks.

Maintains Safe and Secure Prison Capacity. The Budget proposes $8.4 billion for Federal prisons and detention facilities. These funds are provided to maintain secure, controlled detention and prison facilities and to continue bringing newly completed, or acquired, prisons online to protect public safety by alleviating prison overcrowding. Further, the Budget includes resources to support implementation of the Prison Rape Elimination Act in Federal, State, and local prisons and jails and to help inmates successfully transition back into the community.

Combats Financial Fraud, Promotes Innovation, and Protects Civil Rights. Ensuring honest and fair competition and protecting the rights and property of citizens are paramount to the economy and American competitiveness. The Budget maintains support to investigate and prosecute financial and mortgage fraud, and counter intellectual property crimes. In addition, the Budget proposes enhancements to ensure the protection of civil rights, including enforcing Federal prohibitions against racial and ethnic discrimination.

Improves the Way Federal Dollars are Spent

Supports the Smart on Crime Initiative and Enhances Reentry and Recidivism Initiatives. In August of last year, the Attorney General introduced the Smart on Crime initiative, which is designed to promote fundamental reforms to the criminal justice system that will improve public safety, save money, and ensure the fair enforcement of Federal laws. The Budget strongly supports the Smart on Crime

initiative, including $15 million for prisoner reentry programs and for Prevention and Reentry Coordinators in United States Attorneys' offices. The Budget also supports assisting inmates with reentering society and reducing the population of individuals who return to prison after being released, including $15 million for the Bureau of Prisons to expand the Residential Drug Abuse Program at the Federal level and $14 million in the Office of Justice Programs to expand the Residential Substance Abuse Treatment program at the State and local level. In addition, through State and local assistance programs, the Budget provides $115 million for the Second Chance Act Grant program to reduce recidivism and help ex-offenders return to productive lives.

Addresses the Immigration Case Backlog. To help increase efficiency in the immigration courts, the Budget provides enhancements to the Executive Office for Immigration Review to add 35 new immigration judge teams, expand the successful Legal Orientation Program, and establish a pilot program to implement additional efficiencies in the immigration court system.

Supports Program Evaluation and Policy Analysis. Evidence and rigorous evaluation of budget, management, and policy decisions are essential to ensuring that Americans are receiving the maximum value for each Federal dollar spent. The Budget invests $1.7 million to develop new multidisciplinary program evaluation and policy analysis capability within the Department. The objective is to strengthen analysis of the potential impact of policy options and then track and monitor implementation of policy decisions.

Invests in State and Local Public Safety Initiatives that Work

Expands Gun Safety Initiatives and Works to Prevent Mass Casualty Violence. The Budget includes $147 million to help State and local governments continue implementing the Administration's proposals for increasing firearms safety and supporting programs that help keep communities safe from mass casualty violence. Included in these initiatives are $75 million for the Comprehensive School Safety Program, $55 million in grants to improve the submission of State criminal and mental health records to the National Instant Criminal Background Check System, $15 million to improve police officer safety, and $2 million to develop better gun safety mechanisms to prevent the use of firearms by unauthorized users.

Renews Efforts to Promote Juvenile Justice and Fight Youth Violence. The Budget proposes $299 million for the Department's Juvenile Justice Programs and includes evidence-based investments to prevent youth violence. This includes $18 million to fund the Community-Based Violence Prevention Initiative and $4 million for the National Forum on Youth Violence Prevention. Further, the Budget makes available $23 million for research and pilot projects focused on developing appropriate responses for youth exposed to violence.

Continues Efforts to Combat Violence Against Women. The Budget provides $423 million to reinforce efforts to combat and respond to violent crimes against women. This includes $193 million for Services, Training, Officers, and Prosecutors (STOP) Grants to Combat Violence Against Women, $27 million for the Sexual Assault Services Program, and $11 million to reduce violent crimes against women on campuses. The Budget also provides $35 million for a new grant for communities to develop plans to address their untested sexual assault kits at law enforcement agencies or those backlogged at crime labs. These grants play a critical role in helping to create a coordinated community response to this problem. As a result of prior investments in this area, civil and criminal justice systems are more responsive to victims, and crimes of violence committed against women have declined in recent years. Even so, reducing such violence and meeting the needs of the almost 1.3 million women victimized by rape and sexual assault annually, and the nearly seven million victims of intimate partner violence each year, remains a critical priority.

Promotes Community Policing. The Budget includes $274 million to support evidence-based community policing in the Nation's local law enforcement agencies. Of the amount provided, $247 million is for the hiring and retention of approximately 1,300 police officers and sheriffs' deputies across the United States. To help ensure the safety and security of tribal partners, $35 million of the total is set aside for Tribal Law Enforcement.

Promotes Fair and Equal Treatment in the Justice System. The Budget invests in several programs to promote access to justice and to build community trust, including $24 million for indigent defense and civil legal aid initiatives and $9 million to establish a National Center for Building Community Trust and Justice, which will promote procedural fairness in policing, use deterrence strategies to reduce crime, and encourage police departments to track the quality of their interactions with the public.

Prioritizes Evidence-Based Practices that Work at the State and Local Level. The Budget bolsters the Administration's efforts to ensure that more Federal grant funding flows to evidence-based activities that work in State and local criminal justice. The Budget increases set-asides for research, evaluation, and statistics; couples the formula Byrne Justice Assistance Grant and Juvenile Accountability Block Grant programs with competitive incentive grants that provide "bonus" funds to States and localities that adopt evidence-based practices, strategies, and programming that incorporate outcome driven performance measures; expands the Pay for Success initiative, which leverages philanthropic and private dollars to fund services up front, with the Government paying after they generate results; adopts a more evidence-based, data-driven use of competitive grant funds; and invests in the expansion of *CrimeSolutions.gov*, a "what works" clearinghouse for best practices in criminal justice, juvenile justice, and crime victim services.

DEPARTMENT OF LABOR

Funding Highlights:

- Provides $11.8 billion in discretionary funding for the Department of Labor by making targeted investments to improve job training and employment programs; strengthen enforcement of laws that protect workers' wages and working conditions; ensure a strong safety net for workers who lose their jobs or are hurt on the job; and promote a secure retirement for workers at the end of their careers. Activities supported at the Department include:

  o Raising the minimum wage so that hard-working Americans can earn wages that allow them to support their families and make ends meet;

  o Ensuring that Americans have the help and support they need to develop their skills and secure good jobs;

  o Building on proven strategies by providing increased funding for in-person reemployment services to reach unemployed workers who are most at risk of exhausting their benefits and all recently separated veterans;

  o Increasing support for agencies that protect workers' wages and overtime pay, benefits, health and safety, and investing in preventing and detecting the misclassification of employees as independent contractors; and

  o Assisting Americans who need to take time off from work to care for a child or other family member by helping States launch paid leave programs.

Opportunity, Growth, and Security Initiative:

- Through the Opportunity, Growth, and Security Initiative, supports:

  o Investment in a Community College Job-Driven Training Fund, which includes grants that would support doubling the number of apprenticeships in America over the next five years;

  o Increased innovation and performance incentives in the workforce system and additional resources targeted to populations that face significant barriers to employment; and

  o Additional funding to help more States launch paid leave programs.

Reforms:

- Promotes innovative, job-driven approaches to training and employment services and higher performance through the Workforce Innovation Fund and improved Incentive Grants, so American workers can gain the skills to find good jobs and employers can find the workers they need.

- Creates a single program to help all displaced workers as part of a larger effort to modernize the Federal job training system.

- Safeguards workers' pensions by encouraging companies to fully fund their employees' promised benefits and assuring the long-term solvency of the Pension Benefit Guaranty Corporation.

- Strengthens the Unemployment Insurance safety net by supporting work-based reforms, encouraging States to fully fund their Unemployment Insurance systems, and reducing improper payments.

The Department of Labor (DOL) is charged with promoting the welfare of American workers, job seekers, and retirees, a mission critical to America's continued economic recovery and long-term competitiveness. To support this mission, the Budget provides more than $11.8 billion in discretionary funding for DOL. This funding level, coupled with new dedicated mandatory funds, allows for substantial investments in American workers as well as significant reforms to help workers acquire skills, regain their footing after a job loss, and find new employment opportunities. The Budget also makes investments to bolster the enforcement of critical wage and hour, whistleblower, and worker safety laws.

Invests in a Competitive Workforce

Promotes Innovative, Job-Driven Approaches to Training and Employment Services. As the economy changes, training and employment programs must continually innovate and improve to make the most of constrained resources and help American workers gain the skills to find good jobs and move up the career ladder. The Administration believes that government should be doing everything it can to make it easier for people who need help finding a job, or

build their skills for a better one, and for employers who need help finding qualified workers.

- *Invests in Training and Employment Services.* The Budget invests more than $3 billion in formula grants to States and localities to provide training and employment services to more than 20 million Americans at 2,500 American Job Centers across the country. The Opportunity, Growth, and Security Initiative would add another $750 million to restore prior cuts to these grants; increase the investment in innovation, evidence-based practices, and performance in the workforce system; and provide additional funding for programs that serve populations with significant barriers to employment, including Native Americans, ex-offenders, and people with disabilities. This would complement the Budget's new investments through the Social Security Administration in the development of innovative strategies to help people with disabilities remain in the workforce, in partnership with other Federal agencies.

- *Creates New Pathways to Jobs and Careers.* The Budget proposes to include in the Opportunity, Growth, and Security Initiative

$1.5 billion in 2015 to support a four-year, $6 billion Community College Job-Driven Training Fund, which will offer competitive grants to partnerships of community colleges, public and nonprofit training entities, industry groups, and employers to launch new training programs and apprenticeships that will prepare participants for in-demand jobs and careers. The fund will also help to create common credentials and skill assessments to allow employers to more easily identify and hire qualified candidates. Of each year's funding, $500 million will be set aside for grants to States and regional consortia to create new apprenticeships and increase participation in existing apprenticeship programs. This four-year investment will support doubling the number of apprenticeships in America over the next five years. The Budget also invests $2.5 billion in mandatory funding for Summer Jobs Plus, which will fund summer and year-round job opportunities for 600,000 youth as well as innovation grants aimed at improving skills and career options for disadvantaged youth.

- *Drives Better Performance and Innovation.* The Budget invests an amount equal to five percent of the Workforce Investment Act (WIA) formula grants in driving innovation and performance at the State and local level through: $60 million in the Workforce Innovation Fund to support innovative State and regional approaches to service delivery; and $80 million for improved Incentive Grants to reward States that succeed through their WIA programs in serving workers with the greatest barriers to employment. Combined, these funds will fuel innovative approaches to workforce system service delivery and incentivize better program coordination to serve those who need the most help to find high-quality jobs.

- *Streamlines the Delivery of Training.* Today more than 40 Federal programs across the Government deliver job training and related employment services. The Administration is exploring opportunities to streamline access,

more fully engage employers to ensure that training is well matched to jobs, and improve efficiency and employment outcomes. For example, the Budget proposes a New Career Pathways program that will reach as many as one million workers a year with a set of core services, combining the best elements of two existing programs—Trade Adjustment Assistance for Workers and WIA Dislocated Workers. The Administration is proposing strong accountability for outcomes and ensuring that the needs of all job-seekers and workers, including those with barriers to employment, continue to be met.

Reconnects Unemployed Workers to Jobs. As the Nation works to strengthen and rebuild the economy from the worst economic downturn since the Great Depression, it is critical to provide a helping hand and a path back to work for those whose lives have been disrupted by unemployment. The Budget makes an investment of $158 million in reemployment and eligibility assessments and reemployment services, an evidence-based approach to speed the return to work of Unemployment Insurance (UI) beneficiaries. This investment will reach those who are most likely to exhaust their UI benefits, as well as all recently separated veterans transitioning to civilian jobs. The Budget also provides $2 billion in mandatory funding to encourage States to adopt Bridge to Work programs, which would allow individuals to continue receiving their weekly UI check while participating in a short-term work placement and support other strategies for getting UI claimants back to work more quickly. In addition, the Budget provides $4 billion in mandatory funding to support partnerships between businesses and education and training providers to train approximately one million long-term unemployed workers for new jobs. Beyond these investments, the Administration supports extension of emergency unemployment benefits for the long-term unemployed. If not extended, 3.6 million additional people are estimated to lose access to extended UI benefits by the end of the year, despite remaining unemployed and looking for work.

Provides Security for American Workers and Retirees

Maintains Strong Support for Worker Protections. The Budget includes nearly $1.8 billion for DOL's worker protection agencies, putting them on sound footing to meet their responsibilities to protect the health, safety, wages, working conditions, and retirement security of American workers.

- *Supports Raising the Minimum Wage.* In a nation as wealthy as the United States, far too many full-time workers are living below the poverty line. Over the past 30 years, modest minimum wage increases have not kept pace with the higher costs of basic necessities for working families. The Administration supports raising the minimum wage so that hard-working Americans can earn wages that allow them to support their families and make ends meet. Many companies, from small businesses to large corporations, also see higher wages as the right way to boost productivity, reduce turnover, and increase profits. Raising the minimum wage is good for workers, their families, and for the economy. The Administration is ready to work with the Congress to pass legislation to increase the minimum wage as soon as possible. The President took an important step in this effort by signing an Executive Order to increase the minimum wage to $10.10 for those working on new and replacement Federal service, construction, and concession contracts.

- *Ensures that Workers Get the Pay and Overtime They Have Earned.* The Budget provides an increase of more than $41 million for DOL's Wage and Hour Division (WHD) to increase enforcement of the laws that ensure that workers receive appropriate wages and overtime pay, as well as the right to take job-protected leave for family and medical purposes. WHD will be able to hire 300 new investigators across the United States to help in this effort, and use risk-based approaches

to target the industries and employers most likely to break the law.

- *Enhances Worker Safety and Protections for Whistleblowers.* The Budget provides $565 million for the Occupational Safety and Health Administration (OSHA), allowing OSHA to inspect hazardous workplaces and work with employers to help them understand and comply with safety and health regulations. The Budget includes an additional $4 million to bolster OSHA's enforcement of the 21 whistleblower laws that protect workers and others who are retaliated against for reporting unsafe and unscrupulous practices.

- *Detects and Deters the Misclassification of Workers as Independent Contractors.* When employees are misclassified as independent contractors, they are deprived of the benefits and protections to which they are legally entitled, such as minimum wage, overtime, unemployment insurance, and anti-discrimination protections. Misclassification also unfairly disadvantages businesses who comply with the law and costs taxpayers money in lost funds for the United States Treasury, and in Social Security, Medicare, the Unemployment Trust Fund, and State programs. The Budget includes nearly $14 million to combat misclassification, including $10 million for grants to States to identify misclassification and recover unpaid taxes and $4 million for personnel at WHD to investigate misclassification.

Encourages State Paid Leave Initiatives. Too many American workers must make the painful choice between the care of their families and a paycheck they desperately need. While the Family and Medical Leave Act allows many workers to take job-protected unpaid time off, millions of families cannot afford to use unpaid leave. A handful of States have enacted policies to offer paid leave, but more States should have the chance to follow their example. The Budget supports a $5 million State Paid Leave Fund to provide technical assistance and support to States that are considering paid leave programs. The Opportunity, Growth, and Security Initiative provides an additional $100 million in support of this effort.

Strengthens the Pension Benefit Guaranty Corporation to Protect Worker Pensions. The Pension Benefit Guaranty Corporation (PBGC) acts as a backstop to insure pension payments for workers whose companies have failed. PBGC's single employer program covers plans that are normally sponsored by an individual company; the multiemployer program covers plans set up by collectively bargained agreements involving more than one unrelated employer. Both programs are underfunded, and PBGC's combined liabilities exceeded its assets by more than $36 billion at the end of 2013.

The Congress has raised premiums twice since 2012, but rates remain much lower than what a private financial institution would charge for insuring the same risk. Although PBGC will be able to pay benefits for years to come, it is still projected to be unable to meet its long-term obligations under current law. Any further premium increases need to be carefully crafted to avoid worsening PBGC's financial condition and harming workers' retirement security by driving healthy plans that pose little risk of presenting a claim to PBGC out of the system.

To address these concerns, the Budget proposes to give the PBGC Board the authority to adjust premiums in both the single employer and multiemployer programs and directs PBGC to take into account the risks that different sponsors pose. In the multiemployer program, these premium increases are crucial to improving solvency but will not be sufficient to address the complex challenges facing these plans. The Administration looks forward to working with the Congress to develop a more comprehensive solution. This proposal is estimated to save $20 billion over the next decade.

Strengthens the UI Safety Net and Improves Program Integrity. The combination of chronically underfunded reserves and the economic downturn has placed a considerable financial strain on States' UI operations. Currently, 16 States owe more than $21 billion to the Federal UI trust fund. As a result, employers in those States are now facing automatic Federal tax increases, and many States have little prospect of paying these loans back in the foreseeable future. At the same time, State UI programs have large improper payment rates. It is important to put the UI system back on the path to solvency and financial integrity while maintaining benefits for job seekers. The Administration proposes to provide immediate relief to employers to encourage job creation now, reestablish State fiscal responsibility going forward, and work closely with States to eliminate improper payments.

Modernizes Federal Workers' Compensation. The Budget acts on longstanding recommendations from the Government Accountability Office, the Congressional Budget Office, and DOL's Inspector General—as well as numerous Securing Americans Value and Efficiency (SAVE) Award nominations—to reform the Federal Employees' Compensation Act (FECA), which has not been substantially updated since 1974. The Budget proposes a series of FECA reforms that will generate Government-wide savings of more than $340 million over 10 years.

DEPARTMENT OF STATE AND OTHER INTERNATIONAL PROGRAMS

Funding Highlights:

- Provides a total of $40.3 billion in base discretionary funding for the Department of State and U.S. Agency for International Development, equal to the 2014 enacted level. In addition, provides $5.9 billion for Overseas Contingency Operations activity. This includes:

  o Dedicating $1.5 billion for the Middle East and North Africa to address the growing humanitarian crisis in Syria and support transitions and reforms in the region;

  o Supporting the rebalance of diplomatic and assistance resources to the Asia-Pacific region;

  o Advancing Power Africa, the President's historic initiative to partner with African countries and the private sector to expand electricity generation and access to power in sub-Saharan Africa;

  o Investing $4.6 billion to secure overseas personnel and facilities, including sufficient funding to support embassy security construction funding of $2.2 billion, as recommended by the Benghazi Accountability Review Board;

  o Providing $3 billion for peacekeeping missions to share global security burdens with other nations and respond to new peacekeeping requirements;

  o Advancing the President's commitment to global health by providing $1 for every $2 committed by other donors to the Global Fund, expanding access to HIV/AIDS treatment and prevention, and scaling up evidence-based child survival interventions to continue progress toward the end of preventable child and maternal deaths; and

  o Continuing a multi-year plan for Feed the Future to make strategic investments addressing the root causes of hunger and poverty and increase food security for millions by 2015.

- Provides $1 billion for the Millennium Challenge Corporation to support poverty reduction through economic growth.

Opportunity, Growth, and Security Initiative:

- Through the Opportunity, Growth, and Security Initiative, supports:

o   Foreign assistance programs that have a proven track record of fostering economic growth, reducing poverty, and improving health, such as contributing to a 70 percent decline in child mortality over the last 20 years and a long-term income gain for millions of people in developing countries; and

o   Reserving $300 million to match more ambitious pledges from other donors to the Global Fund to Fight AIDS, Tuberculosis, and Malaria.

Reforms:

•   Proposes food aid reforms that allow approximately two million more people per year to be helped in emergencies within current resources, ensuring more cost-effective use of taxpayer resources.

The Department of State, the U.S. Agency for International Development (USAID), and other international programs advance the national security interests of the United States by helping to build and sustain a more democratic, secure, and prosperous world. The Budget proposes smart investments in international programs that will advance peace and security, strengthen the U.S. economy, combat global challenges, and support United States citizens and the U.S. presence overseas.

The Budget proposes a total of $46.2 billion for the Department of State and USAID, including costs for Overseas Contingency Operations. The Administration prioritizes responding to the humanitarian crisis in Syria, promoting reforms and transitions in the Middle East and North Africa (MENA), addressing global security challenges and peacekeeping needs, and responsibly funding operations and assistance in Afghanistan. The Budget continues to provide strong support for the Administration's signature development initiatives in global health, food security, and climate change. The Budget provides the necessary base resources to maintain critical diplomatic and development efforts around the world, including necessary investments in the safety and security of U.S. embassies and personnel serving abroad. At the same time, the Department and USAID are committed to managing effectively and driving efficiencies wherever possible in order to give taxpayers the highest possible return on their investment in U.S. global leadership.

Maintains U.S. Global Leadership

Responds to the Crisis in Syria and Supports Democratic Transitions and Reforms in the Middle East and North Africa. Building on the Administration's significant and continuing response to the transformative events in MENA, the Budget includes $1.5 billion to respond to the crisis in Syria and continue to support transitions and reforms in the region. This includes $1.1 billion in humanitarian assistance funding to address the crisis in Syria. The Budget also includes over $400 million to support an anticipated transition in Syria, to respond to new contingencies, and to promote long-term economic and political reforms across MENA, in addition to continuing or expanding ongoing bilateral and regional programs in MENA. The response builds on several initiatives the United States is supporting to respond to regional developments since the beginning of the Arab Spring, including Enterprise Funds, fiscal stabilization support through cash transfers and loan guarantees, and various initiatives through the G8's Deauville Partnership, including technical assistance, trade, and asset recovery initiatives.

Prioritizes the Asia-Pacific Region. The Budget supports the Presidential priority of advancing security, prosperity, and human dignity across the Asia-Pacific region. The Budget provides resources to help deepen U.S. trade and investment in the region, strengthen regional cooperation, and enhance regional and country capabilities to address security, development, and economic challenges. These investments, along with an expanded U.S. diplomatic and public diplomacy presence, are critical to the Government-wide effort to promote regional security and economic cooperation.

Expands Electricity Generation and Access to Power Through Power Africa. The Administration is bringing to bear a wide range of Federal Government tools and expertise to support investment in Africa's energy sector. The Budget supports infrastructure projects through the Millennium Challenge Corporation (MCC) and the U.S. contribution to the African Development Bank, leverages private sector investment through the Export-Import Bank and Overseas Private Investment Corporation, and provides critical technical assistance to African partners through the Department of State, USAID, and the U.S. Trade and Development Agency. Both the investments in the power sector themselves and the resulting economic growth will expand the markets for U.S. goods in sub-Saharan Africa.

Invests in Security Upgrades. The Budget provides $4.6 billion for the Department of State's security programs, including security staff, construction, and infrastructure upgrades. With a sustained level of investment in security upgrades, the Budget provides funding for the construction of new embassy and consulate compounds. These and other investments will ensure that the Administration continues to safeguard over 86,000 Federal Government employees, from more than 30 agency components, in more secure overseas working environments. When combined with contributions from other agencies, the Budget provides $2.2 billion for capital security construction, as recommended by the Benghazi Accountability Review Board.

Supports Peacekeeping Missions. The Budget provides $3 billion to fund continued, sustained support for the United Nations (UN) and non-UN peacekeeping missions, enabling the United States to advance global security while sharing the burden with other nations.

The Budget pursues a new approach to improve U.S. support for complex and urgent peacekeeping needs by proposing a $150 million peacekeeping response account, which enables the United States to support initial urgent and unexpected requirements of new UN and non-UN missions without compromising support for existing U.S. peacekeeping commitments.

Invests in a Long-Term Partnership with Afghanistan. The Budget continues to support U.S. security, diplomatic, and development goals in Afghanistan. The Budget supports a strong, long-term partnership and includes core operational support funding, as well as economic development, health, education, governance, security, and other civilian assistance programs necessary to reinforce development progress and promote stability. The Budget is consistent with the July 2012 Tokyo Conference commitment to request civilian assistance for Afghanistan "at or near levels of the past decade." The Budget provides for near-term development assistance related to stabilization and counterinsurgency programs, extraordinary costs of operating in a high-threat environment, protection of civilian personnel, and oversight activities of the Special Inspector General for Afghanistan Reconstruction.

Supports Global Health by Investing in High Impact Interventions. The Administration is investing in proven interventions to continue progress toward the goals of achieving an AIDS-free generation and an end to preventable child and maternal deaths. The Budget continues the President's pledge to provide $1 for every $2 pledged by other donors to the Global Fund to Fight AIDS, Tuberculosis, and Malaria by providing $1.35 billion in 2015 base funding, which will increase U.S. leverage and accelerate progress against these three diseases. The Opportunity, Growth, and Security Initiative would provide an additional $300 million for the Global Fund to encourage even more ambitious pledges from other donors. On World AIDS Day 2013, the President announced impressive results in the treatment and prevention of HIV, including that the United States was supporting 6.7 million people on antiretroviral therapy, exceeding the goal of putting

6 million people on treatment that he had set two years prior. The Budget supports continued expansion of evidence-based HIV/AIDS prevention and treatment services. The Budget also builds on the momentum of the Child Survival Call to Action by continuing investments in proven child survival interventions. Additional funding for maternal and child survival in the Opportunity, Growth, and Security Initiative would leverage a strong evidence base to expand access to and improve the quality of life-saving interventions for mothers and children. Funds would target the leading causes of death, including diarrhea, pneumonia, malaria, and complications in childbirth.

Fights Hunger by Improving Food Security. The Budget continues to fund a multi-year plan for the President's food security initiative, Feed the Future, to address the root causes of hunger and poverty through agriculture development, resilience, and nutrition programs intended to reduce extreme poverty and malnutrition and increase food security for millions of families by 2015. The Opportunity, Growth, and Security Initiative would provide additional funds for bilateral food security in order to deepen and intensify the impact of the initiative, as well as $80 million for multilateral food security funding. The Budget also maintains strong support for food aid and other humanitarian assistance, providing $4.8 billion to help internally displaced persons, refugees, and others affected by natural or man-made humanitarian disasters.

Supports Efforts to Cut Carbon Pollution, Promote Sustainable Landscapes, and Enhance Climate Change Resilience. Established in 2010, the Global Climate Change Initiative (GCCI) enables the United States to provide international leadership to promote cleaner and more efficient energy, to conserve the world's remaining tropical rainforests, to phase down chemicals with high global warming potential, and to support the most vulnerable communities in their efforts to cope with the adverse impacts of severe weather events and climate change. The Budget advances the goals of the GCCI and the President's Climate Action Plan,

including by supporting bilateral and multilateral engagement with major and emerging economies; reducing emissions from deforestation and forest degradation; and expanding clean energy use as well as energy efficiency.

Engages the Global Community and Empowers the Next Generation of Global Leaders. The Budget advances efforts to make U.S. global engagement and public diplomacy more flexible tools to achieve U.S. foreign policy goals. To engage and empower emerging leaders in key regions, the Budget provides $44 million for youth leadership programs in sub-Saharan Africa and Southeast Asia. Global events and trends now start, spread, and shape countries in an instant. The Budget includes $25 million for a rapid response exchange program to enable immediate engagement with key actors and groups when opportunities for engagement emerge. In addition, the Budget increases funding to promote private educational exchanges, particularly in target areas such as the Western Hemisphere and China, as well as economic opportunity development and the engagement and strengthening of civil society.

Invests in Poverty Reduction Through Economic Growth. The Budget provides $1 billion for MCC, whose core mission is to reduce poverty through economic growth. These resources will be used for programs which address the binding constraints to economic growth in developing countries that have been deemed eligible for MCC assistance based on performance on independent policy indicators. MCC has a robust model for projecting and measuring the impact of its programs, has demonstrated a commitment to evidence-based decision-making from its inception, and anticipates having a large role in the President's Power Africa initiative. MCC has invested nearly two-thirds of its portfolio in increasing global trade and creating enabling environments throughout the developing world where the American private sector can partner, compete, succeed, and bring key benefits, like jobs, back home. The Opportunity, Growth, and Security Initiative would provide an additional $350 million for MCC, which will support at least one additional compact in 2015 or enhancements to multiple compacts with a focus on enduring partner country policy reforms and sustainable development based on robust and transparent evidence and evaluation.

Makes Contributions to Economic Growth, National Security, and Multilateral Poverty Reduction Efforts. The Budget provides $2.6 billion to the Department of the Treasury for economic growth, national security, and multilateral poverty reduction efforts. These resources fund all annual general capital increase and replenishment commitments to the multilateral development banks, as well as critical contributions to international environmental, food security, and technical assistance activities. These programs leverage the resources of other donors to support U.S. and multilateral objectives in key international institutions.

Leverages Science, Technology, Innovation, and Partnerships (STIP) in Development. The Budget invests in USAID's initiative to modernize global development through the expanded use of science, technology, innovation, and partnerships in its programs and to establish the Global Development Lab. The Opportunity, Growth, and Security Initiative would provide additional STIP funding to scale up innovative solutions and fund new programs focused on achieving transformational development results and accelerating progress toward development goals.

Improves Efficiency and Transparency

Reforms Food Aid for More Cost-Effective Use of Taxpayer Resources. The Budget proposes reforms within P.L. 480 Title II, the Nation's largest international food aid program, to make it more cost-effective and increase its impact, while maintaining robust levels of emergency food and development assistance. Most food aid funding would be used to purchase and ship food from the United States. The remaining flexible resources would be used for interventions such as buying food near crises or cash transfers and vouchers. In addition to saving time and money, this type of flexible funding has been critical to reaching those most in need in complex environments such as Syria and fast onset disasters such as the Philippines' Typhoon Haiyan. The reform would allow around two million more people per year to receive food aid without additional funding. The Budget also proposes $25 million per year through the Department of Transportation's Maritime Administration for additional targeted operating subsidies and incentives to facilitate the retention of mariners.

Improves the Efficiency of U.S. International Broadcasting. The Opportunity, Growth, and Security Initiative would provide $29 million to the Broadcasting Board of Governors to enable the use of long-term contracts for satellite services, which will yield a 31 percent savings over current contract levels over a seven-year timeframe.

DEPARTMENT OF TRANSPORTATION

Funding Highlights:

- Provides a total of $91 billion in discretionary and mandatory budgetary resources for the Department of Transportation.

- Includes $302 billion for a four-year, surface transportation reauthorization proposal to support critical infrastructure projects and create jobs while improving America's roads, bridges, transit systems, and railways. This includes:

  o Proposing new performance measures to prioritize Federal transportation funding for "Fix it First" projects that emphasize maintaining existing infrastructure in a state of good repair;

  o Providing $1.25 billion per year for the competitive TIGER Grant program, which helps States and localities support innovative projects that deliver exceptional transportation benefits;

  o Implementing a new four-year, $10 billion freight program designed to eliminate existing freight transportation bottlenecks and improve the efficiency of moving goods in support of the President's National Export Initiative; and

  o Increasing funding for transit and passenger rail programs from $12.3 billion to $22.3 billion in 2015, expanding transit capital investment grants, significantly improving existing and new intercity passenger rail service, and strengthening the economic competitiveness of the Nation's freight rail system.

- Provides $14 billion in discretionary resources to fund air, maritime, rail safety, and pipeline and hazardous material transportation activities, including:

  o $836 million for the Next Generation Air Transportation System, a revolutionary modernization of the Nation's aviation system;

  o $370 million to support a National Airspace System Sustainment Strategy to reduce the Federal Aviation Administration's multi-billion dollar maintenance backlog;

  o $40 million for a multi-modal fund to support safe shipping of crude oil via rail and truck by ramping up inspection resources, research and development and testing, and response capability; and

○ $158 million for a more robust, rigorous, and data-driven pipeline safety program to ensure the highest level of safety for America's pipeline system.

Opportunity, Growth, and Security Initiative:

• Through the Opportunity, Growth, and Security Initiative, supports:

○ An additional $186 million investment in the Next Generation Air Transportation System, which makes the total request roughly $1 billion. This funding provides the Federal Aviation Administration flexibility to aggressively develop and deploy more time and fuel saving capabilities while also addressing serious maintenance backlogs.

Reforms:

• Modernizes the permitting process for infrastructure projects by expanding a Permitting Dashboard to track the timeliness and outcomes of project permits and reviews, and by assigning responsibility for implementing reforms to a new Interagency Infrastructure Permitting Improvement Center, to be housed at the Department of Transportation.

• Focuses airport grants to support smaller airports, while giving larger commercial service airports additional flexibility to raise their own resources.

• Provides $4 billion for a new competitive surface transportation program that would incentivize States and localities to pursue ambitious performance improvements.

A well-functioning transportation system is critical to America's economic future. Americans rely on the transportation system to move people and goods safely, facilitate commerce, attract and retain businesses, and support jobs. The Budget provides a total of $91 billion in discretionary and mandatory funding in 2015 for the Department of Transportation (DOT) to support infrastructure projects critical for long-term growth; improve America's roads, bridges, transit systems, railways, and aviation system; enhance safety; spur job creation; and improve the way Federal dollars are spent.

Invests in Infrastructure Critical for Job Creation and Long-Term Growth

Improves the Nation's Infrastructure While Creating Jobs and Ladders of Opportunity. To spur economic growth and allow States to initiate sound multi-year investments, the Budget proposes a four-year, $302 billion surface transportation reauthorization package. This would support critical infrastructure projects and create jobs, while improving America's roads, bridges, transit systems, and railways. The reauthorization proposal will also include reforms to improve the review process and delivery of infrastructure projects; support American exports by improving movement within the Nation's freight networks; increase economic mobility by linking economically isolated communities to job opportunities; permanently authorize the TIGER grant program to help spur innovation by competitively awarding funding to projects around the Nation; improve regional coordination by Metropolitan Planning Organizations to stimulate economic development; and advance the Climate Action Plan by building more resilient infrastructure, reducing transportation emissions by shifting travel growth from roads to transit, and encouraging sounder transportation planning. The Administration is committed to supporting the ongoing bipartisan dialogue on surface transportation by providing a legislative proposal that reflects this critical blueprint.

Supports New Transit Investments. The Budget nearly doubles annual transit investments over the prior authorization, with resources supporting both existing capacity and expansion through projects involving bus rapid transit, subway, light rail, and commuter rail systems. These investments—driven by data showing that demand for public transit continues to climb—would represent an historic increase in transit funding. Additional funding would enable a major expansion of new transit projects in suburbs, fast-growing cities, small towns, and rural areas across the United States, while meeting the growing needs of established—and aging—transit systems, which will improve the quality of life in United States' neighborhoods and communities by providing affordable transportation options. All of these efforts will help ensure that workers can access jobs, supporting economic mobility and opportunity.

Emphasizes a "Fix it First" Approach for Highway and Transit Grants. Too many elements of the U.S. surface transportation infrastructure—highways, bridges, and transit assets—fall short of a state of good repair. This can impact the capacity, performance, and safety of the Nation's transportation system. At the same time, States and localities have incentives to emphasize new investments over improving the condition of the existing infrastructure. The Administration's reauthorization proposal will underscore the importance of preserving and improving existing assets, encouraging government and industry partners to make optimal use of current capacity, and minimizing life-cycle costs through sound asset management principles. Accountability is a key element of the Administration's approach, as the reauthorization proposal will improve transparency into States' and localities' use of funds by strengthening performance measures that track how the States' choices of projects impact safety and overall highway conditions.

Proposes Dedicated Funding for Multi-Modal Freight and High Performance Rail Investments. The Budget provides $10 billion over four years for a dedicated regional freight infrastructure investment program to support multi-modal, corridor-based projects designed to eliminate existing freight transportation bottlenecks and improve the efficiency of moving goods in support of the President's National Export Initiative. The Budget also provides $19.1 billion over four years to fund the development of high-performance rail and other passenger rail programs as part of an integrated national transportation strategy. The proposal also benefits freight rail and significantly restructures Federal support for Amtrak to increase transparency, accountability, and performance.

Pays for Transportation Investment with Savings from Comprehensive Business Tax Reform. The President is committed to ensuring that critical transportation investments are fiscally sustainable. Because rebuilding the transportation infrastructure is an urgent need, the Budget reinvests the transition revenue from pro-growth business tax reform to fully offset the baseline Highway Trust Fund solvency needs and the out-year surface and rail transportation reauthorization proposal. The President will work with the Congress to develop fiscally responsible solutions to address funding needs beyond the reauthorization window.

Responds to Emerging Concerns with the Transport of Crude Oil by Rail and Truck. As the Nation's ability to extract energy resources increases, one of DOT's priorities is to ensure safe transportation of these materials. The Budget establishes a new fund to provide $40 million in discretionary resources to support prevention and response activities associated with the safe transportation of energy resources. The funds would be available for multiple DOT modes to address risk through data-driven safety interventions, additional safety personnel, training and outreach, collaboration with other Federal stakeholders, and other strategies. Based on the activities supported by this fund, DOT will report on best practices and lessons learned to help with the implementation of safety measures going forward. Because this effort is a partnership with industry, the Budget proposes to give the Secretary additional authority to share costs associated with ensuring that these cargoes move safely.

Enhances Pipeline Safety. In order to ensure the highest safety standards for the U.S. pipeline system, the Budget proposes a Pipeline Safety Reform initiative to enhance the Department's Pipeline Safety program. The need for reform is acute—pipeline safety inspectors, who work in collaboration with State partners, are spread too thinly across the 2.6 million miles of pipeline, and the current staffing levels cannot ensure prompt investigations following incidents. The Budget increases funding for the State Pipeline Safety Grant program and funds the next phase of a multi-year effort to increase the number of Federal pipeline safety inspectors. In addition, the Budget modernizes pipeline data collection, mapping capabilities and analysis, improves Federal investigation of pipeline accidents of all sizes, and expands public education and outreach.

Modernizes and Sustains the Nation's Air Traffic Control System. The Budget provides over $1 billion in 2015 for the Next Generation Air Transportation System (NextGen), the multi-year effort currently underway to improve the efficiency, safety, capacity, and environmental performance of the aviation system. The Budget includes $836 million in the base request for NextGen and an additional $186 million through the Opportunity, Growth, and Security Initiative. These funds will continue to support the transformation from a ground-based radar surveillance system to a more accurate satellite-based surveillance system; the development of a 21st Century data communications capability between air traffic control and aircraft to improve efficiency; and the improvement of aviation weather information. The Budget supports taking a coordinated and targeted approach to deploying readily-available NextGen capabilities, and to developing new operational procedures, systems, and infrastructure that benefit the traveling public and all aviation stakeholders. However, while NextGen is being deployed, the Federal Aviation Administration (FAA) has to balance investments in future capabilities with maintaining currently operational, but aging equipment. Therefore, the Budget also provides $370 million for the National Airspace System Sustainment Strategy to reduce some of FAA's multi-billion dollar maintenance backlog.

Improves the Way Federal Funds are Spent

Modernizes the Infrastructure Permitting Process. In order to accelerate economic growth and improve the competitiveness of the American economy, the Administration is taking action to modernize and improve the efficiency of the Federal permitting process for major infrastructure projects. By cutting through red tape and getting more timely decisions on Federal permits and reviews, the Budget will ensure that projects that are approved lead to better outcomes for communities and the environment. In support of this effort, the Budget includes funding for a new Interagency Infrastructure Permitting Improvement Center and a Permitting Dashboard to be managed by DOT's Office of the Secretary. The Center will spearhead the Administration's reform efforts, including implementing over 80 actions laid out in the implementation plan for the Presidential Memorandum on Modernizing Infrastructure Permitting. Given the highly decentralized nature of the current permitting process, the Center will play an unprecedented role in driving change across nearly 20 Federal agencies and bureaus. The Permitting Dashboard, a publicly available website, will be expanded to track project schedules and metrics for all major infrastructure projects, further improving the transparency and accountability of the permitting process.

Encourages Innovative Solutions Through a New Fixing and Accelerating Surface Transportation Competition. The Administration's four-year reauthorization plan would dedicate approximately $4 billion for a competitive grant program, Fixing and Accelerating Surface Transportation, designed to create incentives for State and local partners to adopt critical reforms in a variety of areas, including safety and peak traffic demand management. Federally-inspired safety reforms, such as seat belt and drunk-driving laws, have saved thousands of American lives and avoided billions in property losses. This initiative will seek to repeat past successes across the complete spectrum of transportation policy priorities. Specifically, the

Department will work with States and localities to set ambitious goals in different areas. For example, implementing distracted driving (safety) requirements or modifying transportation plans to include mass transit, bike, and pedestrian options, and tie resources to goal-achievement.

Reduces Funding in Targeted Areas. The Budget lowers funding for the airport grants program to $2.9 billion, offset in part by eliminating guaranteed funding for large hub airports. The Budget focuses Federal grants on supporting smaller commercial and general aviation airports that do not have access to additional revenue or other outside sources of capital. At the same time, the Budget allows larger airports to increase non-Federal passenger facility charges, thereby giving larger airports greater flexibility to generate their own revenue.

DEPARTMENT OF THE TREASURY

Funding Highlights:

- Provides $13.8 billion for the Department of the Treasury to maintain a strong economy by promoting the conditions that enable economic growth and job creation. This includes:

    o Continuing to implement the Affordable Care Act to provide quality, affordable health care for millions of Americans who would otherwise be uninsured, including through the delivery of tax credits and cost sharing assistance to make coverage affordable while reducing health care costs and the deficit;

    o Continuing to implement the Wall Street Reform and Consumer Protection Act to create a more stable and responsible financial system;

    o Investing $12.5 billion, including a program integrity initiative, in the Internal Revenue Service (IRS) to improve service to taxpayers and reduce the deficit through more effective enforcement of tax laws;

    o Investing $1.5 billion for a new round of the successful State Small Business Credit Initiative, enabling States to support innovative partnerships of their design that increase small business lending and investment; and

    o Investing $225 million in the Community Development Financial Institutions Fund to spur jobs and healthier communities in underserved areas.

Opportunity, Growth, and Security Initiative:

- Through the Opportunity, Growth, and Security Initiative, supports:

    o Additional IRS customer service improvements, including increasing toll-free telephone level of service from about 60 percent to 80 percent when combined with base funding, driving responsiveness to taxpayers through correspondence inventory reduction, and bolstering resources to help tackle more resource-intensive identity theft and refund fraud cases; and

    o An expansion of the level of detail and capabilities of sorting Federal spending data to enable more effective Federal and non-Federal use of this data.

Reforms:

- Provides for a comprehensive review of U.S. currency production and use, including developing alternative options for the penny and the nickel.

- Proposes a multi-year program integrity cap adjustment for the IRS, including $480 million in 2015, to deliver additional resources to critical tax enforcement and compliance functions that reduce the deficit and narrow the tax gap by nearly $6 for every $1 spent once fully implemented, with total savings of $35 billion over the next 10 years.

The Department of the Treasury's (Treasury) mission is to maintain a strong economy and create economic and job opportunities by promoting the conditions that enable economic growth and stability at home and abroad, strengthen national security by combating threats and protecting the integrity of the financial system, and manage the Federal Government's finances and resources effectively. Treasury also performs an array of core Government functions such as tax law enforcement, financial management, and debt collection that are vital to the overall financial integrity of the Federal Government. In support of Treasury's essential and diverse mission, the Budget provides $13.8 billion in total resources, an increase of nearly $1.2 billion—partially funded through the proposed program integrity cap adjustment—or 9.2 percent above the 2014 enacted level.

The Budget enhances the Department's leadership role in ensuring the safety and soundness of the U.S. economy and the global financial system through key investments in Treasury's essential functions: domestic finance and economic policy; international economics; tax policy and administration; financial management; and currency production. The Budget also recognizes the indispensable role that Treasury plays in implementing essential reforms that have been enacted over the past four years to the Nation's healthcare and financial systems. The Budget also invests in upgrading technologies to enable the Department to secure efficiencies and realize savings for taxpayers.

Supports Individuals, Businesses, and Communities, and Strengthens the U.S. Financial System

Continues Successful Implementation of the Affordable Care Act. The Budget provides the resources necessary to carry out key tax-related provisions of the Affordable Care Act. The tax filing season in 2015 is a critical period for ensuring the delivery of healthcare to millions of Americans in a timely and accurate fashion. The Budget makes the investments necessary for the IRS to better respond to taxpayer inquiries, as well as to verify income, provide benefit calculations, and reconcile tax accounts in support of greater access to healthcare for all Americans.

Protects Consumers and Supports Continued Implementation of Wall Street Reform. The Budget continues responsible implementation of the Wall Street Reform and Consumer Protection Act to ensure a stronger and fairer financial system for investors and consumers. The Budget fully supports the efforts of the Financial Stability Oversight Council and Treasury's Office of Financial Research to identify, monitor, and respond to emerging threats to U.S. financial stability. The Budget also provides critical funding increases for the Commodity Futures Trading Commission and the Securities and Exchange Commission, whose funding in the Budget increases 30 percent and 26 percent, respectively, over their 2014 enacted levels. These independent financial regulators have already taken decisive action to rein in excessive risk-taking and market manipulation, and the Budget will allow them to fully execute their responsibilities for financial oversight under the Wall Street Reform Act.

Provides Significant New Support for Small Business Lending and Investment. The Budget provides $1.5 billion for a second round of Treasury's successful State Small Business Credit Initiative (SSBCI) in order to support State-sponsored public-private partnerships to increase lending, investment, and technical assistance to small businesses and manufacturers. SSBCI is already achieving results: the first $271 million in program expenditures supported lending and investments of $1.9 billion to more than 4,600 small businesses across the United States—creating or saving more than 53,000 American jobs. The Budget proposes to improve the targeting of SSBCI funding so that the funds are put to even more effective use. Of the $1.5 billion provided, $1 billion will be competitively awarded to States best able to target underserved groups, leverage Federal funding, and evaluate results. An additional $500 million will be allocated to States according to a need-based formula.

Responsibly Winds Down the Troubled Asset Relief Program (TARP). The Budget supports the effective, transparent, and accountable winding down of TARP programs, as well as Treasury's continuing efforts to help prevent avoidable home foreclosures. Of the $412 billion in support that TARP provided to the financial and automotive sectors, only $12.4 billion remains outstanding. Taxpayer proceeds from repayments, redemptions, and sales of TARP investments continue to exceed expectations. TARP's banking programs have already generated a positive return, with more than $273 billion recovered for taxpayers as of December 31, 2013, compared to the $245 billion originally invested, and in 2013, with the auto industry back on its feet, Treasury sold TARP's remaining shares in General Motors. The Budget estimates that excluding assistance to distressed homeowners, taxpayers will realize a positive net return of $16 billion from TARP investments and additional

Treasury AIG (American International Group) support.

Supports Struggling Homeowners. With the housing sector still healing, the Budget continues to support key programs to assist homeowners. Since April 2009, TARP's Home Affordable Modification Program, the Department of Housing and Urban Development's Federal Housing Administration, and the private sector HOPE Now alliance have initiated more than 7.4 million foreclosure prevention actions for distressed homeowners, which is nearly double the number of foreclosures completed in the same period. In addition, as of December 31, 2013, more than three million borrowers have lowered their monthly payments by refinancing mortgages through the Home Affordable Refinancing Program.

Spurs Jobs, Healthier Communities, and Delivers Healthy Foods to Underserved Communities. The Budget provides a total of $225 million for Treasury's Community Development Financial Institutions Fund (CDFI), which plays a key role in providing financial and technical assistance to advance community development in impoverished or underserved areas. By facilitating capital, credit, and financial services to low-income communities, this unique program helps spur job creation and investments that improve communities and opportunities for their residents. Within CDFI, $35 million is provided to support Treasury's lead role in an interagency effort to reduce "food deserts" that lack nutritious foods such as fresh fruit and vegetables, by supporting businesses that will provide them, and the supply chain to deliver them, to these areas. The Budget also extends by one year the CDFI Bond Guarantee program to provide a source of long-term capital to CDFIs that support lending in underserved communities.

Manages the Federal Government's Finances Effectively and Efficiently

Invests in the IRS to Boost Customer Service and Improve Compliance with Current Laws. The IRS is responsible for securing over 90 percent of the revenue that funds the Federal Government and ensuring the integrity of U.S. tax laws. The Budget provides $12 billion in base funding for the IRS, an increase of 6.3 percent over the 2014 enacted level. The Budget also proposes a $480 million program integrity cap adjustment to support efforts aimed at improving enforcement of current tax laws and reducing the tax gap, currently estimated at $450 billion in gross revenues annually. Research shows that every additional dollar invested in IRS tax enforcement activities returns six times its value in increased revenue, and this enforcement initiative is estimated to yield a net deficit reduction of $35 billion over the next 10 years. The lack of sufficient IRS funding in recent years has caused a deterioration in the service to taxpayers that the IRS can provide, reflected in longer wait times on the phone when taxpayers call in with questions, and in the time it takes to respond to taxpayer correspondence. The Budget begins to reverse this trend through a more than $100 million increase to improve customer service, which will secure rapid and noticeable improvements in taxpayer interactions with the IRS.

The Budget also includes an Opportunity, Growth, and Security Initiative to generate added value for taxpayers and the economy, and one of its areas of particular focus is to improve the efficiency and effectiveness of Government programs. For the IRS, an additional $165 million is proposed through the Opportunity, Growth, and Security Initiative to further enhance the agency's customer service performance across its service offerings, including an increase to the toll-free level of service from an estimated 60 percent to 80 percent when combined with the base discretionary funding request.

Improves Government Operations and Promotes Efficiencies. The Budget proposes a number of initiatives to make Government work more effectively. For example, Treasury will take action to help improve the Government's ability to collect delinquent debt across all agencies, enhance program integrity, and return greater resources to taxpayers. Treasury, given its financial management expertise and leadership, will also work with other agencies to improve *USAspending.gov*, the Government's website designed to track and share data on how Federal funds are spent and promote spending transparency. In addition, the Budget will create a new $300 million Pay for Success Incentive Fund that will encourage State and local governments to support evidence-based programs that will yield Federal savings through improved outcomes in areas such as juvenile justice, workforce development, and homelessness.

Assesses the Future of Currency, Including the Penny. The production and circulation of currency in the United States have been largely unchanged for decades, despite the growth in electronic financial transactions. Treasury is undertaking a comprehensive review of U.S. currency, including a review of both the production and use of coins, in order to efficiently promote commerce in the 21st Century. These studies will analyze alternative metals, the United States Mint facilities, and consumer behavior and preferences, and will result in the development of alternative options for the penny and the nickel.

DEPARTMENT OF VETERANS AFFAIRS

Funding Highlights:

- Provides $65.3 billion in discretionary funding for the Department of Veterans Affairs (VA), to provide needed care and other benefits to veterans and their families. In addition, the Budget includes $3.1 billion in estimated medical care collections, for a total budget authority of approximately $68.4 billion. This includes:

  o Protecting critical funding for VA medical care by providing $56 billion, in addition to requesting $58.7 billion in 2016 advance appropriations for medical care programs, to ensure continuity of veterans' health care services;

  o Funding programs that, along with programs at the Department of Housing and Urban Development and other Federal agencies, aim to end veterans' homelessness; and

  o Supporting continuing improvements in the delivery of mental health care and the development of telehealth technologies, specialized care for women veterans, and benefits for veterans' caregivers.

- Includes $1 billion in mandatory funding to create the Veterans Job Corps program that would put thousands of veterans back to work over the next five years protecting and rebuilding America.

Opportunity, Growth, and Security Initiative:

- Through the Opportunity, Growth, and Security Initiative, supports:

  o An additional $400 million investment in high priority capital projects to address critical safety issues, improve services, and meet increased demand for veterans' services.

Reforms:

- Addresses the VA claims backlog and improves the Department's efficiency by investing $138.7 million in the Veterans Claims Intake Program, continuing to implement the paperless claims system, and undertaking additional efforts to provide faster and more accurate benefits claims processing and improve veterans' access to benefits information.

The Nation has a solemn obligation to take care of its veterans and to honor them for their service and sacrifice on behalf of the United States. To deliver on this commitment, the Budget provides $65.3 billion in discretionary funding for the Department of Veterans Affairs (VA), a three percent increase above the 2014 enacted level. In addition, the Budget includes $3.1 billion in estimated medical care collections, for a total budget authority of approximately $68.4 billion. This funding will continue to drive improvements in efficiency and responsiveness at VA, enabling the Department to better serve veterans and their families. The Budget supports efforts to ensure the needs of today's veteran population are met and invests in the continued modernization of VA to meet 21st Century challenges. The Budget also addresses anticipated growth in the number of veterans, dependents, and survivors projected to use VA services in 2015—an estimated 9.3 million veterans enrolled in VA's health care system and 4.9 million veterans and survivors receiving disability compensation.

Sustains and Strengthens Services for Veterans and Their Families

Protects Critical Funding for VA Medical Care. The Budget provides $56 billion for VA medical care, a 2.7 percent increase above the 2014 enacted level, to provide high-quality and timely health care services to veterans and other eligible beneficiaries. These services include innovative programs to educate and support veterans' caregivers, enhance veterans' access to care through telehealth technologies, and support equitable, high-quality care for women veterans in an appropriate and safe environment. In addition, the Budget proposes $58.7 billion in advance appropriations for the VA medical care program in 2016, which will provide timely and predictable funding for VA's medical care to prevent veterans from being adversely affected by any potential delays in annual appropriations. In addition, the Administration's Opportunity, Growth, and Security Initiative includes a one-time investment of $400 million to support one additional major construction project and other high priority capital projects to address critical safety issues, improve services, and meet increased demand.

Strengthens Mental Health Care Services. The Budget provides over $7 billion to continue VA's focus on expanding and transforming mental health services for veterans to ensure accessible and patient-centered care, including treatment for Post-Traumatic Stress Disorder, ensuring timely access to mental healthcare, and treatment for Military Sexual Trauma. This funding will allow VA to continue its collaborative efforts with the Departments of Defense (DOD) and Health and Human Services, as directed in the President's Executive Order on improving access to mental health services for veterans, servicemembers, and military families, to help veterans receive timely access to mental health services, including through enhanced partnerships with community providers.

Ends Veterans' Homelessness. Between 2010 and 2013, the number of homeless veterans has decreased by 24 percent. The Budget invests $1.6 billion to serve homeless and at-risk veterans, including $500 million for the Supportive Services for Veteran Families program to provide homelessness prevention and rapid re-housing services, and $321 million for the Department of Housing and Urban Development (HUD)-VA Supportive Housing program (HUD-VASH) for VA case management services. The Budget also includes $75 million in HUD funding for 10,000 new HUD-VASH vouchers to permanently house homeless veterans. Through these investments and collaborative partnerships with local governments, non-profit organizations, and Federal agencies, the Administration will continue to make progress toward the President's goal to end veterans' homelessness in 2015.

Addresses VA Claims Backlog and Continues Implementation of the Paperless Claims System. Over the last decade, VA has received an increasing number of disability claims from veterans. Past growth in the disability claims backlog has been due to a variety of circumstances, including the 255,000 claims received because of VA's decision to expand disability compensation eligibility to veterans for their exposure to Agent Orange. To eliminate the backlog, the Budget includes $138.7 million to enhance VA's Veterans Claims Intake Program, allowing the Department to continue to directly receive and convert paper evidence, such as medical records, into a digital format for increased efficiency in claims processing.

The Budget also supports transformation initiatives, including the continued development of a digital, near-paperless environment that allows for greater exchange of information and increased transparency for veterans. Specifically, the Budget includes $173.3 million for the Veterans Benefit Management System, designed to reduce the processing time and the claims backlog, automate claims tracking, and facilitate quality improvements including service-connected disability evaluations.

These overall efforts support VA's efforts to eliminate the claims backlog and achieve the Department's goal of processing all claims within 125 days with 98 percent accuracy in 2015. VA continues to make considerable progress in reducing the disability claims backlog, defined as those claims pending longer than 125 days.

Advances Medical and Prosthetic Research. The Budget includes $589 million for medical and prosthetic research to support veterans wounded in service. As part of the largest integrated health care system in the United States, the VA research program benefits from clinical care and research occurring together, allowing research to be directly coordinated with the care of veterans.

Supports Veteran Employment. To help the newest veterans transition to civilian life and find good jobs, the Budget provides $33 million to continue the Integrated Disability Evaluation System (IDES) and VetSuccess on Campus initiatives. IDES and VetSuccess counselors ensure that veterans, especially wounded warriors and students, receive timely information about education opportunities, job counseling, and placement. The Budget also proposes $1 billion to create the Veterans Job Corps program that would put thousands of veterans back to work over the next five years protecting and rebuilding America. In addition, the Department of the Interior's historic Centennial Initiative will engage hundreds of veterans to upgrade and rebuild national parks.

Improves Access to Comprehensive Services and Benefits. The Budget supports VA's efforts to ensure consistent, personalized, and accurate information about services and benefits, especially in the delivery of compensation and pension claims processing. To improve the speed, effectiveness, and efficiency of benefits service delivery, the joint DOD/VA eBenefits web portal provides veterans with critical self-service capabilities to manage their VA, military and personal information, apply online for benefits, and check the status of a claim.

CORPS OF ENGINEERS—CIVIL WORKS

Funding Highlights:

- Provides $4.5 billion for the Army Corps of Engineers civil works program, focused on investments in areas that will yield high economic and environmental returns or address a significant risk to public safety. This includes:

  o Investing in restoring significant aquatic ecosystems to help promote their ecological sustainability and resilience; and

  o Supporting investment in maintenance work and related activities at the most heavily used coastal ports and inland waterways in the Nation.

Opportunity, Growth, and Security Initiative:

- Through the Opportunity, Growth, and Security Initiative, supports:

  o Improvements in the resiliency of federally developed and managed water resources infrastructure to address a changing climate.

Reforms:

- Reforms how the Federal Government finances capital investments in support of navigation on the inland waterways, including a new user fee.

- Increases the organizational efficiency of the Corps and improves the management, oversight, and performance of ongoing programs to meet water resources needs and achieve savings.

The Army Corps of Engineers civil works program (Corps) develops, manages, and restores water resources to promote economic growth, increase public safety, and protect the environment. The Corps work focuses primarily on the construction, operation and maintenance of water resources projects, studies of potential new projects, and its regulatory program. The Corps also works with other Federal agencies to help States and communities respond to and recover from floods and other natural disasters. To support this work, the Budget provides $4.5 billion, a $934 million, or 17 percent, decrease from the 2014 enacted level. The Budget focuses resources on the highest priority work within the agency's three main missions: flood and storm damage reduction; commercial navigation; and aquatic ecosystem restoration. In addition, the Budget supports reforms within the Corps that will improve its efficiency and ensure projects deliver the highest return for taxpayers.

Invests in Water Resources to Support Economic Growth and Protect the Environment

Emphasizes Investments in Construction Projects with High Economic and Environmental Returns While Addressing Public Safety. The Budget provides $1.1 billion for Corps construction projects with an emphasis on projects that provide high economic and environmental returns to the Nation or address a significant risk to public safety. The Administration's Task Force on Ports continues to develop a national strategy for investment leading to a network of ports and related infrastructure that is more efficient, safe, secure, resilient, and environmentally sustainable. The strategy will be informed by stakeholder input.

Restores High Priority Aquatic Ecosystems. The Budget provides funding to restore significant aquatic ecosystems based on sound science and adaptive management. Funds are provided for work on priority aquatic ecosystems, including the California Bay-Delta, Chesapeake Bay, Everglades, Great Lakes, and Gulf Coast. Funds are also provided for other aquatic ecosystem restoration efforts, such as endangered species recovery in the Columbia River, restoring Puget Sound, and improving environmental outcomes in the Upper Mississippi and Missouri Rivers.

Invests in Existing Water Resources Infrastructure. The Budget includes funding for the operation and maintenance of existing infrastructure and improving its reliability. The Budget prioritizes the operation and maintenance of key infrastructure, including navigation channels that serve the Nation's largest coastal ports and the inland waterways with the most commercial use, such as the Mississippi and Ohio Rivers and the Illinois Waterway.

Improves Funding and Management

Reforms Inland Waterways Funding. The Administration has proposed to reform the laws governing the Inland Waterways Trust Fund, including an annual per vessel fee to sufficiently increase the amount paid by commercial navigation users to meet their share of the costs of activities financed from this fund. The additional revenue would help finance future capital investments in these waterways. The amounts collected would reflect the actual costs incurred, so any cost savings would translate over time directly into lower fees.

Enhances Non-Federal Leadership in Water Resources. Building and maintaining U.S. water resources infrastructure is a shared responsibility between Federal and non-Federal beneficiaries. The Administration supports efforts to encourage States and communities to assume responsibility for the development, management, restoration, and protection of water resources, including two new navigation studies that will allow local sponsors to assume greater ownership. This includes removing unnecessary obstacles and streamlining procedures for non-Federal parties to pursue investments independently that are important to their communities, while ensuring appropriate Federal interests are maintained.

Increases Organizational Efficiency. The Administration continues to work to improve the responsiveness, accountability, and operational oversight of the civil works program in order to best meet current and future water resources challenges. For example, as part of the President's Executive Order on Improving Performance of Federal Permitting and Review of Infrastructure Projects, the Corps is working to promote early collaboration and partnership among agencies, project sponsors, affected stakeholders, and the public in project planning, development, and permitting processes. These efforts are intended to lead to more timely decisions while also reducing adverse impacts to communities and the environment or to mitigate effects that may occur. In addition, the Corps is implementing steps to reduce cost overruns and achieve efficiencies through life cycle project cost management.

ENVIRONMENTAL PROTECTION AGENCY

Funding Highlights:

- Provides $7.9 billion for the Environmental Protection Agency (EPA) to protect human health and the environment. This includes:

  o Supporting the President's Climate Action Plan to reduce carbon pollution from power plants, vehicles and other sources and prepare the Nation for the unavoidable impacts of climate change;

  o Improving coordination with other Federal agencies and State, local, and tribal emergency planning and response organizations in assessing and managing chemical facility safety and security; and

  o Increasing support for State and tribal environmental protection by $76 million for implementation of delegated authorities, including support for air and water quality management and building tribal program capacity.

Opportunity, Growth, and Security Initiative:

- Through the Opportunity, Growth, and Security Initiative, supports:

  o A Nation that is better prepared for the impacts of climate change by protecting and enhancing coastal wetlands and supporting urban forest enhancement and protection.

Reforms:

- Reforms processes to increase program effectiveness by implementing the E-Enterprise Initiative, which includes transitioning from paper-based to electronic reporting, and using strategic sourcing for EPA's contract needs.

- Redesigns how EPA does business through realigning its workforce while ensuring staff have the skills they need to address today's environmental protection challenges in partnership with States.

The Environmental Protection Agency's (EPA's) mission is to protect human health and the environment. EPA was formed in 1970 in order to implement major pollution control programs, which were carried out primarily by EPA employees at the Federal level. In the decades that followed, new environmental statutes were enacted that expanded EPA's mandate and workload. Federal environmental programs were designed by the Congress to support strong collaboration with State, tribal, and local partners wherever possible, and most major environmental statutes have since been delegated to, and are largely administered by, States and Tribes. As a result of the successful efforts of these collaborations, environmental quality has improved substantially during this time. In recognition of evolving responsibilities, EPA has strategically evaluated its workforce and facility needs and will undertake a comprehensive effort to modernize its workforce in 2015. By implementing creative, flexible, cost-effective, and sustainable strategies to protect public health and safeguard the environment, EPA will target resources toward development of a workforce and structure that can address current challenges and priorities.

Meets the Climate Change Challenge

Supports the President's Climate Action Plan. EPA will continue to address climate change through careful, cost-effective rulemakings that focus on the largest pollution sources and voluntary programs that encourage businesses to cut carbon pollution. The President's Climate Action Plan focuses on three areas: cutting carbon pollution; preparing the Nation for the impacts of climate change that cannot be avoided; and leading international efforts to address climate change. EPA plays an important role in the plan by setting carbon dioxide (CO_2) standards for power plants and heavy duty trucks, and in partnership with other agencies, taking other actions to address hydrofluorocarbons (HFCs) and methane. The Budget supports implementation of greenhouse gas standards by the States, who will be close partners in successful reduction of carbon pollution from power plants. EPA also has a role in preparing the Nation for the unavoidable impacts of climate change, including through technical assistance to communities and by integrating considerations of climate change impacts and adaptive measures into existing programs.

Builds a High Performing Environmental Protection Enterprise

Redesigns how EPA does Business. Strengthening the partnership with States and increasing the efficiency of EPA's core functions are both key to building a high performing environmental protection enterprise. EPA will redesign its business processes, including contracts and grants management, the regulation development process, and records management, and implement approaches such as strategic sourcing in order to increase EPA's effectiveness in an environment of constrained resources. This redesign effort has been largely developed through an EPA-State workgroup.

At the center of EPA's redesign effort is E-Enterprise. Through E-Enterprise, EPA will modernize business processes and systems to reduce reporting burden on States and regulated facilities and improve the effectiveness and efficiency of regulatory programs for EPA, States, and Tribes. The Budget includes an additional $7 million to support the e-Manifest program to provide information on hazardous waste shipments electronically, rather than the current cumbersome, paper-based approach. When fully implemented, the e-Manifest program will result in annual savings of $75 million for over 146,000 waste handlers.

Modernizes EPA's Workforce. In 2015, EPA will undertake a focused examination of its workforce needs in conjunction with efforts to modernize its processes through the use of innovative tools and approaches. The restructuring effort will focus on implementing best management practices and identifying needed skills for the streamlined EPA. Some positions will be consolidated and reconfigured to reflect the current era of data driven analysis.

Strengthens Partnerships to Protect the Environment

Supports State and Tribal Governments. The Budget increases support for EPA's partnership with States and Tribes. Under the Clean Water Act (CWA), the Clean Air Act and other Federal environmental laws, EPA sets standards and enforceable pollution limits and establishes best practices to ensure human health and the environment are protected. States and localities implement the rules while taking into account each State's specific needs, and address the public health and environmental standards and requirements. Categorical grants to States and Tribes to implement their delegated authorities are funded at $1.1 billion, $76 million above the 2014 enacted level. Within these totals, funding is increased in priority areas including $20 million for State implementation of the President's Climate Action Plan, $31 million to build tribal capacity and assist Tribes in leveraging other EPA and Federal funding, and $18 million for activities including water permitting and improving nutrient management.

Invests in Accident Prevention. EPA's responsibilities include working to prevent and prepare for catastrophic accidental chemical releases at industrial facilities through a combination of regulation, technical assistance, outreach, and inspections. Following the explosion of an ammonium nitrate facility in West, Texas last year, the President signed an Executive Order directing EPA and other Federal agencies to, among other things, review and appropriately modernize their operating practices and regulations and seek improvements in coordination with other Federal, State, and local regulators and first responders. To assist in this effort, the Budget includes $13 million above the 2014 enacted level to support upgrades and enhancements to the CAMEO (Computer Aided Management of Emergency Operations) IT system. This funding also provides for additional technical assistance and inspection support, as well as the establishment of a pilot program for local responders to develop tools for emergency notification systems and planning.

Enhances Efforts to Improve Water Quality. The Budget builds on existing collaboration between EPA and its partners to improve water quality across the United States while utilizing new approaches. In 2015, EPA will work to develop tools to improve measurement of water quality and expand technical assistance efforts for communities to develop effective stormwater plans. Through its water quality programs and through the Clean Water State Revolving Fund, EPA will promote green infrastructure approaches such as green roofs, rain gardens, and wetlands and forest buffers, all of which can help to effectively meet CWA requirements and protect and restore the Nation's resources for safe drinking water, recreation, and economic development—now and into the future.

Supports Interagency Partnerships in Local Watersheds. The Budget maintains strong support for interagency efforts in key ecosystems of economic importance and in watersheds throughout the Nation. The Budget includes $275 million to continue the Great Lakes Restoration Initiative under a new Action Plan beginning in 2015. While continuing efforts to address high priority pollution problems in the Great Lakes, EPA and its Federal partners will build on lessons learned in the initiative's first five years to improve performance measurement and the effectiveness of Federal funds. The Budget similarly maintains support for Chesapeake Bay restoration, including $16 million to support State partners in implementing plans to reduce nutrient and sediment pollution. The Budget builds on the significant collaboration already underway between EPA and the Department of Agriculture (USDA) to demonstrate water quality improvements through conservation. By coordinating across EPA's Nonpoint Source Grants and USDA's Farm Bill conservation programs, the agencies will ensure effective, targeted investments to support continued improvements in water quality during times of constrained budgets.

Makes Targeted Reductions

Reduces Funding for State Revolving Funds. The Budget provides $1.8 billion for the Clean Water and Drinking Water State Revolving Funds (SRFs), $581 million below the 2014 enacted level. The Budget proposes a reduction to focus on communities most in need of assistance and continuing to allow financing of approximately $6 billion annually in wastewater and drinking water infrastructure projects. Nearly $60 billion has been provided for the programs to date, including over $21 billion since 2009. Going forward, EPA will continue efforts to target assistance to small and underserved communities that have a limited ability to repay loans, including Tribes.

NATIONAL AERONAUTICS AND SPACE ADMINISTRATION

Funding Highlights:

- Provides $17.5 billion in discretionary funding for the National Aeronautics and Space Administration (NASA) by prioritizing the research and development that lays the foundation for future long-term growth and exploration, as well as the key commercial partnerships that will enable the efficient long-term operations of the International Space Station. This includes:

  o Extending the life of the Space Station to 2024;

  o Allowing NASA and its international partners to continue the research and technology development work that holds promise to improve life on Earth, advance human capability to live and work in space, and allow long-term human exploration missions;

  o Partnering with the commercial space industry to regain the capability to send astronauts into space cost-effectively from U.S. soil;

  o Investing in space technologies, such as advanced in-space propulsion, which is necessary to increase America's capabilities in space, bring the cost of space exploration down, and pave the way for other Federal Government and commercial space activities;

  o Keeping the development of the James Webb Space Telescope, the more powerful successor to the Hubble Space Telescope, on track for a 2018 launch; and

  o Supporting robust development of NASA's longer-term human space exploration programs.

Opportunity, Growth, and Security Initiative:

- Through the Opportunity, Growth, and Security Initiative, supports:

  o The development of game-changing space technologies that will lower the cost and increase the capabilities of future space activities;

  o The ability of American companies to carry people to space;

  o Science missions and research that will enhance human understanding of the Earth and solar system; and

  o NASA's investment in a heavy lift rocket and crew capsule for deep space exploration.

Reforms:

- Contributes to the Government-wide effort to restructure and improve the effectiveness of science, technology, engineering, and mathematics education programs.

- Achieves savings by reducing funding for lower priority programs, such as the Stratospheric Observatory for Infrared Astronomy. These savings enable continued support for higher priority programs, including lower cost, competitive science missions, and extended operations for the Cassini Saturn mission.

The National Aeronautics and Space Administration's (NASA) mission is to drive advances in science, technology, and exploration to enhance knowledge, education, innovation, economic vitality, and stewardship of Earth. To achieve this mission, NASA develops aeronautics and space technologies, studies the Earth from space, and pioneers the exploration of space. The Budget provides $17.5 billion for NASA to support investments that will ensure continued U.S. leadership in space, while helping to create new industries and capabilities. The Budget supports research and development to drive advances in space capabilities and strengthens NASA's ability to answer increasingly important scientific questions about the Earth. The Budget also prioritizes the "seed corn" of technology development, as well as innovative commercial programs that promise to reduce costs and increase U.S. capabilities.

Leads the World in Space Exploration

Extends the Life of the International Space Station. The Budget extends the planned life of the International Space Station to 2024. The Space Station provides a unique environment for the research on human health and space operations necessary for future long-term human missions. In addition, the Space Station has served as a tool for promoting science, technology, engineering, and mathematics (STEM) education and inspiring the public. The Opportunity, Growth, and Security Initiative provides an additional $100 million to enable the Space Station's research facilities to be fully utilized.

Partners with American Commercial Space Enterprises. In order to reduce U.S. reliance on foreign providers for transporting U.S. astronauts to and from the International Space Station, the Budget invests in private industry-based solutions that will create competitive transport capabilities at a lower cost than previous systems. After the successful completion of the commercial cargo development program, NASA is now purchasing services from two U.S. providers who have successfully conducted cargo resupply missions to the Space Station. Building on the success of these efforts, the Commercial Crew Program is a uniquely American partnership aimed at introducing new efficiencies in space exploration that will strengthen U.S. leadership in space, help produce a more globally competitive U.S. space industry, and enable the Nation to more fully benefit from the International Space Station's research capabilities. The Opportunity, Growth, and Security Initiative provides an additional $250 million to speed development and certification of these systems.

Sustains Investment in Space Technologies. Advanced technology investments will increase the affordability and safety of space activities by NASA, other Federal Government entities, and industry, with the ultimate goal of enabling travel to and exploration of destinations never before visited. From laboratory experiments to technology demonstrations onboard the International Space Station to future in-space missions, the Budget funds the testing and development of technologies that will be crucial to NASA's missions and will help to keep the U.S. aerospace industry competitive with other nations. The Opportunity, Growth, and Security Initiative provides an additional $100 million to develop new space technologies.

Unlocks Mysteries of the Universe. The Budget continues the development of the James Webb Space Telescope, a 100-times more capable successor to the Hubble Telescope, keeping it on track for launch in 2018. Within the current constrained funding environment, the Budget also funds high priority planetary science missions, including efforts to detect and characterize potentially hazardous Earth asteroids, extension of an existing Saturn mission, and multiple missions focused on Mars exploration. The Opportunity, Growth, and Security Initiative provides funding to extend missions that continue to generate valuable science and to accelerate early work on a potential successor to the James Webb Space Telescope.

Continues Human Exploration of the Solar System. The Budget funds the continued development of new systems that will support crewed missions to deep space. The Space Launch System heavy lift rocket will eventually be the world's largest rocket since the Apollo era Saturn V, and its capsule counterpart, the Orion Multi-Purpose Crew Vehicle, is designed to carry crews past the Moon. Both programs leverage NASA's skilled workforce and contractor teams and build upon existing capabilities to push the reach of humans farther into the solar system, with an initial goal of visiting an asteroid in the next decade, followed eventually by a human mission to Mars. The Opportunity, Growth, and Security Initiative provides an additional $100 million to aid the development of the heavy lift rocket and the Orion capsule.

Improves Understanding of the Earth

Advances Science Needed to Improve Prediction of Climate and Weather. The Budget provides $1.8 billion for NASA's Earth Science missions that will allow unprecedented study of climate change and weather modeling and prediction. From global measurements of soil moisture and the ocean to continuation of key

climate and land imaging observations, NASA missions will advance Earth system science and demonstrate technologies for next generation measurements.

Makes Air Travel Safer and More Cost-Effective

Promotes Innovation in Aviation. The Budget continues support for research and development to improve the Nation's air transportation system so that Americans can get where they need to go as safely and efficiently as possible. The Budget funds the second year of an initiative that will make lighter composite materials more easily usable in aviation, and continues to fund myriad research projects aimed at increasing efficiency and reducing environmental impacts in aviation. The Opportunity, Growth, and Security Initiative provides additional funding for research to help increase the efficiency and throughput of the air traffic systems that affect all travelers.

Maximizes Resources

Supports High-Quality STEM Education Programs. The Budget continues NASA's effort to consolidate its education efforts into a more focused portfolio funded through the Office of Education. Additionally, the Budget provides $15 million to NASA's Science Directorate to fund the best application of NASA Science assets to meet the Nation's STEM education goals through a competitive process.

Boosts Sustainability and Energy Efficiency of NASA Facilities. The Budget supports a number of initiatives to help NASA facilities operate in a more efficient and sustainable manner. Today, more than 80 percent of NASA buildings are beyond their design life. The Budget supports NASA's efforts to replace or modernize inefficient buildings, providing jobs to local communities, and leading to increasingly efficient use of taxpayer dollars. For example, the Budget supports cost-saving investments across NASA that will reduce the agency's footprint, co-locate personnel, consolidate data centers, increase energy efficiency, and improve sustainability.

Achieves Savings Through Reducing or Terminating Lower Priority Programs. Recognizing the challenges of the fiscal environment, the Budget focuses on those programs that have the most significant return on investment and reduces funding for lower priority programs. For example, the Budget sharply reduces funds for the Stratospheric Observatory for Infrared Astronomy in order to fund higher priority science missions.

NATIONAL SCIENCE FOUNDATION

Funding Highlights:

- Provides $7.3 billion for the National Science Foundation to expand the frontiers of knowledge and to lay the foundation for long-term economic growth by building an innovation economy and educating a globally competitive workforce. This includes:

  o Building an innovation economy through investments in a broad portfolio of fundamental research, as well as investments in strategic areas such as advanced manufacturing and clean energy; and

  o Preparing a globally competitive workforce by supporting advanced education in science, technology, engineering, and mathematics.

Opportunity, Growth, and Security Initiative:

- Through the Opportunity, Growth, and Security Initiative, supports:

  o An additional 1,000 new research grants in areas such as neuroscience and materials science; and

  o Additional research traineeships to improve advanced education in high priority areas, impacting thousands of graduate students.

Reforms:

- Increases the impact of the Agency's investments and operational efficiency by increasing public access to the results of research and reducing the cost of processing research grant proposals.

The National Science Foundation (NSF) is the key Federal grant-making agency responsible for supporting the full breadth of non-biomedical science and engineering research at the Nation's universities and colleges. The Agency's mission is to promote the progress of science; to advance the national health, prosperity, and welfare; and to secure the national defense. NSF's research and high-tech workforce development programs help lay the foundation for economic growth by building an innovation economy and educating globally competitive American workers. To support this important mission, the Budget provides $7.3 billion for NSF, one percent above the

2014 enacted level, including strong support for cross-cutting research priorities such as advanced manufacturing and clean energy. The Budget also supports efforts to increase the Agency's impact and improve its operations, for example, by increasing public access to the results of research and reducing the cost of processing research grant proposals.

Builds an Innovation Economy

Supports the Fundamental Research that Underpins Progress in Science, Technology, and Innovation. The Budget proposes $5.8 billion for research and related activities at NSF and supports research activities at over 1,900 colleges and universities. The Budget will enable NSF to make about 7,900 research grant awards in 2015.

Lays the Groundwork for the Industries and Jobs of the Future. NSF links the results of fundamental research to societal needs, including building human capacity through educating tomorrow's technical workforce. To encourage interdisciplinary research for a future bioeconomy, the Budget provides $29 million for innovative proposals at the intersection of biology, mathematics, the physical sciences, and engineering. The Budget provides $125 million for a cyber-infrastructure initiative that will accelerate the pace of discovery in all research disciplines by advancing high performance computing—increasingly essential to developments in fields such as climate science and clean energy—by creating new research networks and data repositories, and by developing new systems to visualize data.

Invests in the Long-Term Competitiveness of American Manufacturing. The Budget provides $151 million for fundamental research on revolutionary new manufacturing technologies in partnership with other Federal agencies and the private sector. This advanced manufacturing research is part of a larger $213 million NSF research initiative aimed at transforming static systems, processes, and infrastructure into adaptive, pervasive "smart" systems with embedded computational intelligence that can sense, adapt, and react. This larger research effort also provides $29 million for NSF's contribution to the National Robotics Initiative, which will accelerate the development and use of robots in the United States. The Budget also provides $22 million for NSF's contribution to the Materials Genome Initiative, which is designed to discover, manufacture, and deploy advanced materials twice as fast as the current state of the art, at a fraction of the cost.

Supports the Long-Term Development of a Clean Energy Economy. The Budget provides $362 million for fundamental research that is directly relevant to future clean energy technologies such as solar power generation and energy efficiency. In coordination with other Federal agencies, this clean energy research is a key component of an integrated approach to increasing U.S. energy independence, enhancing environmental stewardship, reducing energy and carbon intensity, and generating sustainable economic growth.

Accelerates Innovations Moving From the Laboratory to the Market. While the knowledge gained from NSF-supported fundamental research frequently advances a particular field of science or engineering, some results also show immediate potential for broader applicability and impact in the business world. The Budget proposes $25 million for the public-private Innovation Corps program at NSF aimed at bringing together the technological, entrepreneurial, and business know-how necessary to bring discoveries ripe for innovation out of the university lab.

Educates a Globally Competitive American Workforce

Promotes Advanced Education for the Jobs of Tomorrow. In line with the Federal plan for science, technology, engineering, and mathematics education, the Budget promotes graduate education for tomorrow's workforce. The Budget provides $333 million to support thousands of outstanding graduate student researchers, who will become tomorrow's leaders in science and engineering research. The Budget also supports opportunities for graduate students to receive training for the range of jobs needed in the future. In addition, the Budget provides $7 million for a new program to spark innovation in graduate education by providing awards to universities to explore novel ideas in student training.

Improves Undergraduate Education for Science and Engineering. The Budget provides $118 million for a consolidated program to implement evidence-based instructional practices, expand the evidence base, and support research on how new technologies can facilitate adoption and use of new approaches to instruction. The Budget also proposes $75 million for NSF's Research Experiences for Undergraduates to provide early opportunities to conduct research, which can be especially influential in maintaining a student's interest in science, engineering, and mathematics.

Accelerates Innovation Through the Opportunity, Growth, and Security Initiative

Deepens the Nation's Knowledge and Human Capital. The Budget includes $552 million for NSF in the Opportunity, Growth, and Security Initiative. This funding will increase research to expand knowledge across disciplines and accelerate innovation across industries. The Opportunity, Growth, and Security Initiative will support 1,000 additional research grants. It will also expand graduate research traineeships, promoting improved advanced education in targeted, high-priority disciplines, impacting the training of thousands of graduate students.

Improves Impact and Efficiency

Increases the Impact of the Agency's Investments. NSF will increase the impact of its investments by making the results of the research it supports more accessible to the public. For example, NSF will develop a repository where the public can access articles by NSF-funded researchers. The Agency will also continue to strengthen its ability to evaluate its activities, making programs more effective at increasing scientific knowledge, supporting long-term economic growth, and laying the groundwork for the industries and jobs of the future.

Increases the Efficiency of the Agency's Operations. NSF will increase the efficiency of its operations by increasing the automation of research grant proposal processing and the use of virtual review panels. Increasing the automation of proposal processing will allow the Agency to reduce related personnel costs. Increasing the use of virtual review panels will reduce travel costs, as well as broaden the range of potential reviewers. The Agency will also increase the operational efficiency of U.S. activities in the Antarctic by implementing the highest payoff recommendations of a blue ribbon panel of outside experts.

SMALL BUSINESS ADMINISTRATION

Funding Highlights:

- Provides $710 million for the Small Business Administration (SBA) to create jobs, invest in competitiveness, and grow America's small businesses. This includes:

  o Supporting more than $36 billion in loan guarantees to enable more than 55,000 loans to entrepreneurs to start up and expand small businesses and create jobs;

  o Supporting equity investments in underserved markets;

  o Continuing fee waivers put in place in 2014 on small business loans to support lower-cost financing to veterans and populations underserved by the credit market;

  o Continuing the expansion of financing available for Small Business Investment Companies including helping innovative small businesses obtain early-stage financing through the Impact Investment Fund and Early-Stage Innovation Fund;

  o Supporting more than $1 billion in low-cost direct loans for homeowners, renters, and businesses of all sizes that are available in the event of disaster, ensuring that the agency can continue to fulfill its critical role in the Federal Government's disaster response efforts; and

  o Expanding entrepreneurship training opportunities through continued support for the Emerging Leaders program, which trains and develops existing small business owners with growth potential. The Budget also expands entrepreneurship education for veterans transitioning to civilian life through the Administration's Boots to Business initiative.

Opportunity, Growth, and Security Initiative:

- Through the Opportunity, Growth, and Security Initiative, supports:

  o Public-private investment funding to support the scaling-up of new advanced manufacturing firms into full-scale commercial production to help ensure that if it is invented here it can be made here.

> **Reforms:**
>
> • Creates a single, streamlined application for SBA loan products called SBA ONE, which will reduce the time and cost for lenders to process loans and encourage lenders to make more loans.

Small businesses play a vital role in supporting job creation, economic growth, and U.S. global competitiveness. They create two out of every three net new jobs in the United States and half of all working Americans own, or are employed, by a small business. The Small Business Administration's (SBA) mission is to help Americans start, build, and grow businesses, which in turn fuels the growth of a strong middle class. To achieve this mission, the Budget provides $710 million through appropriations and an additional $155 million in disaster relief funding. Small business loan guarantees are funded at levels sufficient to meet expected demand, but continue at a reduced subsidy cost relative to the 2014 enacted level, largely due to improving economic conditions and lower estimated loan defaults. The savings realized through lower credit subsidy costs allow investments to be made in SBA's technical assistance programs and other initiatives aimed at growing America's small businesses, thus delivering impact to more communities across the United States.

Provides Small Businesses with Access to Capital and Disaster Assistance

Spurs Economic Growth and Job Creation by Providing Access to Capital. To encourage economic growth and job creation, the Budget provides $47.5 million in subsidy for SBA's business loan programs. This funding supports $17.5 billion in 7(a) loan guarantees for operating expenses and other purposes, which supports more than 45,000 loans to help small businesses operate and grow their businesses; $7.5 billion in guaranteed lending under the 504 Certified Development Company (CDC) program to finance more than 10,000 loans to small businesses for commercial real estate development and heavy machinery

purchases; and $25 million in direct microloans to assist more than 3,500 small businesses in getting started and expanding.

In addition, the Budget supports guarantees for the Small Business Investment Company (SBIC) program at the program level of $4 billion at no cost to the taxpayer, to enable SBICs to continue to invest in high-growth and impact-oriented small businesses that create jobs and strengthen communities, as well as to support early financing of innovative startups via the Impact Investment Fund and the Early-Stage Innovation Fund. Within these funds, the Budget also includes an emphasis on supporting lending to young and innovative U.S. manufacturing firms to enable their scale-up to a full commercial production facility.

Strengthens U.S. Manufacturing and Innovation. In addition to the efforts within existing SBIC funds, the Budget also calls on the Congress to work together with the President to launch a public-private investment fund as part of the Administration's manufacturing initiative. This will help emerging advanced manufacturing technologies reach commercial viability, ensuring that if a technology is invented in the United States, it can be made in the United States. To address the gap in financing for these new manufacturing firms, the Budget proposes, in the Opportunity, Growth, and Security Initiative, a fund of funds to support transformative manufacturing technologies in the United States by helping entrepreneurial firms secure capital to scale from idea to prototype and into full commercial production. Once fully deployed, this fund could eventually leverage up to $10 billion in total public-private investment to build first-of-a-kind manufacturing production capabilities here.

Waives Fees for Small Dollar and Veteran-Owned Business Loans. The Budget waives fees on loans of $150,000 and less in SBA's 7(a) loan program to promote lending to small businesses that face the greatest constraints on credit access. For veteran-owned businesses, upfront fees are fully waived on all 7(a) SBA Express loans up to $350,000 and waived by 50 percent for all non-SBA Express loans above $150,000 to support the entrepreneurial efforts of veterans, a group comprised of individuals who are well-positioned to be successful entrepreneurs as they transition from their military careers to working as a civilian.

Expands Refinancing Opportunities for Small Businesses. Consistent with the Administration's plan to help responsible homeowners refinance their mortgages, the Budget proposes to reauthorize the 504 Loan Refinancing program through September 30, 2015, to provide up to $7.5 billion in guaranteed loans. The successful program, originally established in 2010, has been temporarily suspended since its authorization expired at the end of 2012, and will resume at no cost to taxpayers. This will help small businesses lock in low, long-term interest rates on commercial mortgage and equipment debts and free up resources that can be re-invested in their businesses.

Fully Funds Disaster Assistance Loans. SBA's Disaster Loan Program provides low-interest disaster loans to homeowners, renters, and businesses of all sizes whose property is damaged or destroyed in a disaster. The Budget supports more than $1 billion in direct disaster assistance loans for 2015, the normalized 10-year average demand for these loans. In the continued wake of Hurricane Sandy and to prepare for future major disasters, the Budget provides $187 million for loan administrative expenses to operate the Disaster Loans Program. Of this total, $155 million is designated as qualifying disaster funding under the Budget Control Act's cap adjustment.

Streamlines and Simplifies Loan Applications for SBA Lenders. The Budget supports SBA ONE, a reformed lending platform that will streamline and simplify the loan process by using one set of forms for all 7(a) loans. The platform will serve as a single entry point for all steps of the loan process, from determining eligibility through closing out the loan, and provide one data management system to measure and evaluate loan trends and performance. SBA ONE will simplify the lending process by lowering the cost of underwriting small dollar loans, thereby increasing the expected total number of lenders offering SBA financing and expanding small business access to capital.

Fosters Entrepreneurship and Expands Opportunities for Small Business Growth

Invests in Small Business Leadership Program. The Budget provides $15 million to expand the Emerging Leaders program, an entrepreneurial education initiative, to 1,750 more small business owners who have growth potential. The program has a proven track record of helping small businesses in increasing their revenue, creating jobs, and spurring economic growth in their communities. The expanded program will become a public-private partnership to support a small business leadership model built on the best practices of private sector and non-profit models.

Invests in Entrepreneurship Training for America's Transitioning Veterans. The Budget provides $7 million to support SBA's Boots to Business initiative, which is expected to reach an estimated 25,000 veterans across all military branches and build upon SBA's successful pilot program that provides veterans transitioning to civilian life with the training and tools they need to start their own businesses.

Supports Entrepreneurship Counseling and Regional Economic Development. The Budget includes $198 million for SBA's technical assistance programs, including $114 million for

63 Small Business Development Center grants to support 940 locations and $20 million in technical assistance for microloan programs, to help businesses get started. The Budget also includes $5 million for SBA's growth accelerators program and $6 million for the Regional Innovation Clusters program, which help connect small businesses with universities, venture capitalists, and regional industry leaders to leverage a region's unique assets to turn entrepreneurial ideas into sustainable high-growth small businesses.

Provides a One-Stop Shop for Federal Business Assistance Resources. The Budget provides $6 million for SBA's contribution to BusinessUSA, a one-stop shop for businesses looking for assistance from, or business opportunities with, the Federal Government. In 2015, SBA will continue scaling BusinessUSA into a robust, customer friendly system that supports U.S. small businesses and exporters to access the broad range of Federal, State, and local business-facing resources. As the website continues to mature, BusinessUSA will further enhance the customer experience by incorporating a more personalized web design that will adapt the layout presented to users based on their preferences. BusinessUSA will also aim to create a leaner, more performance-focused website, enabling SBA to more closely monitor small business trends and increase relevant content on the website. BusinessUSA will seek to achieve interoperability across all platforms, browsers, and operating systems. BusinessUSA also plans to upgrade the Content Management System, allowing better maintenance and management of the content presented to website users. In addition, BusinessUSA will ensure that only the best and most relevant content is integrated into the site by assigning subject matter experts from other agencies to manage key business areas such as taxes and healthcare.

SOCIAL SECURITY ADMINISTRATION

Funding Highlights:

- Provides $12.1 billion in funding for the operations of the Social Security Administration to provide services to the American public, including workers, retirees, surviving spouses and children, and people with disabilities. This includes:

  o Investing in customer service, including $100 million in a new modernization initiative to improve online and in-person services; and

  o Establishing a dependable mandatory source of funding for Continuing Disability Reviews and Supplemental Security Income Redeterminations, which reduce program costs and enhance program integrity by ensuring that only those eligible for benefits receive them.

Opportunity, Growth, and Security Initiative:

- Through the Opportunity, Growth, and Security Initiative, supports:

  o Expanding on the new customer service modernization initiative, investing an additional $150 million to further reduce wait times and enhance services for the public.

Reforms:

- Funds pilot projects to test innovative strategies to help people with disabilities remain in the workforce, in partnership with other Federal agencies.

- Prevents duplicative or excessive benefit payments through a series of targeted reforms.

The Social Security Administration (SSA) administers the Old Age, Survivors, and Disability Insurance program and the Supplemental Security Income (SSI) program. The President believes that Social Security is critical to ensuring that all Americans have the opportunity to retire with dignity and that Americans with disabilities do not have to experience economic hardship. To fund this commitment, the Budget includes $12.1 billion for SSA operations. The Budget also supports pilot programs to improve employment outcomes for people with disabilities and enhancements to program integrity.

Protects Social Security for Future Generations

The President believes that Social Security is indispensable to workers, retirees, survivors, and people with disabilities and that it is one of the most important and successful programs ever established in the United States. Although current forecasts indicate that Social Security can pay full benefits until 2033, the Administration is committed to making sure that the program is solvent and viable for the American people, now and in the future. The President is strongly opposed to privatizing Social Security and looks forward to working in a bipartisan way to strengthen the program for future generations.

Improves Customer Service. As part of the Administration's second term management agenda's focus on improving key citizen- and business-facing transactions, the Budget includes $100 million for a new customer service modernization initiative to significantly improve internet and in-person services at SSA. These investments will save time for the agency as well as for the public. In addition, the Opportunity, Growth, and Security Initiative includes $150 million in additional funding to further reduce wait times and enhance services for the public.

Enhances Program Integrity in Disability Programs and Pilots Pro-Work Interventions

Reduces Program Costs by Providing Reliable Funding for Program Integrity Work. The Budget proposes to establish a dependable source of mandatory funding in 2016 for Continuing Disability Reviews (CDRs) and SSI Redeterminations, which ensure that only those eligible for benefits continue to receive them. SSA estimates that each $1 spent on CDRs would save the Federal Government $9. SSA could save an estimated $35 billion over 10 years through this proposal and reduce the current backlog of 1.3 million overdue CDRs.

Prevents Duplicative or Excessive Benefit Payments. The Budget enhances collection of delinquent debts owed to the Government by applying the Treasury Offset Program to retroactive Disability Insurance (DI) payments, and proposes to automate coordination of disability benefit payments between the Office of Personnel

Management (OPM) and SSA, which would substantially reduce overpayments. Further, the Budget proposes to reduce an individual's DI benefit in any month in which that person also receives a State or Federal unemployment benefit. In addition, the Budget proposes to eliminate aggressive Social Security claiming strategies, which allow upper-income beneficiaries to manipulate the timing of collection of Social Security benefits in order to maximize delayed retirement credits.

Improves Tax Administration by Restructuring Federal Wage Reporting. The Budget proposes to restructure the Federal wage reporting process by moving from annual to quarterly wage reporting. Increasing the timeliness of wage reporting will enhance tax administration and improve program integrity for a range of programs. The Administration will work with States to ensure that the overall reporting burden on employers is not increased. The Budget also proposes to lower the Electronic Wage Reporting Threshold for W-2s/W-3s from 250 employees to 25. The vast majority of employers with between 25 and 250 employees already choose to report electronically.

Tests New Ways to Boost Employment. The Budget provides new authority and $400 million in new resources for SSA, in partnership with other Federal agencies, to test innovative strategies to help people with disabilities remain in the workforce. Early-intervention measures, such as supportive employment services for individuals with mental impairments, targeted incentives for employers to help workers with disabilities remain on the job, and incentives and opportunities for States to better coordinate services, have the potential to achieve long-term gains in the employment and the quality of life of people with disabilities, and the proposed demonstration authority will help build the evidence base for future program improvements. The cost of the demonstrations could be offset by the proposal to automate coordination of disability benefit payments between OPM and SSA and other program integrity measures.

Corporation for
NATIONAL &
COMMUNITY
SERVICE ★★★

CORPORATION FOR NATIONAL AND COMMUNITY SERVICE

Funding Highlights:

- Provides $1.05 billion for the Corporation for National and Community Service to support efforts to address national and local challenges. This includes:

  o Supporting the service of a record 114,000 AmeriCorps members across the United States, and encouraging people of all ages and backgrounds to serve; and

  o Investing in promising new approaches to major community challenges through the Social Innovation Fund, and continuing to allow the use of up to 20 percent of the funds for Pay for Success projects.

Reforms:

- Incorporates the Senior Companion and Foster Grandparent models into AmeriCorps to achieve administrative efficiencies, increase competition, and more effectively engage older Americans in national service.

- Integrates RSVP, a program that supports senior volunteer opportunities, into the Volunteer Generation Fund to improve the Corporation for National and Community Service's ability to support older Americans in volunteer activities.

Through national service, volunteering, and other forms of civic participation, millions of Americans each year help to address the Nation's greatest challenges, accelerate economic recovery, and strengthen our communities. The Corporation for National and Community Service (CNCS) provides opportunities for Americans of all ages to serve their community and country in sustained and effective ways, from tutoring at-risk youth to responding to natural disasters to building homes for low-income families. Many of the most creative solutions to America's challenges have been developed at the grassroots level in cities and towns across the Nation, where

citizens work hand in hand to make a difference. The Budget proposes $1.05 billion for CNCS, which reflects the Administration's continuing commitment to providing opportunities for Americans to address local challenges through service.

Invests in Community Solutions

Supports National Service. The Budget supports a record 114,000 AmeriCorps members, 34,000 more members than projected for 2014. These members support the efforts of nonprofit organizations to address a wide range of critical community challenges, from disaster response to homelessness to low-performing schools. The Budget encourages people of all ages and backgrounds to serve in AmeriCorps, and provides more positions for disconnected and low-income youth that can serve as pathways to higher education and employment. The Budget maximizes the total number of members by providing only the education awards and loan forgiveness benefits for programs in which another entity pays the full cost of the members' service stipends. The Budget uses these savings to expand opportunities for others to serve.

Engages Older Americans in High-Impact Service. The Budget simplifies and maximizes the impact of national service programs by transitioning the Senior Companion and Foster Grandparent models to AmeriCorps and expanding the Volunteer Generation Fund to support the most competitive RSVP grantees. These reforms will support an over 40 percent expansion in the number of AmeriCorps members and align and integrate CNCS's service and volunteering programs. The Administration continues to believe strongly in the value of engaging older Americans in addressing the needs of their communities and will preserve this commitment in its implementation of this reform. In 2015, the AmeriCorps program will surpass the goal of reserving at least 10 percent of member positions for seniors, as established in the 2009 Edward M. Kennedy Serve America Act. This reform will continue CNCS's efforts to ensure that all national service programs are competitive, effective, and accountable for achieving results, which has become a central focus of the AmeriCorps program.

Increases Capacity of Nonprofits to Support Volunteers. The Budget provides approximately $19 million for the Volunteer Generation Fund. The Fund will focus on strengthening the ability of nonprofits and other organizations to recruit, retain, and manage volunteers, especially senior volunteers. In particular, the Fund will support organizations as they help volunteers build skills and match volunteers with opportunities that take advantage of their existing skills.

Invests in Evidence-Based and Innovative Solutions. Nonprofits cannot seed and scale effective innovative solutions to critical national challenges without adequate capital to develop, evaluate, and replicate what works. The Budget invests $70 million in the Social Innovation Fund (SIF) to test promising new approaches to major challenges, leverage private and philanthropic capital to meet these needs, and expand evidence-based programs that demonstrate measurable outcomes. The Budget continues to allow the use of up to 20 percent of SIF funds to support Pay for Success projects. Pay for Success models leverage philanthropic and private dollars to fund services up front, with the Government paying only after they generate results. This funding level also includes $4 million for a pilot to improve grantee access to State and Federal administrative data. This investment has the potential to make it easier and less costly for grantees to track performance, conduct rigorous evaluation, and demonstrate measurable impact.

CUTS, CONSOLIDATIONS, AND SAVINGS

As part of the President's Management Agenda, the Administration will build upon the successful efforts started in the first term to maximize the value of every taxpayer dollar while increasing productivity and the quality of services.

The Budget continues efforts from the President's first-term Campaign to Cut Waste, such as reducing administrative overhead, cutting improper payments, saving on real estate costs, reforming military acquisition, and consolidating data centers. Further detail on these initiatives is provided in the Creating a 21ˢᵗ Century Government chapter.

The Budget also continues efforts to reorganize and consolidate Federal programs to reduce duplication and improve efficiency. The President is again asking the Congress to revive an authority that Presidents had for almost the entire period from 1932 through 1984—the ability to submit proposals to reorganize the Executive Branch via a fast-track procedure. In effect, the President is asking to have the same authority that any business owner has to reorganize or streamline operations to meet changing circumstances and customer demand.

The Budget specifically proposes a fresh Government-wide reorganization of science, technology, engineering, and mathematics (STEM) education programs designed to enable more strategic investment in STEM education and more critical evaluation of outcomes. In 2012, there were more than 200 STEM education programs across Government. Already, a substantial number of program consolidations and eliminations have been implemented or will be completed in 2014, through actions by the Congress or internal consolidations or eliminations undertaken by the Administration. The Budget continues to reduce STEM fragmenta-

tion by proposing 31 additional program consolidations or eliminations, and focuses ongoing efforts around the five key areas identified by the Federal STEM Education 5-Year Strategic Plan.

The Budget also continues to target unnecessary or lower priority programs for reduction or elimination. For example, at the Department of Defense, based on recommendations from uniformed military leadership, the Budget would cancel the Ground Combat Vehicle Program, which is no longer needed under the current defense strategy, saving $51 million in 2015. The Budget would also close or consolidate 250 offices at the Department of Agriculture as part of streamlining Farm Service Agency operations that would save a total of $39 million in 2015.

In each of the President's first three Budgets, the Administration identified, on average, more than 150 terminations, reductions, and savings proposals, totaling nearly $25 billion each year. In the 2013 and 2014 Budgets, the Administration detailed more than 200 cuts, consolidations, and savings proposals, again totaling roughly $25 billion each year. This year's Budget shows the tradeoffs and choices the Administration is making to adhere to the funding levels established in the Bipartisan Budget Act of 2013. It includes 136 cuts, consolidations, and savings proposals, which are projected to save nearly $17 billion in 2015. The cuts, consolidation, and savings proposals this year reflect the deep spending reductions that occurred in 2013, some of which have continued in 2014, and the fact that many of the Administration's previous cuts, consolidations, and savings proposals have now been implemented. Discretionary and mandatory cuts, consolidations, and savings proposals in this year's Budget are detailed on the following tables, as well as internal efficiencies agencies are undertaking that require no further action by the Congress, many of which were suggested through the President's SAVE Award program.

Savings from the Administration's program integrity proposals, totaling $99 billion through 2024, are detailed in the Budget Process chapter of the *Analytical Perspectives* volume. As these tables show, the Budget includes a robust package of proposals that modify Medicare provider payments totaling about $354 billion over the next 10 years. These include a number of measures detailed in Table S-9 (see Summary Tables section of this volume), including a proposal to align Medicare drug payment policies with Medicaid rebate policies for low-income beneficiaries, reducing the net cost of this valuable benefit. This change alone will save about $117 billion over the next 10 years. The Budget takes other critical steps to save money, such as preventing individuals from collecting disability and unemployment benefits for the same period of time. This reform will save $3.2 billion over 10 years.

DISCRETIONARY CUTS, CONSOLIDATIONS, AND SAVINGS
(Budget authority in millions of dollars)

	2014	2015	2015 Change from 2014
Cuts			
317 Immunization Program, Department of Health and Human Services	612	561	−51
Access to Recovery, Department of Health and Human Services	50	....	−50
Area Health Education Centers, Department of Health and Human Services	30	....	−30
Beach Grants, Environmental Protection Agency	10	....	−10
Brownfields Projects, Environmental Protection Agency	90	85	−5
C–130 Avionics Modernization, Department of Defense	47	....	−47
Capacity Building, Department of Housing and Urban Development	35	20	−15
Centers for Disease Control and Prevention Direct Healthcare Screenings, Department of Health and Human Services	251	209	−42
Christopher Columbus Fellowship Foundation[1]	....	....	....
Clean Water and Drinking Water State Revolving Funds, Environmental Protection Agency	2,356	1,775	−581
Community Development Block Grant - Formula Funds Only, Department of Housing and Urban Development	3,030	2,800	−230
Community Services Block Grant, Department of Health and Human Services	674	350	−324
Diesel Emissions Reduction Grant Program, Environmental Protection Agency	20	....	−20
Divestiture of the A–10 Fleet, Department of Defense	1,049	737	−312
Economic Impact Grants, Department of Agriculture[1]	6	....	−6
Education Research Centers and Agricultural Research, Department of Health and Human Services[1]	52	....	−52
Effective Teacher and Leader State Grants (Title II), Department of Education	2,350	2,000	−350
Enhancing the Mathematical Sciences Workforce in the 21st Century, National Science Foundation	10	6	−4
Foreign Military Financing, Department of State	5,919	5,648	−271
Fossil Energy Research and Development, Department of Energy	562	476	−86
Grants for Abstinence-Only Programs, Department of Health and Human Services	5	....	−5
Grants-in-Aid for Airports, Department of Transportation[1]	3,350	2,900	−450
Great Lakes Restoration Initiative, Environmental Protection Agency	300	275	−25
Ground Combat Vehicle, Department of Defense	100	49	−51
Harry S. Truman Scholarship Foundation[1]	1	....	−1
Health Care Services Grant Program, Department of Agriculture[1]	3	....	−3
Health Careers Opportunity Program, Department of Health and Human Services	14	....	−14
High Energy Cost Grants, Department of Agriculture[1]	10	....	−10
High Intensity Drug Trafficking Areas, Office of National Drug Control Policy	239	193	−46
HOME Investment Partnerships Program, Department of Housing and Urban Development	1,000	950	−50
Impact Aid - Payments for Federal Property, Department of Education[1]	1,289	1,222	−67
International Forestry, Department of Agriculture[1]	8	....	−8
International Narcotics Control and Law Enforcement, Department of State	1,350	1,118	−232
Investigator-Initiated Research Grants, Department of Health and Human Services	46	40	−6
Low Income Home Energy Assistance Program, Department of Health and Human Services	3,425	2,800	−625
Low Priority Studies and Construction, Corps of Engineers[1]	1,781	1,205	−576
Low Priority Work, Bureau of Reclamation, Department of the Interior[1]	1,060	986	−74
Mine Safety and Health Administration State Grants, Department of Labor	8	....	−8
National Heritage Areas, Department of the Interior[1]	18	9	−9
National Wildlife Refuge Fund, Department of the Interior[1]	13	....	−13
Network for Earthquake Engineering Simulation, National Science Foundation	20	12	−8
Nuclear Energy, Department of Energy	888	863	−25

DISCRETIONARY CUTS, CONSOLIDATIONS, AND SAVINGS—Continued
(Budget authority in millions of dollars)

	2014	2015	2015 Change from 2014
Office of the Assistant Secretary Grant Programs, Department of Health and Human Services	91	66	−25
Office of the Federal Coordinator for Alaska Natural Gas Transportation Projects[1]	1	....	−1
Operation and Maintenance Work, Corps of Engineers	2,861	2,600	−261
Prevention and Care Management Research, Department of Health and Human Services	23	11	−12
Preventive Health and Health Services Block Grant, Department of Health and Human Services[1]	160	....	−160
PRIME Technical Assistance, Small Business Administration[1]	4	....	−4
Public Broadcasting Grants, Department of Agriculture[1]	2	....	−2
REACH, Department of Health and Human Services	51	....	−51
Rehabilitation Act Programs, Department of Education[1]	32	....	−32
Research, Education and Extension Grants, Department of Agriculture:			
Animal Health (Sec. 1433)[1]	4	....	−4
Capacity Building: Non-Land Grant Colleges[1]	5	....	−5
Critical Agricultural Materials[1]	1	....	−1
Farm Business Management and Benchmarking[1]	1	....	−1
Food Animal Residue Avoid Database[1]	1	....	−1
Methyl Bromide Transition Program[1]	2	....	−2
Potato Breeding Research (Competitive)[1]	1	....	−1
Rural Health and Safety[1]	2	....	−2
Sungrants[1]	3	....	−3
Supplemental and Alternative Crops[1]	1	....	−1
Water Quality[1]	5	....	−5
Rural Access to Emergency Devices, Department of Health and Human Services[1]	3	....	−3
Rural Community Facilities, Department of Health and Human Services[1]	6	....	−6
Rural Hospital Flexibility Grant Programs, Department of Health and Human Services	41	26	−14
Rural Multifamily Housing Preservation Grants, Department of Agriculture[1]	4	....	−4
Rural Single Family Housing Grant Programs, Department of Agriculture	57	35	−22
Science of Learning Centers, National Science Foundation	19	7	−12
Senior Community Service Employment Program, Department of Health and Human Services	434	380	−54
State Criminal Alien Assistance Program, Department of Justice	180	....	−180
State Indoor Radon Grant Program, Environmental Protection Agency	8	....	−8
Stratospheric Observatory for Infrared Astronomy, National Aeronautics and Space Administration[1]	84	12	−72
Sunwise, Environmental Protection Agency	1	....	−1
Tactical Tomahawk, Department of Defense	313	194	−119
University Radio Observatories, National Science Foundation	1	....	−1
Urban and Community Forestry, Department of Agriculture	28	24	−4
Virtual Astronomy Observatory, National Science Foundation[1]	1	....	−1
Water and Wastewater and Community Facilities Loan Guarantees, Department of Agriculture[1]	4	....	−4
Water and Wastewater Grants and Loans, Department of Agriculture	462	304	−158
Water Quality Research and Support Grants, Environmental Protection Agency	17	....	−17
Watershed Rehabilitation Program, Department of Agriculture[1]	12	....	−12
Women in Apprenticeship in Non-Traditional Occupations, Department of Labor[1]	1	....	−1
Total, Discretionary Cuts	**37,007**	**30,948**	**−6,059**

DISCRETIONARY CUTS, CONSOLIDATIONS, AND SAVINGS—Continued
(Budget authority in millions of dollars)

	2014	2015	2015 Change from 2014
Consolidations			
Central Utah Project, Department of the Interior	9	7	–2
Community Economic Development Program, Department of Health and Human Services	30	....	–30
Elementary and Secondary Education Act, Department of Education	....	....	....
Kiowa Warrior, Department of Defense	108	....	–108
Rural Business and Cooperative Grants, Department of Agriculture	....	....	....
Science, Technology, Engineering, and Mathematics (STEM) Reorganization, Multi-Agency			
Consolidated and Eliminated Programs Total - 31 Programs			
Department of Agriculture - 4 Programs	*[11]*		
Department of Commerce - 6 Programs	*[13]*		
Department of Defense - 2 Programs	*[26]*		
Department of Energy - 1 Program	*[9]*		
Department of Health and Human Services - 2 Programs	*[2]*		
Environmental Protection Agency - 3 Programs	*[13]*		
National Aeronautics and Space Administration - 11 Programs	*[7]*		
National Science Foundation - 1 Program	*[49]*		
Nuclear Regulatory Commission - 1 Program	*[15]*		
Senior Service Consolidation, Corporation for National and Community Service	....	....	....
Streamline Farm Service Agency Operations, Department of Agriculture	1,178	1,139	–39
Streamline Federal Air Marshals, Department of Homeland Security	817	815	–2
Total, Discretionary Consolidations	**2,142**	**1,961**	**–181**
Savings			
Census Bureau Operations, Department of Commerce	252	243	–9
Immigration Detention Prioritization, Department of Homeland Security	2,085	1,886	–199
Senate Campaign Finance Reports Electronic Submission, Federal Election Commission	....	....	....
Total, Discretionary Savings	**2,337**	**2,129**	**–208**
Total, Discretionary Cuts, Consolidations, and Savings	**41,486**	**35,038**	**–6,448**

[1] This cut has been identified as a lower priority program activity for purposes of the GPRA Modernization Act, at 31 U.S.C. 1115(b)(10). Additional information regarding this proposed cut is included in the respective agency's Congressional Justification submission, where applicable.

MANDATORY CUTS AND SAVINGS

(Outlays and receipts in millions of dollars)

	2015	2016	2017	2018	2019	2015–2019	2015–2024
Cuts							
Coal Tax Preferences, Department of Energy							
Domestic Manufacturing Deduction for Hard Mineral Fossil Fuels[1]	−36	−63	−67	−70	−73	−309	−726
Expensing of Exploration and Development Costs[1]	−39	−66	−69	−73	−77	−324	−679
Percent Depletion for Hard Mineral Fossil Fuels[1]	−167	−173	−182	−195	−203	−920	−2,052
Royalty Taxation[1]	−20	−43	−47	−49	−52	−211	−508
Crop Insurance Program, Department of Agriculture	−691	−1,232	−1,435	−1,466	−1,507	−6,331	−14,280
Geothermal Payments to Counties, Department of the Interior[2]	−4	−4	−4	−4	−4	−20	−42
Oil and Gas Company Tax Preferences, Department of Energy							
Increase Geological and Geophysical Amortization Period for Independent Producers to Seven Years[1]	−103	−382	−596	−581	−463	−2,125	−3,081
Repeal Credit for Oil and Gas Produced from Marginal Wells[1]	....	....	....	....	....	....	....
Repeal Deduction for Tertiary Injectants[1]	−10	−10	−10	−10	−10	−50	−100
Repeal Domestic Manufacturing Tax Deduction for Oil and Natural Gas Companies[1]	−963	−1,614	−1,585	−1,522	−1,453	−7,137	−14,218
Repeal Enhanced Oil Recovery Credit[1]	....	....	....	....	....	....	....
Repeal Exception to Passive Loss Limitations for Working Interests in Oil and Natural Gas Properties[1]	−5	−7	−7	−7	−6	−32	−59
Repeal Expensing of Intangible Drilling Costs[1]	−2,317	−3,244	−2,348	−1,803	−1,469	−11,181	−14,350
Repeal Percentage Depletion for Oil and Natural Gas Wells[1]	−1,502	−1,568	−1,469	−1,375	−1,306	−7,220	−13,030
Offset Disability Benefits for Period of Concurrent Unemployment Insurance Receipt[2]	....	−56	−254	−390	−414	−1,114	−3,231
Unrestricted Abandoned Mine Lands Payments, Department of the Interior[2]	−48	−35	−28	−34	−36	−181	−295
Total, Mandatory Cuts	**−5,905**	**−8,497**	**−8,101**	**−7,579**	**−7,073**	**−37,155**	**−66,651**
Savings							
FECA Reform, Department of Labor	−11	−1	−8	−16	−24	−60	−309
Federal Employees Health Benefits Program Reforms, Office of Personnel Management	....	−52	−113	−147	−182	−494	−2,243
Health Care (Medicaid Proposals), Department of Health and Human Services	−532	−932	−1,022	−1,072	−1,137	−4,695	−14,955
Health Care (Pharmaceuticals), Department of Health and Human Services[3]	−770	−830	−970	−1,220	−1,450	−5,240	−15,260
Medicare Provider Payment Modifications, Department of Health and Human Services[3, 4]	−3,480	−10,590	−19,820	−24,810	−30,700	−89,400	−353,720
Total, Mandatory Savings	**−4,793**	**−12,405**	**−21,933**	**−27,265**	**−33,493**	**−99,889**	**−386,487**
Total, Mandatory Cuts and Savings	**−10,698**	**−20,902**	**−30,034**	**−34,844**	**−40,566**	**−137,044**	**−453,138**

[1] This cut has been identified as a lower priority program activity for purposes of the GPRA Modernization Act, at 31 U.S.C. 1115(b)(10). Additional information regarding this proposed cut is included in the Governmental Receipts chapter of the Analytical Perspectives volume.

[2] This cut has been identified as a lower priority program activity for purposes of the GPRA Modernization Act, at 31 U.S.C. 1115(b)(10). Additional information regarding this proposed cut is included in the respective agency's Congressional Justification submission, where applicable.

[3] Medicare savings estimates do not include interactions.

[4] In addition to the savings reported on this table, the Budget includes an additional $68.3 billion in 10-year savings for Medicare Structural Reforms, as detailed on Table S-9.

The SAVE Award logo denotes a proposal that was suggested by a Federal employee through the SAVE Award program.

ADMINISTRATIVELY IMPLEMENTED SAVINGS
(In millions of dollars)

	2014	2015	2014–2018
Department of Agriculture			
Reduce Mailings at the Food Safety Inspection Service	-0.002	-0.003	-0.009
Sync the Link	0.000	0.000	-0.138
Department of Homeland Security			
Collect Custom Fines and Penalties Online	0.000	0.000	-1.000
Department of Labor			
Curtail Bureau of Labor Statistics' International Price Program	0.000	-4.500	-18.000
Curtail Bureau of Labor Statistics' Quarterly Census of Employment and Wages	-1.700	-4.800	-20.900
Department of State			
Use E-Mail for Follow-Up Passport Information Requests	0.000	-0.140	-1.821
Department of Veterans Affairs			
Online Tracking of Veterans Mail Prescription Deliveries	0.036	-0.638	-3.700
Multi-Agency			
Share Employee Training Certifications Across Agencies	*	*	*

Note: Amounts in this table include estimated savings from actions agencies are implementing to reduce costs that require no further action by the Congress.
* Savings estimates under development.

The SAVE Award logo denotes this savings action was suggested by a Federal employee through the SAVE Award program.

SUMMARY TABLES

Table S–1. Budget Totals
(In billions of dollars and as a percent of GDP)

	2013	2014	2015	2016	2017	2018	2019	2020	2021	2022	2023	2024	Totals 2015-2019	Totals 2015-2024
Budget Totals in Billions of Dollars:														
Receipts	2,775	3,002	3,337	3,568	3,811	4,030	4,226	4,452	4,706	4,954	5,212	5,478	18,972	43,775
Outlays	3,455	3,651	3,901	4,099	4,269	4,443	4,729	4,964	5,209	5,485	5,694	5,912	21,441	48,705
Deficit	680	649	564	531	458	413	503	512	504	530	482	434	2,468	4,930
Debt held by the public	11,983	12,903	13,592	14,257	14,843	15,370	15,982	16,603	17,213	17,850	18,441	18,986		
Debt net of financial assets	10,926	11,575	12,138	12,669	13,127	13,540	14,043	14,555	15,058	15,588	16,070	16,503		
Gross domestic product (GDP)	16,619	17,332	18,219	19,181	20,199	21,216	22,196	23,200	24,225	25,280	26,381	27,531		
Budget Totals as a Percent of GDP:														
Receipts	16.7%	17.3%	18.3%	18.6%	18.9%	19.0%	19.0%	19.2%	19.4%	19.6%	19.8%	19.9%	18.8%	19.2%
Outlays	20.8%	21.1%	21.4%	21.4%	21.1%	20.9%	21.3%	21.4%	21.5%	21.7%	21.6%	21.5%	21.2%	21.4%
Deficit	4.1%	3.7%	3.1%	2.8%	2.3%	1.9%	2.3%	2.2%	2.1%	2.1%	1.8%	1.6%	2.5%	2.2%
Debt held by the public	72.1%	74.4%	74.6%	74.3%	73.5%	72.4%	72.0%	71.6%	71.1%	70.6%	69.9%	69.0%		
Debt net of financial assets	65.7%	66.8%	66.6%	66.1%	65.0%	63.8%	63.3%	62.7%	62.2%	61.7%	60.9%	59.9%		

Table S–2. Effect of Budget Proposals on Projected Deficits

(Deficit increases (+) or decreases (–) in billions of dollars)

	2014	2015	2016	2017	2018	2019	2020	2021	2022	2023	2024	Totals 2015–2019	Totals 2015–2024
Projected deficits in the adjusted baseline[1]	628	561	568	560	558	657	707	741	887	914	942	2,905	7,097
Percent of GDP	3.6%	3.1%	3.0%	2.8%	2.6%	3.0%	3.0%	3.1%	3.5%	3.5%	3.4%	2.9%	3.1%
Proposals in the 2015 Budget:[2]													
Investments in growing the economy and creating opportunity:													
Opportunity, Growth, and Security Initiative		33	14	4	2	1	1	*	*	......	......	54	55
Spending cuts		–1	–2	–3	–3	–3	–3	–3	–3	–3	–3	–11	–28
Tax loophole closers		–1	–2	–2	–3	–3	–3	–3	–3	–4	–4	–11	–28
Surface transportation reauthorization		4	9	12	14	12	7	5	3	2	1	51	70
Transition revenue from business tax reform[3]		–38	–38	–38	–38	......	......	......	......	......	......	–150	–150
Early childhood investments		*	1	4	6	8	10	11	12	12	11	19	76
Tobacco tax financing		–8	–10	–9	–9	–8	–8	–7	–7	–6	–6	–44	–78
Earned Income Tax Credit expansion for workers without qualifying children		*	6	6	6	6	7	7	7	7	7	26	60
High-income tax loophole closers	–*	–5	–5	–6	–6	–6	–6	–6	–7	–7	–7	–27	–60
Additional investments in education, innovation, infrastructure, and security		–*	47	60	58	51	43	34	–32	–58	–63	216	140
Additional mandatory and tax proposals	20	33	24	–2	–14	–31	–35	–39	–45	–52	–52	9	–215
Debt service	*	*	1	2	4	5	7	7	6	3	–2	12	32
Total, investments	20	18	45	29	18	33	18	4	–69	–106	–117	143	–127
Additional deficit reduction from health, tax, and immigration reform:													
Health savings	1	2	–8	–18	–25	–33	–44	–53	–63	–72	–89	–81	–402
Revenue proposals		–37	–42	–50	–58	–64	–70	–75	–80	–85	–91	–251	–651
Immigration reform		6	–1	–10	–15	–17	–18	–20	–23	–29	–31	–37	–158
Debt service	*	–*	–1	–2	–7	–12	–18	–25	–32	–41	–50	–22	–188
Total, additional deficit reduction	1	–29	–51	–80	–105	–126	–150	–173	–198	–227	–260	–391	–1,399

Table S–2. Effect of Budget Proposals on Projected Deficits—Continued

(Deficit increases (+) or decreases (–) in billions of dollars)

	2014	2015	2016	2017	2018	2019	2020	2021	2022	2023	2024	Totals 2015–2019	Totals 2015–2024
Other changes to deficits:													
Reductions in Overseas Contingency Operations	....	–7	–41	–59	–65	–69	–71	–74	–94	–105	–110	–241	–695
Replacement of mandatory sequestration[4]	....	10	17	17	17	18	19	20	21	27	6	79	171
Proposed Budget Control Act cap adjustment for disaster relief and wildfires	....	3	3	4	1	1	1	1	1	1	1	12	19
Outlay effects of discretionary policy	....	8	–10	–12	–8	–6	–3	–5	–4	–5	–6	–29	–52
Debt service and indirect interest effects	....	*	–*	–1	–3	–6	–8	–11	–14	–18	–22	–10	–84
Total, additional deficit reduction	....	13	–31	–51	–58	–62	–63	–69	–90	–99	–131	–189	–641
Total proposals in the 2015 Budget	20	2	–37	–103	–145	–155	–195	–238	–357	–432	–509	–437	–2,167
Resulting deficits in 2015 Budget	649	564	531	458	413	503	512	504	530	482	434	2,468	4,930
Percent of GDP	3.7%	3.1%	2.8%	2.3%	1.9%	2.3%	2.2%	2.1%	2.1%	1.8%	1.6%	2.5%	2.2%

* $500 million or less.

[1] See Tables S–4 and S–8 for information on the adjusted baseline.

[2] For total deficit reduction since January 2011, see Table S–3.

[3] Business tax reform transition revenue finances the $70 billion cost of above-baseline surface transportation investments (the PAYGO cost of the reauthorization proposal) plus $78 billion in cash transfers necessary to ensure Transportation Trust Fund solvency over the four-year reauthorization period.

[4] Reverses mandatory sequestration for 2015–2023. Extension of mandatory sequestration to 2024 was enacted subsequent to the completion of the 2015 Budget baseline and policy estimates.

Table S-3. Cumulative Deficit Reduction

(Deficit reduction (–) or increase (+) in billions of dollars)

	2015–2024
Deficit reduction achieved through March 2014, excluding Overseas Contingency Operations (OCO):	
Enacted deficit reduction excluding pending Joint Committee enforcement:	
Discretionary savings[1]	–1,622
Mandatory savings	–80
Revenues	–723
Debt service	–690
Subtotal, enacted deficit reduction excluding pending Joint Committee enforcement	–3,115
Pending Joint Committee enforcement:[2]	
Discretionary cap reductions	–533
Mandatory sequestration	–171
Debt service	–158
Subtotal, pending Joint Committee enforcement	–862
Total, deficit reduction achieved, excluding OCO	–3,977
Investments in growing the economy and creating opportunity:	
Investment proposals and offsets[3]	–159
Debt service	32
Total, investments in growing the economy and creating opportunity	–127
Additional deficit reduction from tax and entitlement reform:	
Health savings	–402
Revenue proposals	–651
Immigration reform	–158
Debt service	–188
Total, additional deficit reduction	–1,399
Other changes to deficits:[1]	
Replacement of mandatory sequestration	171
Proposed Budget Control Act cap adjustment for disaster relief and wildfires	19
Outlay effects of discretionary policy	–52
Debt service and indirect interest effects	30
Total, other changes to deficits	168
Grand total, achieved and proposed deficit reduction, excluding OCO	–5,335
Memorandum: revenue and outlay effects of achieved and proposed deficit reduction:	
Enacted outlay reductions and 2015 Budget spending proposals	–3,370
Enacted receipt increases and 2015 Budget tax proposals	–1,807
Immigration reform	–158

Table S–3.   Cumulative Deficit Reduction—Continued

(Deficit reduction (–) or increase (+) in billions of dollars)

	2015–2024
Memorandum, savings in Overseas Contingency Operations (OCO):	
Enacted reduction in OCO funding	–780
Proposed reductions in OCO	–695
Debt service	–334
Total, savings in overseas contingency operations (OCO)	–1,809

[1] Excludes savings from reductions in OCO.
[2] Consists of mandatory sequestration for 2015–2023 and discretionary cap reductions for 2016–2021. Excludes extension of mandatory sequestration to 2024 enacted subsequent to the completion of the 2015 Budget estimates.
[3] See Table S–2 for details on investment proposals.

Table S–4. Adjusted Baseline by Category[1]

(In billions of dollars)

	2013	2014	2015	2016	2017	2018	2019	2020	2021	2022	2023	2024	Totals 2015-2019	Totals 2015-2024
Outlays:														
Appropriated ("discretionary") programs:														
Defense	626	612	606	653	675	687	700	711	728	745	763	781	3,321	7,050
Non-defense	522	562	543	542	552	559	569	581	592	605	618	632	2,766	5,795
Subtotal, appropriated programs	1,147	1,174	1,150	1,195	1,227	1,246	1,270	1,292	1,321	1,350	1,381	1,414	6,088	12,845
Mandatory programs:														
Social Security	808	852	896	947	1,003	1,063	1,127	1,195	1,264	1,337	1,415	1,499	5,037	11,748
Medicare	492	513	529	580	596	617	682	734	790	879	914	947	3,003	7,268
Medicaid	265	308	331	353	373	393	416	440	466	493	522	556	1,868	4,345
Other mandatory programs	521	560	659	697	712	704	752	778	807	847	852	858	3,524	7,666
Subtotal, mandatory programs	2,086	2,234	2,415	2,577	2,684	2,777	2,977	3,147	3,326	3,556	3,704	3,861	13,432	31,026
Net interest	221	223	251	318	393	480	563	635	697	761	827	886	2,005	5,812
Adjustments for disaster costs[2]	......	2	6	8	9	9	9	10	10	10	10	10	40	90
Joint Committee enforcement[3]	......	......	–10	–73	–96	–102	–105	–107	–107	–54	–38	–10	–387	–704
Total outlays	3,455	3,633	3,812	4,025	4,217	4,409	4,714	4,978	5,247	5,623	5,884	6,160	21,178	49,069
Receipts:														
Individual income taxes	1,316	1,389	1,498	1,606	1,727	1,854	1,971	2,094	2,223	2,353	2,487	2,622	8,656	20,435
Corporation income taxes	274	333	412	463	488	501	512	524	538	552	566	585	2,376	5,141
Social insurance and retirement receipts:														
Social Security payroll taxes	673	732	756	808	848	896	942	984	1,039	1,090	1,139	1,191	4,251	9,693
Medicare payroll taxes	209	219	231	248	261	276	291	304	320	336	352	368	1,307	2,987
Unemployment insurance	57	60	59	59	58	54	54	56	56	58	59	61	283	572
Other retirement	8	9	9	10	10	11	11	12	13	13	14	15	51	118
Excise taxes	84	94	99	100	105	108	114	118	123	129	135	143	526	1,174
Estate and gift taxes	19	16	18	19	20	22	23	24	26	27	29	31	102	240
Customs duties	32	35	38	41	44	48	51	54	58	61	65	70	222	529
Deposits of earnings, Federal Reserve System	76	90	88	58	34	20	25	34	43	47	54	58	225	462
Other miscellaneous receipts	27	27	43	45	61	62	63	66	67	68	70	74	274	620
Total receipts	2,775	3,005	3,251	3,457	3,656	3,851	4,057	4,271	4,505	4,736	4,970	5,218	18,273	41,973
Deficit	680	628	561	568	560	558	657	707	741	887	914	942	2,905	7,097
Net interest	221	223	251	318	393	480	563	635	697	761	827	886	2,005	5,812
Primary deficit	459	405	310	250	167	79	94	72	44	126	87	56	900	1,285
On-budget deficit	719	648	558	569	548	538	623	651	676	800	800	799	2,837	6,563
Off-budget deficit / surplus (–)	–39	–19	3	–1	12	20	34	56	66	87	114	143	68	534

Table S–4.　Adjusted Baseline by Category¹—Continued

(In billions of dollars)

	2013	2014	2015	2016	2017	2018	2019	2020	2021	2022	2023	2024	Totals 2015-2019	Totals 2015-2024
Memorandum, budget authority for appropriated programs:⁴														
Defense	600	606	608	666	681	696	711	727	743	760	779	798	3,362	7,170
Non-defense	536	521	496	532	544	556	569	581	593	608	623	638	2,696	5,739
Total, appropriated funding	1,136	1,127	1,104	1,199	1,225	1,252	1,280	1,308	1,336	1,368	1,402	1,436	6,059	12,909

* $500 million or less.

¹ See Table S-8 for information on adjustments to the Balanced Budget and Emergency Deficit Control Act (BBEDCA) baseline.

² These amounts represent a placeholder for major disasters requiring Federal assistance for relief and reconstruction. Such assistance might be provided in the form of discretionary or mandatory outlays or tax relief. These amounts are included as outlays for convenience.

³ Includes discretionary cap reduction for 2016 through 2021 and mandatory sequestration for 2015 through 2023.

⁴ Excludes discretionary cap reductions for Joint Committee enforcement.

Table S–5. Proposed Budget by Category

(In billions of dollars)

	2013	2014	2015	2016	2017	2018	2019	2020	2021	2022	2023	2024	Totals 2015-2019	Totals 2015-2024
Outlays:														
Appropriated ("discretionary") programs:														
Defense	626	612	623	584	570	570	577	583	592	602	615	630	2,925	5,946
Non-defense	522	562	563	569	576	579	585	593	599	588	591	604	2,871	5,845
Subtotal, appropriated programs	1,147	1,174	1,186	1,153	1,146	1,149	1,162	1,176	1,191	1,190	1,206	1,233	5,796	11,791
Mandatory programs:														
Social Security	808	852	896	947	1,003	1,063	1,126	1,193	1,262	1,335	1,413	1,496	5,035	11,734
Medicare	492	513	526	569	575	589	648	690	737	817	843	863	2,906	6,855
Medicaid	265	309	336	355	372	392	415	439	464	492	521	552	1,870	4,337
Other mandatory programs	521	577	691	739	754	744	790	812	841	879	882	890	3,719	8,024
Allowance for immigration reform	....	....	8	11	18	24	28	29	35	41	48	56	89	298
Subtotal, mandatory programs	2,086	2,251	2,458	2,621	2,723	2,811	3,007	3,163	3,339	3,563	3,707	3,856	13,620	31,248
Net interest	221	223	252	318	392	474	551	616	669	721	772	812	1,985	5,576
Adjustments for disaster costs[1]	....	2	6	8	8	9	9	10	10	10	10	10	40	90
Total outlays	3,455	3,651	3,901	4,099	4,269	4,443	4,729	4,964	5,209	5,485	5,694	5,912	21,441	48,705
Receipts:														
Individual income taxes	1,316	1,386	1,534	1,648	1,781	1,920	2,047	2,179	2,314	2,451	2,592	2,733	8,930	21,197
Corporation income taxes	274	333	449	502	528	540	514	527	542	557	571	592	2,533	5,322
Social insurance and retirement receipts:														
Social Security payroll taxes	673	732	758	811	850	898	945	987	1,042	1,094	1,143	1,195	4,262	9,723
Medicare payroll taxes	209	219	232	249	263	278	293	306	323	339	355	372	1,315	3,009
Unemployment insurance	57	60	57	57	71	69	64	67	68	69	71	72	319	665
Other retirement	8	9	9	10	10	11	11	12	13	13	14	15	51	118
Excise taxes	84	94	111	115	119	122	127	130	135	140	146	154	594	1,299
Estate and gift taxes	19	16	18	20	21	23	39	42	46	49	53	57	120	368
Customs duties	32	35	37	41	44	48	51	54	58	61	65	70	221	528
Deposits of earnings, Federal Reserve System	76	90	88	58	34	20	25	34	43	47	54	58	225	462
Other miscellaneous receipts	27	27	43	45	62	63	64	67	68	69	71	74	278	627
Allowance for immigration reform	....	....	2	12	28	39	45	47	55	64	77	87	126	456
Total receipts	2,775	3,002	3,337	3,568	3,811	4,030	4,226	4,452	4,706	4,954	5,212	5,478	18,972	43,775
Deficit	680	649	564	531	458	413	503	512	504	530	482	434	2,468	4,930
Net interest	221	223	252	318	392	474	551	616	669	721	772	812	1,985	5,576
Primary deficit / surplus (–)	459	425	312	214	66	–60	–48	–103	–166	–191	–290	–379	483	–646
On-budget deficit	719	670	564	535	448	395	472	458	440	449	374	298	2,414	4,433
Off-budget deficit / surplus (–)	–39	–21	–*	–4	10	18	31	54	64	81	108	136	55	497

Table S–5. Proposed Budget by Category—Continued

(In billions of dollars)

	2013	2014	2015	2016	2017	2018	2019	2020	2021	2022	2023	2024	Totals 2015-2019	Totals 2015-2024
Memorandum, budget authority for appropriated programs:														
Defense	600	606	628	561	569	578	586	595	604	614	629	646	2,922	6,010
Non-defense	536	521	531	557	564	573	582	590	598	578	593	610	2,807	5,777
Total, appropriated funding	1,136	1,127	1,159	1,118	1,133	1,151	1,168	1,185	1,202	1,192	1,222	1,256	5,730	11,787

* $500 million or less.

[1] These amounts represent a placeholder for major disasters requiring Federal assistance for relief and reconstruction. Such assistance might be provided in the form of discretionary or mandatory outlays or tax relief. These amounts are included as outlays for convenience.

Table S-6. Proposed Budget by Category as a Percent of GDP

(As a percent of GDP)

	2013	2014	2015	2016	2017	2018	2019	2020	2021	2022	2023	2024	Averages 2015–2019	Averages 2015–2024
Outlays:														
Appropriated ("discretionary") programs:														
Defense	3.8	3.5	3.4	3.0	2.8	2.7	2.6	2.5	2.4	2.4	2.3	2.3	2.9	2.7
Non-defense	3.1	3.2	3.1	3.0	2.9	2.7	2.6	2.6	2.5	2.3	2.2	2.2	2.9	2.6
Subtotal, appropriated programs	6.9	6.8	6.5	6.0	5.7	5.4	5.2	5.1	4.9	4.7	4.6	4.5	5.8	5.3
Mandatory programs:														
Social Security	4.9	4.9	4.9	4.9	5.0	5.0	5.1	5.1	5.2	5.3	5.4	5.4	5.0	5.1
Medicare	3.0	3.0	2.9	3.0	2.8	2.8	2.9	3.0	3.0	3.2	3.2	3.1	2.9	3.0
Medicaid	1.6	1.8	1.8	1.8	1.8	1.8	1.9	1.9	1.9	1.9	2.0	2.0	1.9	1.9
Other mandatory programs	3.1	3.3	3.8	3.9	3.7	3.5	3.6	3.5	3.5	3.5	3.3	3.2	3.7	3.5
Allowance for immigration reform	....	....	*	0.1	0.1	0.1	0.1	0.1	0.1	0.2	0.2	0.2	0.1	0.1
Subtotal, mandatory programs	12.6	13.0	13.5	13.7	13.5	13.3	13.5	13.6	13.8	14.1	14.1	14.0	13.5	13.7
Net interest	1.3	1.3	1.4	1.7	1.9	2.2	2.5	2.7	2.8	2.9	2.9	3.0	1.9	2.4
Adjustments for disaster costs[1]	....	*	*	*	*	*	*	*	*	*	*	*	*	*
Total outlays	20.8	21.1	21.4	21.4	21.1	20.9	21.3	21.4	21.5	21.7	21.6	21.5	21.2	21.4
Receipts:														
Individual income taxes	7.9	8.0	8.4	8.6	8.8	9.0	9.2	9.4	9.6	9.7	9.8	9.9	8.8	9.2
Corporation income taxes	1.6	1.9	2.5	2.6	2.6	2.5	2.3	2.3	2.2	2.2	2.2	2.1	2.5	2.4
Social insurance and retirement receipts:														
Social Security payroll taxes	4.1	4.2	4.2	4.2	4.2	4.2	4.3	4.3	4.3	4.3	4.3	4.3	4.2	4.3
Medicare payroll taxes	1.3	1.3	1.3	1.3	1.3	1.3	1.3	1.3	1.3	1.3	1.3	1.4	1.3	1.3
Unemployment insurance	0.3	0.3	0.3	0.3	0.4	0.3	0.3	0.3	0.3	0.3	0.3	0.3	0.3	0.3
Other retirement	0.1	0.1	0.1	0.1	0.1	0.1	0.1	0.1	0.1	0.1	0.1	0.1	0.1	0.1
Excise taxes	0.5	0.5	0.6	0.6	0.6	0.6	0.6	0.6	0.6	0.6	0.6	0.6	0.6	0.6
Estate and gift taxes	0.1	0.1	0.1	0.1	0.1	0.1	0.2	0.2	0.2	0.2	0.2	0.2	0.1	0.2
Customs duties	0.2	0.2	0.2	0.2	0.2	0.2	0.2	0.2	0.2	0.2	0.2	0.3	0.2	0.2
Deposits of earnings, Federal Reserve System	0.5	0.5	0.5	0.3	0.2	0.1	0.1	0.1	0.2	0.2	0.2	0.2	0.2	0.2
Other miscellaneous receipts	0.2	0.2	0.2	0.2	0.3	0.3	0.3	0.3	0.3	0.3	0.3	0.3	0.3	0.3
Allowance for immigration reform	....	....	*	0.1	0.1	0.2	0.2	0.2	0.2	0.3	0.3	0.3	0.1	0.2
Total receipts	16.7	17.3	18.3	18.6	18.9	19.0	19.0	19.2	19.4	19.6	19.8	19.9	18.8	19.2
Deficit	4.1	3.7	3.1	2.8	2.3	1.9	2.3	2.2	2.1	2.1	1.8	1.6	2.5	2.2
Net interest	1.3	1.3	1.4	1.7	1.9	2.2	2.5	2.7	2.8	2.9	2.9	3.0	1.9	2.4
Primary deficit / surplus (–)	2.8	2.5	1.7	1.1	0.3	–0.3	–0.2	–0.4	–0.7	–0.8	–1.1	–1.4	0.5	–0.2
On-budget deficit	4.3	3.9	3.1	2.8	2.2	1.9	2.1	2.0	1.8	1.8	1.4	1.1	2.4	2.0
Off-budget deficit / surplus (–)	–0.2	–0.1	–*	–*	*	0.1	0.1	0.2	0.3	0.3	0.4	0.5	0.1	0.2

Table S–6. Proposed Budget by Category as a Percent of GDP—Continued

(As a percent of GDP)

	2013	2014	2015	2016	2017	2018	2019	2020	2021	2022	2023	2024	Averages 2015–2019	2015–2024
Memorandum, budget authority for appropriated programs:														
Defense	3.6	3.5	3.4	2.9	2.8	2.7	2.6	2.6	2.5	2.4	2.4	2.3	2.9	2.7
Non-defense	3.2	3.0	2.9	2.9	2.8	2.7	2.6	2.5	2.5	2.3	2.2	2.2	2.8	2.6
Total, appropriated funding	6.8	6.5	6.4	5.8	5.6	5.4	5.3	5.1	5.0	4.7	4.6	4.6	5.7	5.2

*0.05 percent of GDP or less.

[1] These amounts represent a placeholder for major disasters requiring Federal assistance for relief and reconstruction. Such assistance might be provided in the form of discretionary or mandatory outlays or tax relief. These amounts are included as outlays for convenience.

Table S–7. Proposed Budget in Population- and Inflation-Adjusted Dollars

(In billions of constant dollars, adjusted for population growth)

	2015	2016	2017	2018	2019	2020	2021	2022	2023	2024
Outlays:										
Appropriated ("discretionary") programs:										
Defense	623	567	537	520	511	500	492	485	480	477
Non-defense	563	552	542	528	517	508	497	474	462	458
Subtotal, appropriated programs	1,186	1,119	1,079	1,049	1,028	1,008	990	959	942	935
Mandatory programs:										
Social Security	896	920	944	970	996	1,023	1,048	1,076	1,104	1,135
Medicare	526	552	541	537	573	591	612	658	659	654
Medicaid	336	344	350	358	367	376	386	396	407	418
Other mandatory programs	691	718	710	679	699	696	699	708	690	675
Allowance for immigration reform	8	11	17	22	25	25	29	33	38	42
Subtotal, mandatory programs	2,458	2,545	2,564	2,565	2,659	2,712	2,775	2,872	2,898	2,924
Net interest	252	308	369	432	487	528	556	581	603	616
Adjustments for disaster costs[1]	6	7	8	8	8	8	8	8	8	8
Total outlays	3,901	3,980	4,019	4,054	4,182	4,256	4,330	4,420	4,451	4,483
Receipts:										
Individual income taxes	1,534	1,600	1,677	1,752	1,810	1,868	1,923	1,975	2,026	2,073
Corporation income taxes	449	487	497	493	455	451	450	449	447	449
Social insurance and retirement receipts										
Social Security payroll taxes	758	788	800	819	836	846	866	882	893	906
Medicare payroll taxes	232	242	247	254	259	262	268	273	277	282
Unemployment insurance	57	55	67	63	57	57	56	55	56	54
Other retirement	9	9	10	10	10	10	10	11	11	12
Excise taxes	111	112	112	111	112	112	112	113	114	116
Estate and gift taxes	18	19	20	21	35	36	38	40	42	43
Customs duties	37	39	42	44	45	46	48	49	51	53
Deposits of earnings, Federal Reserve System	88	56	32	18	22	29	36	38	42	44
Other miscellaneous receipts	43	44	59	57	57	57	56	56	55	56
Allowance for immigration reform	2	12	26	36	40	40	46	52	60	66
Total receipts	3,337	3,464	3,588	3,677	3,737	3,817	3,911	3,993	4,074	4,154
Deficit	564	516	431	377	445	439	419	427	377	329
Net interest	252	308	369	432	487	528	556	581	603	616
Primary deficit / surplus (–)	312	207	62	–55	–42	–89	–138	–154	–227	–287
On-budget deficit	564	520	422	361	417	393	366	362	292	226
Off-budget deficit / surplus (–)	–*	–4	9	16	27	46	53	65	84	103

Table S–7. Proposed Budget in Population- and Inflation-Adjusted Dollars—Continued

(In billions of constant dollars, adjusted for population growth)

	2015	2016	2017	2018	2019	2020	2021	2022	2023	2024
Memorandum, budget authority for appropriated programs:										
Defense	628	545	536	527	518	510	502	495	492	490
Non-defense	531	541	531	523	515	506	497	466	464	463
Subtotal, appropriated programs	1,159	1,086	1,067	1,050	1,033	1,016	999	961	955	953
Memorandum, index of population growth and inflation	1.00	1.03	1.06	1.10	1.13	1.17	1.20	1.24	1.28	1.32

*$500 million or less.

[1] These amounts represent a placeholder for major disasters requiring Federal assistance for relief and reconstruction. Such assistance might be provided in the form of discretionary or mandatory outlays or tax relief. These amounts are included as outlays for convenience.

Table S–8. Bridge From Balanced Budget and Emergency Control Act (BBEDCA) Baseline to Adjusted Baseline

(Deficit increases (+) or decreases (–) in billions of dollars)

	2013	2014	2015	2016	2017	2018	2019	2020	2021	2022	2023	2024	Totals 2015–2019	Totals 2015–2024
BBEDCA baseline deficit	680	617	568	617	629	637	721	773	812	907	918	918	3,171	7,498
Adjustments for current policy:														
Continue tax benefits provided under the American Taxpayer Relief Act [1]		....	....	....	....	1	24	26	26	26	25	25	25	154
Prevent reduction in Medicare physician payments		6	14	12	10	7	7	9	11	12	13	14	50	110
Reflect incremental cost of funding existing Pell maximum grant award		–*	–*	–*	4	2	2	2	2	2	2	2	7	17
Reflect Postal Service default on 2014 retiree health benefit payment		3	1	1	*	–*	–*	–*	–*	–*	–*	–*	1	–*
Subtotal		9	14	13	14	11	33	37	38	40	40	41	84	280
Adjustments for provisions contained in the Budget Control Act:														
Set discretionary budget authority at cap levels[2]			–24	1	13	15	14	13	9	8	8	8	19	65
Reflect Joint Committee enforcement[3]				–66	–96	–102	–105	–107	–107	–54	–38	–10	–370	–687
Subtotal			–24	–65	–83	–88	–91	–94	–98	–46	–30	–2	–351	–622
Adjustments for disaster costs:														
Remove non-recurring emergency costs		–2	–2	–4	–6	–6	–7	–7	–7	–7	–8	–8	–24	–61
Add placeholder for future emergency costs[4]		2	6	8	8	9	9	10	10	10	10	10	40	90
Reclassify surface transportation outlays:														
Remove outlays from appropriated category	–55	–58	–59	–60	–60	–59	–60	–61	–61	–62	–63	–64	–298	–609
Add outlays to mandatory category	55	58	59	60	60	59	60	61	61	62	63	64	298	609
Subtotal														
Total program adjustments		11	–6	–49	–67	–74	–55	–54	–57	–4	12	40	–251	–313
Debt service on adjustments		*	*	–*	–2	–5	–8	–11	–14	–16	–16	–16	–15	–88
Total adjustments		11	–6	–49	–68	–79	–63	–66	–71	–20	–4	25	–266	–401
Adjusted baseline deficit	680	628	561	568	560	558	657	707	741	887	914	942	2,905	7,097

*$500 million or less.

[1] The baseline permanently continues the tax benefits provided to individuals and families that were extended only through taxable year 2017 under ATRA.

[2] Includes adjustments for program integrity.

[3] Consists of mandatory sequestration for 2016-2023 and discretionary cap reductions for 2016-2021. Excludes extension of mandatory sequestration to 2024 enacted subsequent to the completion of the 2015 Budget estimates.

[4] These amounts represent a placeholder for major disasters requiring Federal assistance for relief and reconstruction.

Table S–9. Mandatory and Receipt Proposals

(Deficit increases (+) or decreases (–) in millions of dollars)

	2014	2015	2016	2017	2018	2019	2020	2021	2022	2023	2024	Totals 2015–2019	Totals 2015–2024
Opportunity, Growth, and Security Initiative:													
Discretionary funding (non-add)	......	32,588	13,842	4,485	1,993	1,108	553	221	55	......	......	54,016	54,845
Spending and tax offsets:													
Reduce subsidies for crop insurance companies and farmer premiums	......	–691	–1,232	–1,435	–1,466	–1,507	–1,539	–1,566	–1,598	–1,621	–1,625	–6,331	–14,280
Reform the aviation passenger security user fee to more accurately reflect the costs of aviation security		......	–200	–425	–650	–660	–670	–680	–690	–695	–700	–1,935	–5,370
Offset Disability Insurance (DI) benefits for period of concurrent Unemployment Insurance (UI) receipt [1]		......	–56	–254	–390	–414	–416	–419	–426	–441	–415	–1,114	–3,231
Enact Spectrum License User Fee and allow the FCC to auction predominantly domestic satellite services		–225	–325	–425	–550	–550	–550	–550	–550	–550	–550	–2,075	–4,825
Limit the total accrual of tax-favored retirement benefits		–1,482	–2,157	–2,334	–2,512	–2,697	–2,940	–3,233	–3,479	–3,638	–3,905	–11,182	–28,377
Total, spending and tax offsets		–2,398	–3,970	–4,873	–5,568	–5,828	–6,115	–6,448	–6,743	–6,945	–7,195	–22,637	–56,083
Surface Transportation Reauthorization:													
Invest in surface transportation reauthorization		3,534	9,244	12,436	14,057	11,914	7,225	4,565	3,295	2,349	1,489	51,185	70,108
Transfer to achieve trust fund solvency (non-add)		22,000	18,000	19,000	19,000							78,000	78,000
Transition to a reformed business tax system		–37,500	–37,500	–37,500	–37,500							–150,000	–150,000
Early Childhood Investments:													
Support Preschool for All		130	1,235	3,110	5,456	7,360	8,773	9,787	10,560	10,275	9,356	17,291	66,042
Extend and expand voluntary home visiting		20	115	400	575	900	1,075	1,400	1,575	1,900	2,075	2,010	10,035
Subtotal, investments		150	1,350	3,510	6,031	8,260	9,848	11,187	12,135	12,175	11,431	19,301	76,077
Increase tobacco taxes and index for inflation [2]		–7,797	–9,936	–9,350	–8,738	–8,203	–7,721	–7,267	–6,840	–6,438	–5,927	–44,024	–78,217
Earned Income Tax Credit (EITC) Expansion:													
Expand EITC for workers without qualifying children [3]		490	6,308	6,335	6,362	6,444	6,536	6,653	6,760	6,874	6,978	25,939	59,740
High-income tax loophole closers:													
Tax carried (profits) interests as ordinary income		–2,153	–1,951	–1,762	–1,474	–1,403	–1,443	–1,219	–972	–765	–655	–8,743	–13,797
Conform SECA taxes for professional service businesses		–2,151	–3,009	–3,227	–3,461	–3,691	–3,936	–4,207	–4,470	–4,691	–4,836	–15,539	–37,679
Impose liability on shareholders to collect unpaid income taxes of applicable corporations	–309	–325	–450	–474	–497	–521	–544	–568	–593	–619	–647	–2,267	–5,238
Require that the cost basis of stock that is a covered security must be determined using an average cost basis method		......	–53	–162	–279	–406	–481	–501	–522	–544	–567	–900	–3,515
Total, high-income tax loophole closers	–309	–4,629	–5,463	–5,625	–5,711	–6,021	–6,404	–6,495	–6,557	–6,619	–6,705	–27,449	–60,229

Table S-9. Mandatory and Receipt Proposals—Continued

(Deficit increases (+) or decreases (−) in millions of dollars)

	2014	2015	2016	2017	2018	2019	2020	2021	2022	2023	2024	Totals 2015–2019	Totals 2015–2024
Other Mandatory Initiatives and Savings:													
Agriculture:													
Reauthorize Secure Rural Schools	....	178	188	105	63	40	7	....	....	....	....	574	581
Enact Food Safety and Inspection Service (FSIS) fee	....	−4	−4	−4	−5	−5	−5	−5	−5	−5	−5	−22	−47
Enact biobased labeling fee	....	....	....	....	....	....	....	....	....	....	....	....	....
Enact Grain Inspection, Packers, and Stockyards Administration (GIPSA) fee	....	−28	−28	−29	−29	−29	−30	−30	−31	−32	−33	−143	−299
Enact Animal Plant and Health Inspection Service (APHIS) fee	....	−20	−27	−27	−28	−29	−30	−31	−32	−33	−34	−131	−291
Total, Agriculture	....	126	129	45	1	−23	−58	−66	−68	−70	−72	278	−56
Education:													
Recognize Educational Success, Professional Excellence, and Collaborative Teaching (RESPECT)	....	2,750	1,750	500	....	....	....	....	....	....	....	5,000	5,000
Reform and expand Perkins loan program	....	−395	−1,084	−890	−744	−663	−607	−552	−487	−458	−443	−3,776	−6,323
Provide mandatory appropriation to sustain recent Pell Grant increases	....	....	890	2,599	317	−28	128	582	600	613	625	3,778	6,326
Expand and reform student loan income-based repayment	....	7,640	308	−10	−244	−420	−659	−687	−798	−768	−810	7,274	3,552
Implement College Opportunity and Graduation Bonus Program	....	123	362	482	671	684	693	702	710	719	727	2,322	5,873
Establish State Higher Education Performance Fund	....	20	370	720	970	980	630	280	30	....	....	3,060	4,000
Total, Education	....	10,138	2,596	3,401	970	553	185	325	55	106	99	17,658	18,428
Energy:													
Reauthorize special assessment from domestic nuclear utilities [1]	....	−200	−204	−209	−213	−218	−223	−229	−234	−239	−245	−1,044	−2,214
Establish Energy Security Trust Fund	....	60	140	180	200	200	200	200	200	200	200	780	1,780
Enact nuclear waste management program	....	....	....	....	90	170	400	520	760	−1,394	764	260	1,310
Total, Energy	....	−140	−64	−29	77	152	377	491	726	−1,433	719	−4	876
Health and Human Services (HHS):													
HHS health savings:													
Medicare providers:													
Bad debts:													
Reduce Medicare coverage of bad debts	....	−340	−1,310	−2,460	−3,070	−3,330	−3,550	−3,790	−4,050	−4,320	−4,600	−10,510	−30,820

Table S–9. Mandatory and Receipt Proposals—Continued

(Deficit increases (+) or decreases (−) in millions of dollars)

	2014	2015	2016	2017	2018	2019	2020	2021	2022	2023	2024	Totals 2015–2019	Totals 2015–2024
Graduate medical education:													
Better align graduate medical education payments with patient care costs	......	−960	−1,160	−1,210	−1,320	−1,400	−1,500	−1,600	−1,710	−1,830	−1,950	−6,050	−14,640
Better align payments to rural providers with the cost of care:													
Reduce Critical Access Hospital (CAH) payments from 101% of reasonable costs to 100% of reasonable costs		−110	−130	−140	−150	−160	−180	−180	−200	−220	−220	−690	−1,690
Prohibit CAH designation for facilities that are less than 10 miles from the nearest hospital		−40	−60	−60	−70	−70	−70	−80	−80	−90	−100	−300	−720
Cut waste, fraud, and improper payments in Medicare:													
Reduce fraud, waste, and abuse in Medicare	......	......	−20	−20	−30	−50	−50	−50	−60	−60	−60	−120	−400
Drug rebates and additional Part D savings:													
Align Medicare drug payment policies with Medicaid policies for low-income beneficiaries	......	......	−2,830	−7,960	−9,500	−10,760	−12,520	−14,580	−16,390	−19,480	−23,230	−31,050	−117,250
Accelerate manufacturer discounts for brand drugs to provide relief to Medicare beneficiaries in the coverage gap	......	......	40	−190	−380	−740	−1,190	−1,300	−1,430	−1,380	−1,280	−1,270	−7,850
Suspend coverage and payment for questionable Part D prescriptions and incomplete clinical information												......	......
Establish quality bonus payments for high-performing Part D plans												......	......
Encourage efficient post-acute care:													
Adjust payment updates for certain post-acute care providers	......	−1,450	−3,250	−4,830	−6,330	−8,200	−10,180	−12,440	−15,220	−17,090	−18,870	−24,060	−97,860
Equalize payments for certain conditions commonly treated in inpatient rehabilitation facilities (IRFs) and skilled nursing facilities (SNFs)	......	−110	−130	−140	−150	−160	−170	−180	−190	−190	−200	−690	−1,620
Encourage appropriate use of inpatient rehabilitation hospitals by requiring that 75 percent of IRF patients require intensive rehabilitation services		−170	−210	−220	−230	−240	−250	−260	−270	−280	−290	−1,070	−2,420
Adjust SNF payments to reduce hospital readmissions	......	......	......	......	......	−230	−280	−300	−320	−350	−380	−230	−1,860

Table S-9. Mandatory and Receipt Proposals—Continued

(Deficit increases (+) or decreases (−) in millions of dollars)

	2014	2015	2016	2017	2018	2019	2020	2021	2022	2023	2024	Totals 2015–2019	Totals 2015–2024
Implement bundled payment for post-acute care	.....	.....	.....	.....	.....	−430	−960	−1,570	−1,760	−1,900	−2,060	−430	−8,680
Additional provider efficiencies:													
Exclude certain services from the in-office ancillary services exception	.....	.....	−350	−540	−590	−640	−680	−730	−780	−830	−890	−2,120	−6,030
Modify the documentation requirement for face-to-face encounters for durable medical equipment, prosthetics, orthotics, and supplies (DMEPOS) claims	.....	.....	.....	.....	.....	.....	.....	.....	.....	.....	.....	.....	.....
Modify reimbursement of Part B drugs	.....	−300	−530	−570	−610	−650	−700	−760	−810	−870	−950	−2,660	−6,750
Modernize payments for clinical laboratory services	.....	.....	−80	−220	−380	−560	−780	−1,030	−1,310	−1,650	−1,880	−1,240	−7,890
Expand sharing Medicare data with qualified entities	.....	.....	.....	.....	.....	.....	.....	.....	.....	.....	.....	.....	.....
Clarify the Medicare DSH Fraction in the Medicare DSH statute	.....	.....	.....	.....	.....	.....	.....	.....	.....	.....	.....	.....	.....
Implement Value-Based Purchasing for SNFs, Home Health Agencies (HHAs), Ambulatory Surgical Centers (ASCs), and Hospital Outpatient Departments (HOPDs)	.....	.....	.....	.....	.....	.....	.....	.....	.....	.....	.....	.....	.....
Improve payment accuracy for Medicare Advantage (MA):													
Increase the minimum MA coding intensity adjustment	.....	.....	−390	−1,000	−1,700	−2,760	−3,990	−4,620	−5,050	−5,500	−5,950	−5,850	−30,960
Align employer group waiver plan payments with average MA plan bids	.....	.....	−200	−280	−330	−370	−420	−470	−510	−550	−610	−1,180	−3,740
Strengthen the Independent Payment Advisory Board (IPAB) to reduce long-term drivers of Medicare cost growth	.....	.....	.....	.....	.....	.....	.....	.....	−2,180	−2,980	−7,780	.....	−12,940
Total, Medicare providers	.....	−3,480	−10,610	−19,840	−24,840	−30,750	−37,470	−43,940	−52,320	−59,570	−71,300	−89,520	−354,120
Medicare structural reforms:													
Increase income-related premium under Medicare Parts B and D	.....	.....	.....	.....	−1,720	−2,600	−5,760	−7,870	−9,540	−11,530	−13,770	−4,320	−52,790
Modify Part B deductible for new enrollees	.....	.....	.....	.....	−50	−60	−260	−360	−810	−910	−960	−110	−3,410
Introduce home health co-payments for new beneficiaries	.....	.....	.....	.....	−20	−50	−80	−110	−140	−190	−230	−70	−820
Introduce a Part B premium surcharge for new beneficiaries who purchase near first-dollar Medigap coverage	.....	.....	.....	.....	−70	−160	−270	−380	−510	−640	−710	−230	−2,740
Encourage the use of generic drugs by low-income beneficiaries	.....	.....	−680	−710	−790	−840	−920	−1,000	−1,090	−1,180	−1,280	−3,020	−8,490
Total, Medicare structural reforms	.....	.....	−680	−710	−2,650	−3,710	−7,290	−9,720	−12,090	−14,450	−16,950	−7,750	−68,250
Interactions	.....	38	93	145	198	1,452	2,114	2,314	4,189	5,086	6,420	1,926	22,049

Table S-9. Mandatory and Receipt Proposals—Continued

(Deficit increases (+) or decreases (−) in millions of dollars)

	2014	2015	2016	2017	2018	2019	2020	2021	2022	2023	2024	Totals 2015–2019	Totals 2015–2024
Medicaid and other:													
Medicaid and Children's Health Insurance Program:													
Limit Medicaid reimbursement of durable medical equipment based on Medicare rates	......	−195	−250	−265	−285	−305	−325	−345	−365	−390	−410	−1,300	−3,135
Rebase future Medicaid Disproportionate Share Hospital (DSH) allotments	......										−3,260	......	−3,260
Reduce fraud, waste, and abuse in Medicaid	......		−38	−66	−76	−85	−84	−85	−85	−86	−87	−265	−692
Strengthen the Medicaid drug rebate program	......	−307	−612	−647	−677	−722	−777	−827	−892	−982	−1,077	−2,965	−7,520
Exclude brand-name and authorized generic drug prices from Medicaid Federal upper limit (FUL)	......	−30	−70	−110	−110	−110	−120	−120	−120	−120	−130	−430	−1,040
Increase access to and transparency for Medicaid drug pricing data	......	6	6	6	6	6	......					30	30
Improve and extend the Money Follows the Person Rebalancing Demonstration through 2020	......											......	......
Provide home and community-based services to children eligible for psychiatric residential treatment facilities	......	75	158	168	179	190	202	214	227	240	255	770	1,908
Create demonstration to address over-prescription of psychotropic medications for children in foster care	......	130	215	230	240	250	100					1,065	1,165
Permanently extend Express Lane Eligibility (ELE) option for children	......	30	55	80	100	115	120	135	145	160	175	380	1,115
Expand State flexibility to provide benchmark benefit packages	......											......	......
Extend the Qualified Individuals (QI) program through CY 2015	365	760	200									960	960
Extend the Transitional Medical Assistance (TMA) program through CY 2015	175	920	615	15								1,550	1,550
Total, Medicaid and Children's Health Insurance Program	540	1,389	279	−589	−623	−661	−884	−1,028	−1,090	−1,178	−4,534	−205	−8,919
Pharmaceutical savings:													
Prohibit brand and generic drug companies from delaying the availability of new generic drugs and biologics	......	−770	−830	−890	−960	−1,040	−1,120	−1,220	−1,310	−1,400	−1,510	−4,490	−11,050

Table S–9. Mandatory and Receipt Proposals—Continued

(Deficit increases (+) or decreases (–) in millions of dollars)

	2014	2015	2016	2017	2018	2019	2020	2021	2022	2023	2024	Totals 2015–2019	Totals 2015–2024
Modify length of exclusivity to facilitate faster development of generic biologics	....	....	....	–80	–260	–410	–540	–580	–680	–820	–840	–750	–4,210
Total, pharmaceutical savings	....	–770	–830	–970	–1,220	–1,450	–1,660	–1,800	–1,990	–2,220	–2,350	–5,240	–15,260
Medicare-Medicaid enrollees:													
Ensure retroactive Part D coverage of newly-eligible low-income beneficiaries	....	....	....	....	....	....	....	....	....	....	....	....	....
Establish integrated appeals process for Medicare-Medicaid enrollees	....	....	....	....	....	....	....	....	....	....	....	....	....
Create pilot to expand PACE eligibility to individuals between ages 21 and 55	....	....	....	....	....	....	....	....	....	....	....	....	....
Total, Medicare-Medicaid enrollees	....	....	....	....	....	....	....	....	....	....	....	....	....
Accelerate the issuance of State innovation waivers	....	....	....	....	....	....	....	....	....	....	....	....	....
Enact survey and certification revisit fees	....	....	....	....	....	....	....	....	....	....	....	....	....
Invest in CMS Quality Measurement	....	10	30	30	20	....	....	....	....	....	....	90	90
Allow CMS to reinvest civil monetary penalties recovered from home health agencies	....	1	1	1	1	1	1	1	1	1	1	5	10
Allow CMS to assess a fee on Medicare providers subject to the Federal Payment Levy Program	....	....	....	....	....	....	....	....	....	....	....	....	....
Extend special diabetes program at National Institutes of Health and Indian Health Services (IHS)	....	180	266	291	116	35	9	5	....	....	....	888	902
Permit IHS/Tribal/Urban Indian Health programs to pay Medicare like rates for outpatient services funded through the Purchased and Referred Care program	....	....	....	....	....	....	....	....	....	....	....	....	....
Extend Health Centers	....	....	1,269	2,619	2,673	1,431	81	27	....	....	....	7,992	8,100
Total, Medicaid and other	540	810	1,015	1,382	967	–644	–2,453	–2,795	–3,079	–3,397	–6,883	3,530	–15,077
Health workforce investments:													
Create a competitive, value-based graduate medical education grant program funded through the Medicare Hospital Insurance Trust Fund	....	530	500	450	450	500	500	550	550	600	600	2,430	5,230
Extend the Medicaid primary care payment increase through CY 2015 with modifications to expand provider eligibility and better target primary care services	....	4,060	1,380	....	....	....	....	....	....	....	....	5,440	5,440

Table S-9. Mandatory and Receipt Proposals—Continued

(Deficit increases (+) or decreases (−) in millions of dollars)

	2014	2015	2016	2017	2018	2019	2020	2021	2022	2023	2024	Totals 2015–2019	Totals 2015–2024
Invest in the National Health Services Corps	......	200	527	676	697	707	710	355	50	21	7	2,807	3,950
Total, health workforce investments	......	4,790	2,407	1,126	1,147	1,207	1,210	905	600	621	607	10,677	14,620
Program management implementation funding	......	25	300	75	......	......	......	......	......	......	......	400	400
Total, HHS health savings	540	2,183	−7,475	−17,822	−25,178	−32,445	−43,889	−53,236	−62,700	−71,710	−88,106	−80,737	−400,378
Provide dedicated, mandatory funding for Health Care Fraud and Abuse Control Program (HCFAC) program integrity:													
Administrative costs	......	378	706	725	745	765	786	807	829	852	876	3,319	7,469
Benefit savings	......	−552	−610	−646	−684	−725	−758	−791	−825	−861	−899	−3,217	−7,351
Subtotal, provide dedicated, mandatory funding for HCFAC program integrity	......	−174	96	79	61	40	28	16	4	−9	−23	102	118
Annual reduction to discretionary spending limits (non-add)	......	......	−294	−294	−294	−294	−294	−294	−294	−294	−294	−1,176	−2,646
Continue funding for the Personal Responsibility Education Program and Health Profession Opportunity Grants	......	4	62	115	145	160	156	98	44	15	......	486	799
Repurpose Temporary Assistance for Needy Families (TANF) Contingency Fund to support Pathways to Jobs initiative	......	......	......	......	......	......	......	......	......	......	......	......	......
Establish hold harmless for Federal poverty guidelines	......	......	......	......	......	......	......	......	......	......	......	......	......
Expand access to quality child care	......	600	922	1,064	1,332	1,790	2,039	2,247	2,449	2,691	2,939	5,708	18,073
Modernize child support	......	7	47	173	195	285	334	392	384	378	240	707	2,435
Supplemental Security Income (SSI) effects	......	......	−1	−5	−5	−7	−9	−10	−10	−10	−10	−18	−67
Supplemental Nutrition Assistance Program (SNAP) effects	......	−2	−4	−37	−40	−62	−78	−93	−92	−91	−89	−145	−588
Provide funding for Aging and Disability Resource Centers	......	20	20	20	20	20	......	......	......	......	......	100	100
Reauthorize Family Connection Grants	......	......	10	15	5	......	......	......	......	......	......	30	30
Support demonstration to address over-prescription of psychotropic medications for children in foster care (funding in Administration for Children and Families)	......	1	20	55	71	52	28	16	6	1	1	199	251
Total, Health and Human Services	540	2,639	−6,303	−16,343	−23,394	−30,167	−41,391	−50,570	−59,915	−68,735	−85,048	−73,568	−379,227
Homeland Security:													
Permanently extend and reallocate the travel promotion surcharge [1]	......	......	......	......	......	......	......	......	......	......	......	......	......
Housing and Urban Development:													
Provide funding for Project Rebuild	......	50	4,650	7,100	3,200	......	......	......	......	......	......	15,000	15,000
Provide funding for the Affordable Housing Trust Fund	......	10	140	290	230	190	100	20	20	20	20	860	1,000

Table S-9. Mandatory and Receipt Proposals—Continued

(Deficit increases (+) or decreases (−) in millions of dollars)

	2014	2015	2016	2017	2018	2019	2020	2021	2022	2023	2024	Totals 2015–2019	Totals 2015–2024
Total, Housing and Urban Development	......	60	4,790	7,390	3,430	190	100	20	20	20	......	15,860	16,000
Interior:													
Establish dedicated funding for Land and Water Conservation Fund (LWCF) programs	......	177	536	1,012	969	915	900	900	900	900	900	3,609	8,109
Provide funding for a National Park Service Centennial Initiative	......	75	295	400	325	105	......	......	......	......	......	1,200	1,200
Extend funding for Payments in Lieu of Taxes (PILT)	......	442	......	......	......	......	......	......	......	......	......	442	442
Enact Federal oil and gas management reforms	......	−50	−120	−125	−150	−170	−185	−200	−215	−225	−240	−615	−1,680
Reform hardrock mining on public lands	......	......	−2	−4	−5	−5	−6	−6	−11	−17	−24	−16	−80
Repeal geothermal payments to counties	......	−4	−4	−4	−4	−4	−4	−4	−4	−5	−5	−20	−42
Terminate Abandoned Mine Lands (AML) payments to certified States	......	−48	−35	−28	−34	−36	−31	−36	−38	−9	......	−181	−295
Establish an AML hardrock reclamation fund[1]	......	......	−200	−150	−100	−50	−50	......	......	......	......	−500	−500
Increase coal AML fee to pre–2006 levels[1]	......	−52	−34	−27	−16	−10	−3	−2	53	38	28	−139	−25
Reauthorize the Federal Land Transaction Facilitation Act of 2000 (FLTFA)	......	−4	−6	−9	−12	−3	......	......	......	......	......	−34	−34
Permanently reauthorize the Federal Lands Recreation Enhancement Act (FLREA)	......	......	......	......	......	......	......	......	......	......	......	......	......
Increase duck stamp fees[1]	......	−4	......	......	......	......	......	......	......	......	......	−4	−4
Extend the Palau Compact of Free Association	......	42	30	24	19	17	16	10	9	6	4	132	177
Total, Interior	......	574	460	1,089	992	759	687	662	694	688	663	3,874	7,268
Labor:													
Create Back to Work Partnerships for the long-term unemployed	......	2,000	2,000	......	......	......	......	......	......	......	......	4,000	4,000
Establish a New Career Pathways program for displaced workers	......	3,698	3,305	2,875	2,622	2,406	2,250	2,029	1,908	1,699	1,520	14,906	24,312
Establish Summer Jobs Plus program for youth	......	1,000	1,250	250	......	......	......	......	......	......	......	2,500	2,500
Support Bridge to Work and other work-based UI program reforms	......	200	300	400	400	400	300	......	......	......	......	1,700	2,000
Enhance UI program integrity[1,2]	......	−5	−9	−13	−13	−12	−11	−10	−11	−12	−10	−52	−106
Extend Emergency Unemployment Compensation	14,979	4,718	......	......	......	......	......	......	......	......	......	4,718	4,718
Implement cap adjustments for UI program integrity activities[1,2]	......	−27	−79	−92	−103	−108	−118	−128	−143	−155	−132	−409	−1,085
Outlays from discretionary cap adjustment (non-add)	......	*25*	*30*	*35*	*40*	*45*	*50*	*55*	*60*	*65*	*70*	*175*	*475*
Strengthen UI system solvency[1,2]	403	2,960	3,118	−9,344	−10,818	−6,987	−7,295	−8,081	−7,154	−8,036	−7,047	−21,071	−58,684
Improve Pension Benefit Guaranty Corporation (PBGC) solvency	......	......	......	−1,318	−1,648	−2,003	−2,332	−2,662	−3,016	−3,346	−3,676	−4,969	−20,001
Provide the Secretary of the Treasury authority to access and disclose prisoner data to prevent and identify improper payments[1,2]	......	−4	−8	−9	−8	−7	−7	−7	−6	−6	−6	−36	−68

Table S–9. Mandatory and Receipt Proposals—Continued

(Deficit increases (+) or decreases (−) in millions of dollars)

	2014	2015	2016	2017	2018	2019	2020	2021	2022	2023	2024	Totals 2015–2019	Totals 2015–2024
Reform the Federal Employees' Compensation Act (FECA)	......	−11	−1	−8	−16	−24	−32	−41	−49	−59	−68	−60	−309
Total, Labor	15,382	14,529	9,876	−7,259	−9,584	−6,335	−7,245	−8,900	−8,471	−9,915	−9,419	1,227	−42,723
Transportation:													
Establish a mandatory surcharge for air traffic services [1]	......	−725	−756	−787	−816	−844	−870	−894	−921	−947	−973	−3,928	−8,533
Establish a co-insurance program for aviation war risk insurance	......	−19	−10	−3	−1	......	......	1	1	2	2	−33	−27
Total, Transportation	......	−744	−766	−790	−817	−844	−870	−893	−920	−945	−971	−3,961	−8,560
Treasury:													
Establish a Pay for Success Incentive Fund	......	1	1	10	24	40	56	49	42	24	15	76	262
Reauthorize and reform the Terrorism Risk Insurance Program	......	......	......	......	......	......	......	......	......	......	......	......	......
Authorize Treasury to locate and recover assets of the United States and to retain a portion of amounts collected to pay for the costs of recovery	......	−3	−3	−3	−3	−3	−3	−3	−3	−3	−3	−15	−30
Increase delinquent Federal non-tax debt collections by authorizing administrative bank garnishment for non-tax debts	......	−32	−32	−32	−32	−32	−32	−32	−32	−32	−32	−160	−320
Increase levy authority for payments to Medicare providers with delinquent tax debt [1]	......	−50	−71	−74	−76	−76	−77	−78	−80	−80	−81	−347	−743
Allow offset of Federal income tax refunds to collect delinquent State income taxes for out-of-state residents	......	......	......	......	......	......	......	......	......	......	......	......	......
Reduce costs for States collecting delinquent income tax obligations	......	......	......	......	......	......	......	......	......	......	......	......	......
Implement tax enforcement program integrity cap adjustment [1]	......	−370	−1,265	−2,584	−3,978	−5,426	−6,620	−7,431	−7,850	−8,137	−8,343	−13,623	−52,004
Outlays from discretionary cap adjustment (non-add)	......	*451*	*834*	*1,200*	*1,581*	*1,973*	*2,062*	*2,113*	*2,175*	*2,239*	*2,306*	*6,039*	*16,934*
Provide authority to contact delinquent debtors via their cell phones	......	−12	−12	−12	−12	−12	−12	−12	−12	−12	−12	−60	−120
Reauthorize the State Small Business Credit Initiative	......	277	626	539	38	8	7	5	......	......	......	1,488	1,500
Total, Treasury	......	−189	−756	−2,156	−4,039	−5,501	−6,681	−7,502	−7,935	−8,240	−8,456	−12,641	−51,455
Veterans Affairs:													
Establish Veterans Job Corps	......	50	237	237	238	238	......	......	......	......	......	1,000	1,000
Extend round-down of cost of living adjustments (compensation)	......	−30	−69	−107	−148	−191	−206	−215	−225	−236	−246	−545	−1,673
Extend round-down of cost of living adjustments (education)	......	......	−1	−1	−2	−3	−3	−3	−3	−4	−4	−7	−24

Table S–9. Mandatory and Receipt Proposals—Continued

(Deficit increases (+) or decreases (–) in millions of dollars)

												Totals	
	2014	2015	2016	2017	2018	2019	2020	2021	2022	2023	2024	2015–2019	2015–2024
Provide burial receptacles for certain new casketed gravesites	....	3	3	4	1	6	....	....	3	3	4	17	27
Make permanent the pilot for certain work-study activities	....	1	1	1	1	1	1	1	1	1	1	5	10
Increase cap on vocational rehabilitation contract counseling	....	1	1	1	1	1	1	1	1	1	1	5	10
Increase annual limitation on new Independent Living cases	....	....	....	....	....	....	4	4	4	4	4	....	20
Improve housing grant program	....	11	12	12	13	13	15	15	17	17	17	61	142
Extend supplemental service disabled veterans insurance coverage [4]	....	....	....	....	....	....	....	....	....	....	....	....	....
Total, Veterans Affairs	....	36	185	146	104	65	–188	–197	–202	–214	–223	536	–488
Corps of Engineers:													
Reform inland waterways funding [1]	....	–82	–113	–113	–113	–113	–113	–113	–113	–113	–114	–534	–1,100
Environmental Protection Agency:													
Enact pre-manufacture notice fee	....	–4	–8	–8	–8	–8	–8	–8	–8	–8	–8	–36	–76
Establish Confidential Business Information management fee	....	....	....	....	....	....	....	....	....	....	....	....	....
Total, Environmental Protection Agency	....	–4	–8	–8	–8	–8	–8	–8	–8	–8	–8	–36	–76
International Assistance Programs:													
Mandatory effects of discretionary proposal to implement 2010 International Monetary Fund (IMF) agreement (non-scoreable)	....	46	....	....	....	....	....	....	....	....	....	46	46
Other Defense -- Civil Programs:													
Increase TRICARE pharmacy copayments	....	–3	–4	–6	–66	–125	–394	–483	–586	–692	–821	–204	–3,180
Increase annual premiums for TRICARE-For-Life (TFL) enrollment	....	....	–4	–21	–54	–81	–110	–140	–172	–204	–238	–160	–1,024
Increase TRICARE pharmacy copayments (accrual effects)	....	668	698	721	750	785	831	879	930	985	1,041	3,622	8,288
Increase annual premiums for TFL enrollment (accrual effects)	....	80	84	87	92	96	101	107	113	119	127	439	1,006
Total, Other Defense -- Civil Programs	....	745	774	781	722	675	428	363	285	208	109	3,697	5,090
Office of Personnel Management (OPM): Modernize the Federal Employees Health Benefits Program (FEHBP):													
Streamline FEHBP pharmacy benefit contracting	....	....	–53	–101	–111	–117	–124	–133	–139	–151	–162	–382	–1,091

Table S-9. Mandatory and Receipt Proposals—Continued

(Deficit increases (+) or decreases (−) in millions of dollars)

	2014	2015	2016	2017	2018	2019	2020	2021	2022	2023	2024	Totals 2015–2019	Totals 2015–2024
Provide FEHBP benefits to domestic partners			−8	5	12	18	27	38	45	57	71	27	265
Expand FEHBP plan types			−1	−2	−3	−4	−7	−8	−12	−16	−17	−10	−70
Adjust FEHBP premiums for wellness			2	−10	−33	−61	−93	−128	−176	−247	−337	−102	−1,083
Total, modernize FEHBP			−60	−108	−135	−164	−197	−231	−282	−357	−445	−467	−1,979
Social Security Administration (SSA):													
Provide dedicated, mandatory funding for program integrity:													
Administrative costs			1,750	1,800	1,710	1,625	1,543	1,543	1,543	1,543	1,543	6,885	14,600
Benefit savings			−264	−2,269	−3,204	−4,096	−4,777	−5,400	−6,239	−6,526	−6,738	−9,833	−39,513
Subtotal, provide dedicated, mandatory funding for program integrity			1,486	−469	−1,494	−2,471	−3,234	−3,857	−4,696	−4,983	−5,195	−2,948	−24,913
Annual reduction to discretionary spending limits (non-add)			−273	−273	−273	−273	−273	−273	−273	−273	−273	−1,092	−2,457
Allow SSA to electronically certify certain RRB payments													
Conform treatment of State and local government EITC and child tax credit (CTC) for SSI [5]													
Eliminate aggressive Social Security claiming strategies													
Establish Workers Compensation Information Reporting		5	5									10	10
Extend SSI time limits for qualified refugees		43	49									92	92
Medicaid effects		11	12									23	23
SNAP effects		−8	−9									−17	−17
Improve collection of pension information from States and localities		18	28	24	−307	−675	−907	−986	−935	−924	−905	−912	−5,569
Lower electronic wage reporting threshold to 25 employees													
Move from annual to quarterly wage reporting		20	30	90								140	140
Reauthorize and expand demonstration authority for DI and SSI		22	44	67	98	111	58					342	400
Terminate step-child benefits in the same month as step-parent [6]													
Use the Death Master File to prevent Federal improper payments													
Total, Social Security Administration		111	1,645	−288	−1,703	−3,035	−4,083	−4,843	−5,631	−5,907	−6,100	−3,270	−29,834
Other Independent Agencies:													
Civilian Property Realignment Board:													
Dispose of unneeded real property		−87	−203	−376	−990	−130	−100	−120	−120	−120	−120	−1,786	−2,366

Table S-9. Mandatory and Receipt Proposals—Continued

(Deficit increases (+) or decreases (–) in millions of dollars)

	2014	2015	2016	2017	2018	2019	2020	2021	2022	2023	2024	Totals 2015–2019	Totals 2015–2024
National Infrastructure Bank:													
Create infrastructure bank	......	33	153	373	595	831	1,058	1,158	1,233	1,207	1,062	1,985	7,703
Postal Service:													
Enact Postal Service financial relief and reform:													
PAYGO effects	1,653	1,568	–2,028	–4,999	–4,999	–4,999	–4,999	–4,999	–4,999	–4,999	–4,999	–15,457	–40,452
Non-scoreable effects	......	3,097	5,650	3,451	4,453	5,582	6,526	7,576	4,758	4,647	4,647	22,233	50,387
Total, enact Postal Service financial relief and reform	1,653	4,665	3,622	–1,548	–546	583	1,527	2,577	–241	–352	–352	6,776	9,935
Multi-Agency:													
Enact immigration reform [1]	......	6,000	–1,000	–10,000	–15,000	–17,000	–18,000	–20,000	–23,000	–29,000	–31,000	–37,000	–158,000
Auction or assign via fee 1675–1680 megahertz	......	......	......	–80	–150	......	......	......	......	......	......	–230	–230
Reconcile OPM/SSA retroactive disability payments	......	6	......	–38	–41	–41	–41	–41	–41	–41	–41	–114	–319
Establish a consolidated TRICARE program (mandatory effects in Coast Guard, Public Health Service, and National Oceanic and Atmospheric Administration)	......	1	–10	–17	–17	–18	–19	–20	–21	–22	–23	–61	–166
Outyear mandatory effects of Special Immigrant Visa extension:													
Medicaid	......	......	3	5	5	4	4	4	4	3	4	17	36
SNAP	......	......	4	4	4	4	4	4	4	5	5	16	38
SSI	......	......	5	5	5	5	5	5	5	5	5	20	45
Subtotal, outyear mandatory effects of Special Immigrant Visa extension	......	......	12	14	14	13	13	13	13	13	14	53	119
Total, multi-agency	......	6,007	–998	–10,121	–15,194	–17,046	–18,047	–20,048	–23,049	–29,050	–31,050	–37,352	–158,596
Total, other mandatory initiatives and savings	17,575	38,463	14,959	–25,914	–49,632	–59,558	–74,619	–87,895	–103,942	–123,250	–139,726	–81,682	–611,114
Other Tax Proposals:													
Incentives for job creation, clean energy, and manufacturing:													
Provide additional tax credits for investment in qualified property used in a qualifying advanced energy manufacturing project	......	......	86	398	660	641	285	8	–61	–66	–55	1,785	1,896
Designate Promise Zones [3]	......	366	693	641	609	594	588	582	583	598	622	2,903	5,876
Provide new Manufacturing Communities tax credit	......	20	104	275	454	589	676	737	749	646	414	1,442	4,664
Provide a tax credit for the production of advanced technology vehicles	......	705	675	753	875	984	850	537	21	–281	–294	3,992	4,825

Table S–9. Mandatory and Receipt Proposals—Continued

(Deficit increases (+) or decreases (–) in millions of dollars)

	2014	2015	2016	2017	2018	2019	2020	2021	2022	2023	2024	Totals 2015–2019	Totals 2015–2024
Provide a tax credit for medium- and heavy-duty alternative-fuel commercial vehicles	....	54	86	71	64	65	47	14	....	....	....	340	401
Modify tax-exempt bonds for Indian tribal governments	....	4	12	12	12	12	12	12	12	12	12	52	112
Extend the tax credit for cellulosic biofuel	30	70	121	157	178	204	236	237	210	171	114	730	1,698
Modify and extend the tax credit for the construction of energy-efficient new homes	78	127	137	163	182	199	215	231	246	261	287	808	2,048
Reduce excise taxes on LNG to bring into parity with diesel [2]	....	2	2	2	2	2	2	2	2	2	2	10	20
Total, incentives for job creation, clean energy, and manufacturing	108	1,348	1,916	2,472	3,036	3,290	2,911	2,360	1,762	1,343	1,102	12,062	21,540
Incentives for investment in infrastructure:													
Provide America Fast Forward Bonds and expand eligible uses [3]	....	....	1	....	....	....	–1	1	1	....	–1	1	1
Allow eligible uses of America Fast Forward Bonds to include financing all qualified private activity bond categories [3]	....	1	4	10	14	21	27	32	39	46	52	50	246
Allow current refundings of State and local governmental bonds	....	3	5	5	5	5	5	5	5	5	5	23	48
Repeal the $150 million non-hospital bond limitation on all qualified 501(c)(3) bonds	....	....	1	3	5	7	9	11	13	16	17	16	82
Increase national limitation amount for qualified highway or surface freight transfer facility bonds	....	....	3	16	34	52	72	92	113	133	154	105	669
Eliminate the volume cap for private activity bonds for water infrastructure	....	....	3	5	9	14	20	27	33	41	49	31	201
Increase the 25-percent limit on land acquisition restriction on private activity bonds	....	....	2	4	8	11	15	19	23	27	32	25	141
Allow more flexible research arrangements for purposes of private business use limits	....	....	....	....	1	1	1	1	3	3	3	2	13
Repeal the government ownership requirement for certain types of exempt facility bonds	....	14	66	140	216	290	364	437	509	579	644	726	3,259
Exempt foreign pension funds from the application of FIRPTA	....	114	196	205	216	227	238	250	262	275	289	958	2,272
Total, incentives for investment in infrastructure	....	132	281	388	508	628	750	875	1,001	1,125	1,244	1,937	6,932
Tax cuts for families and individuals:													
Provide for automatic enrollment in IRAs, including a small employer tax credit, and double the tax credit for small employer plan start-up costs [3]	....	....	817	1,276	1,309	1,410	1,552	1,728	1,902	2,137	2,376	4,812	14,507
Expand child and dependent care tax credit [3]	....	287	1,064	1,060	1,056	1,045	1,039	1,030	1,021	1,011	997	4,512	9,610
Extend exclusion from income for cancellation of certain home mortgage debt	2,687	3,497	3,343	825	....	....	....	....	....	....	....	7,665	7,665

Table S-9. Mandatory and Receipt Proposals—Continued

(Deficit increases (+) or decreases (−) in millions of dollars)

	2014	2015	2016	2017	2018	2019	2020	2021	2022	2023	2024	Totals 2015–2019	Totals 2015–2024
Provide exclusion from income for student loan forgiveness for students in certain income-based or income-contingent repayment programs who have completed payment obligations	......	......	......	......	......	......	......	......	......	2	3	......	5
Provide exclusion from income for student loan forgiveness and for certain scholarship amounts for participants in the IHS Health Professions Programs	......	6	14	14	15	16	18	19	20	21	22	65	165
Make Pell Grants excludable from income [3]	......	23	768	1,184	1,116	1,068	1,019	977	938	904	867	4,159	8,864
Total, tax cuts for families and individuals	2,687	3,813	6,006	4,359	3,496	3,539	3,628	3,754	3,881	4,075	4,265	21,213	40,816
Upper-income revenue proposals for deficit reduction:													
Reduce the value of certain tax expenditures	......	−26,587	−43,356	−47,943	−53,259	−58,632	−63,750	−68,720	−73,649	−78,581	−83,589	−229,777	−598,066
Implement the Buffett Rule by imposing a new "Fair Share Tax"	......	−10,536	1,241	−1,609	−4,383	−5,598	−5,874	−6,173	−6,427	−6,645	−7,022	−20,885	−53,026
Total, upper-income revenue proposals for deficit reduction	......	−37,123	−42,115	−49,552	−57,642	−64,230	−69,624	−74,893	−80,076	−85,226	−90,611	−250,662	−651,092
Modify estate and gift tax provisions:													
Restore the estate, gift, and GST tax parameters in effect in 2009	......	......	......	......	......	−15,930	−17,309	−18,846	−20,412	−22,250	−23,535	−15,930	−118,282
Require consistency in value for transfer and income tax purposes	......	......	−215	−228	−242	−257	−272	−290	−310	−333	−354	−942	−2,501
Require a minimum term for grantor retained annuity trusts (GRATs)	......	......	−244	−325	−411	−504	−602	−711	−843	−1,004	−1,067	−1,484	−5,711
Limit duration of generation-skipping transfer (GST) tax exemption	......	......	......	......	......	......	......	......	......	......	......	......	......
Coordinate certain income and transfer tax rules applicable to grantor trusts	......	......	−59	−77	−97	−125	−157	−201	−256	−326	−346	−358	−1,644
Extend the lien on estate tax deferrals where estate consists largely of interest in closely held business	......	......	−19	−20	−21	−22	−23	−24	−26	−28	−30	−82	−213
Modify GST tax treatment of Health and Education Exclusion Trusts	......	......	30	29	27	26	24	23	21	20	18	112	218
Simplify gift tax exclusion for annual gifts	......	......	−70	−138	−205	−268	−328	−358	−435	−517	−605	−681	−2,924
Expand applicability of definition of executor	......	......	......	......	......	......	......	......	......	......	......	......	......
Total, modify estate and gift tax provisions	......	......	−577	−759	−949	−17,080	−18,667	−20,407	−22,261	−24,438	−25,919	−19,365	−131,057
Reform treatment of financial industry institutions and products:													
Impose a financial crisis responsibility fee	......	......	−3,058	−6,142	−6,271	−6,395	−6,507	−6,673	−6,830	−6,993	−7,155	−21,866	−56,024
Require current inclusion in income of accrued market discount and limit the accrual amount for distressed debt	......	−14	−38	−47	−46	−44	−41	−36	−32	−28	−24	−189	−350

Table S–9. Mandatory and Receipt Proposals—Continued

(Deficit increases (+) or decreases (–) in millions of dollars)

	2014	2015	2016	2017	2018	2019	2020	2021	2022	2023	2024	Totals 2015–2019	Totals 2015–2024
Total, reform treatment of financial industry institutions and products	....	–14	–3,096	–6,189	–6,317	–6,439	–6,548	–6,709	–6,862	–7,021	–7,179	–22,055	–56,374
Other revenue raisers and loophole closers:													
Require non-spouse beneficiaries of deceased IRA owners and retirement plan participants to take inherited distributions over no more than five years	....	–91	–235	–388	–543	–702	–735	–693	–642	–591	–539	–1,959	–5,159
Increase Oil Spill Liability Trust Fund financing rate by one cent and update the law to include other sources of crudes[2]		–60	–82	–88	–92	–94	–99	–102	–108	–111	–115	–416	–951
Reinstate Superfund taxes[2]		–1,602	–2,185	–2,285	–2,337	–2,380	–2,403	–2,444	–2,495	–2,545	–2,594	–10,789	–23,270
Make unemployment insurance surtax permanent[2]	....	–1,051	–1,461	–1,493	–1,524	–1,551	–1,575	–1,599	–1,623	–1,649	–1,674	–7,080	–15,200
Enhance and modify the conservation easement deduction:													
Enhance and make permanent incentives for the donation of conservation easements	....	....	5	8	12	16	28	51	67	70	74	41	331
Eliminate the deduction for contributions of conservation easements on golf courses ...	....	–37	–53	–55	–59	–61	–64	–68	–71	–74	–77	–265	–619
Restrict deductions and harmonize the rules for contributions of conservation easements for historic preservation	....	–8	–11	–16	–22	–26	–27	–28	–31	–32	–33	–83	–234
Subtotal, enhance and modify the conservation easement deduction ...	....	–45	–59	–63	–69	–71	–63	–45	–35	–36	–36	–307	–522
Eliminate the deduction for dividends on stock of publicly-traded corporations held in certain ESOPs	....	–618	–767	–777	–788	–798	–808	–818	–827	–837	–845	–3,748	–7,883
Total, other revenue raisers and loophole closers	....	–3,467	–4,789	–5,094	–5,353	–5,596	–5,683	–5,701	–5,730	–5,769	–5,803	–24,299	–52,985
Reduce the tax gap and make reforms:													
Expand information reporting:													
Require information reporting for private separate accounts of life insurance companies		....	....	–1	–1	–1	–1	–1	–1	–1	–1	–3	–8
Require a certified Taxpayer Identification Number (TIN) from con-tractors and allow certain withholding		–26	–61	–103	–141	–147	–154	–161	–168	–176	–184	–478	–1,321
Modify reporting of tuition expenses and scholarships on Form 1098-T[3]		–5	–65	–65	–65	–65	–66	–67	–68	–70	–70	–265	–606

Table S–9. Mandatory and Receipt Proposals—Continued

(Deficit increases (+) or decreases (–) in millions of dollars)

	2014	2015	2016	2017	2018	2019	2020	2021	2022	2023	2024	Totals 2015–2019	Totals 2015–2024
Provide for reciprocal reporting of information in connection with the implementation of FATCA													
Provide authority to readily share beneficial ownership information of U.S. companies with law enforcement			–1	–1	–6	–4	–3	–2	–2	–2	–2	–12	–23
Improve compliance by businesses:													
Require greater electronic filing of returns													
Implement standards clarifying when employee leasing companies can be held liable for their clients' Federal employment taxes		–4	–5	–6	–6	–6	–7	–7	–7	–8	–8	–27	–64
Increase certainty with respect to worker classification	–4	–79	–386	–759	–914	–1,000	–1,091	–1,187	–1,289	–1,396	–1,509	–3,138	–9,610
Increase information sharing to administer excise taxes [2]		–4	–9	–13	–14	–15	–17	–18	–19	–19	–20	–55	–148
Strengthen tax administration:													
Streamline audit and adjustment procedures for large partnerships		–144	–192	–191	–188	–183	–177	–177	–180	–182	–184	–898	–1,798
Revise offer-in-compromise application rules		–1	–1	–1	–2	–2	–2	–2	–2	–2	–2	–7	–17
Expand IRS access to information in the National Directory of New Hires for tax administration purposes													
Make repeated willful failure to file a tax return a felony					–1	–1	–1	–1	–2	–2	–2	–2	–10
Facilitate tax compliance with local jurisdictions		–1	–1	–1	–1	–2	–2	–2	–2	–2	–2	–6	–16
Extend statute of limitations where State adjustment affects Federal tax liability					–1	–4	–4	–4	–4	–4	–4	–5	–25
Improve investigative disclosure statute					–1	–1	–1	–1	–2	–2	–2	–2	–10
Require taxpayers who prepare their returns electronically but file their returns on paper to print their returns with a scannable code													
Allow the IRS to absorb credit and debit card processing fees for certain tax payments		–1	–2	–2	–2	–2	–2	–2	–2	–2	–2	–9	–19
Provide the IRS with greater flexibility to address correctable errors [3]		–7	–15	–16	–17	–17	–19	–19	–20	–21	–22	–72	–173
Make e-filing mandatory for exempt organizations													

Table S–9. Mandatory and Receipt Proposals—Continued

(Deficit increases (+) or decreases (−) in millions of dollars)

	2014	2015	2016	2017	2018	2019	2020	2021	2022	2023	2024	Totals 2015–2019	Totals 2015–2024
Authorize the Department of the Treasury to require additional information to be included in electronically filed Form 5500 Annual Reports and electronic filing of certain other employee benefit plan reports	......	......	......	......	......	......	......	......	......	......	......	......	......
Impose a penalty on failure to comply with electronic filing requirements					−1	−1	−1	−1	−2	−2	−2	−2	−10
Provide whistleblowers with protection from retaliation	......	......	......	......	......	......		......	......	......	......	......	......
Provide stronger protection from improper disclosure of taxpayer information in whistleblower actions	......	......	......	......	......	......	......	......	......	......	......	......	......
Index all penalties for inflation		−45	−60	−61	−62	−63	−65	−66	−68	−70	−71	−291	−631
Extend paid preparer EITC due diligence requirements to the child tax credit	......	......	......	......	......	......	......	......	......	......	......	......	......
Extend IRS authority to require truncated Social Security Numbers on Form W–2	......	......	......	......	......	......	......	......	......	......	......	......	......
Add tax crimes to the Aggravated Identity Theft Statute	......	......	......	......	......	......	......	......	......	......	......	......	......
Impose a civil penalty on tax identity theft crimes	......	......	......	......	......	......	......	......	......	......	......	......	......
Allow States to send notices of intent to offset Federal tax refunds to collect State tax obligations by regular first-class mail instead of certified mail	......	......	......	......	......	......		......	......	......	......	......	......
Explicitly provide that the Department of the Treasury and IRS have authority to regulate all paid return preparers	......	......	......	......	......	......	......	......	......	......	......	......	......
Rationalize tax return filing due dates so they are staggered [3]		−210	−220	−230	−242	−252	−263	−273	−285	−297	−309	−1,154	−2,581
Increase the penalty applicable to paid tax preparers who engage in willful or reckless conduct	......	......	......	−1	−1	−1	−1	−1	−1	−1	−1	−3	−8
Enhance administrability of the appraiser penalty	......	......	......	......	......	......	......	......	......	......	......	......	......
Total, reduce the tax gap and make reforms	−4	−527	−1,018	−1,451	−1,666	−1,767	−1,877	−1,992	−2,124	−2,259	−2,397	−6,429	−17,078
Simplify the tax system:													
Simplify the rules for claiming the EITC for workers without qualifying children [3]		44	587	599	612	598	609	621	632	598	609	2,440	5,509
Modify adoption credit to allow tribal determination of special needs						1	1	1	1	1	1	1	6

Table S-9. Mandatory and Receipt Proposals—Continued

(Deficit increases (+) or decreases (−) in millions of dollars)

	2014	2015	2016	2017	2018	2019	2020	2021	2022	2023	2024	Totals 2015–2019	Totals 2015–2024
Simplify MRD rules	......	5	5	3	−5	−19	−38	−60	−88	−122	−165	−11	−484
Allow all inherited plan and IRA balances to be rolled over within 60 days	......	......	......	......	......	......	......	......	......	......	......	......	......
Repeal non-qualified preferred stock designation	......	−31	−52	−51	−50	−47	−44	−39	−34	−30	−27	−231	−405
Repeal preferential dividend rule for publicly traded and publicly offered REITs	......	......	......	......	......	......	......	......	......	......	......	......	......
Reform excise tax based on investment income of private foundations	......	......	4	4	5	5	5	5	6	6	7	18	47
Remove bonding requirements for certain taxpayers subject to Federal excise taxes on distilled spirits, wine, and beer	......	......	......	......	......	......	......	......	......	......	......	......	......
Simplify arbitrage investment restrictions	......	2	10	18	28	38	46	58	68	76	87	96	431
Simplify single-family housing mortgage bond targeting requirements	......	1	3	5	7	10	12	17	20	22	24	26	121
Streamline private business limits on governmental bonds	......	1	3	5	7	9	11	13	15	17	19	25	100
Exclude self-constructed assets of small taxpayers from the uniform capitalization rules	......	47	50	68	71	90	95	98	103	107	112	326	841
Repeal technical terminations of partnerships	......	−16	−20	−21	−22	−23	−23	−24	−25	−25	−26	−102	−225
Repeal anti-churning rules of section 197	......	25	106	209	278	313	328	331	331	331	331	931	2,583
Repeal special estimated tax payment provision for certain insurance companies	......	......	......	......	......	......	......	......	......	......	......	......	......
Repeal the telephone excise tax [2]	......	419	357	302	253	213	178	148	122	102	83	1,544	2,177
Increase the standard mileage rate for automobile use by volunteers	......	16	47	45	44	44	44	45	46	48	49	196	428
Total, simplify the tax system	......	513	1,100	1,186	1,228	1,232	1,224	1,214	1,197	1,131	1,104	5,259	11,129
Trade initiative:													
Extend GSP [2]	372	696	161	......	......	......	......	......	......	......	......	857	857
Other initiatives:													
Authorize the limited sharing of business tax return information to improve the accuracy of important measures of the economy	......	......	......	......	......	......	......	......	......	......	......	......	......
Eliminate certain reviews conducted by the U.S. Treasury Inspector General for Tax Administration (TIGTA)	......	......	......	......	......	......	......	......	......	......	......	......	......

Table S-9. Mandatory and Receipt Proposals—Continued

(Deficit increases (+) or decreases (−) in millions of dollars)

	2014	2015	2016	2017	2018	2019	2020	2021	2022	2023	2024	Totals 2015–2019	Totals 2015–2024
Modify indexing to prevent deflationary adjustments	......	......	......	......	......	......	......	......	......	......	......	......	......
Total, other initiatives	......	......	......	......	......	......	......	......	......	......	......	......	......
Total, other tax proposals	3,163	−34,629	−42,131	−54,640	−63,659	−86,423	−93,886	−101,499	−109,212	−117,039	−124,194	−281,482	−827,312
Grand Total	20,429	−44,316	−67,139	−115,621	−144,358	−139,415	−165,136	−187,199	−211,104	−238,893	−263,849	−510,849	−1,577,030
Addendum, Reserve for Long-Run Revenue-Neutral Business Tax Reform:													
Incentives for manufacturing, research, clean energy, and insourcing and creating jobs:													
Provide tax incentives for locating jobs and business activity in the United States and remove tax deductions for shipping jobs overseas	......	14	18	19	21	21	22	23	24	24	26	93	212
Enhance and make permanent the R&E tax credit	3,259	6,524	7,731	8,671	9,591	10,483	11,309	12,148	13,019	13,894	14,776	43,000	108,146
Extend and modify certain employment tax credits, including incentives for hiring veterans	382	747	821	885	928	964	994	1,029	1,072	1,115	1,159	4,345	9,714
Modify and permanently extend renewable electricity production tax credit [3]	......	141	499	848	1,193	1,584	2,002	2,458	2,963	3,509	4,089	4,265	19,286
Modify and permanently extend the deduction for energy-efficient commercial building property	61	190	371	515	607	675	720	738	745	751	756	2,358	6,068
Total, incentives for manufacturing, research, clean energy, and insourcing and creating jobs	3,702	7,616	9,440	10,938	12,340	13,727	15,047	16,396	17,823	19,293	20,806	54,061	143,426
Tax relief for small business:													
Extend increased expensing for small business	6,712	9,321	7,197	6,246	5,563	4,981	4,703	4,586	4,622	4,735	4,874	33,308	56,828
Eliminate capital gains taxation on investments in small business stock	......	......	......	......	......	227	719	1,245	1,762	2,310	2,939	227	9,202
Increase the limitations for deductible new business expenditures and consolidate provisions for start-up and organizational expenditures	......	360	449	446	440	434	431	428	427	424	419	2,129	4,258
Expand and simplify the tax credit provided to qualified small employers for non-elective contributions to employee health insurance [3]	219	313	322	219	133	95	66	52	50	48	28	1,082	1,326
Total, tax relief for small business	6,931	9,994	7,968	6,911	6,136	5,737	5,919	6,311	6,861	7,517	8,260	36,746	71,614

Table S-9. Mandatory and Receipt Proposals—Continued

(Deficit increases (+) or decreases (−) in millions of dollars)

	2014	2015	2016	2017	2018	2019	2020	2021	2022	2023	2024	Totals 2015–2019	Totals 2015–2024
Incentives to promote regional growth:													
Permanently extend and modify the New Markets tax credit	17	77	191	351	548	772	1,013	1,245	1,429	1,529	1,558	1,939	8,713
Restructure assistance to New York City, provide tax incentives for transportation infrastructure	....	200	200	200	200	200	200	200	200	200	200	1,000	2,000
Reform and expand the Low-Income Housing tax credit	....	28	66	96	127	147	168	178	188	196	196	464	1,390
Total, incentives to promote regional growth	17	305	457	647	875	1,119	1,381	1,623	1,817	1,925	1,954	3,403	12,103
Reform U.S. international tax system:													
Defer deduction of interest expense related to deferred income of foreign subsidiaries	....	−2,976	−5,028	−5,219	−5,444	−5,651	−5,864	−4,051	−2,850	−2,962	−3,093	−24,318	−43,138
Determine the foreign tax credit on a pooling basis	....	−3,963	−6,697	−6,952	−7,251	−7,527	−7,810	−8,115	−8,436	−8,766	−9,155	−32,390	−74,672
Tax currently excess returns associated with transfers of intangibles offshore	....	−1,578	−2,693	−2,787	−2,832	−2,798	−2,718	−2,664	−2,636	−2,626	−2,633	−12,688	−25,965
Limit shifting of income through intangible property transfers	....	−71	−137	−172	−207	−244	−283	−325	−373	−427	−489	−831	−2,728
Disallow the deduction for excess non-taxed reinsurance premiums paid to affiliates	....	−366	−632	−682	−721	−755	−794	−833	−882	−928	−975	−3,156	−7,568
Restrict deductions for excessive interest of members of financial reporting groups	....	−1,944	−3,434	−3,778	−4,156	−4,571	−5,028	−5,531	−6,084	−6,693	−7,362	−17,883	−48,581
Modify tax rules for dual capacity taxpayers	....	−527	−906	−953	−1,002	−1,049	−1,096	−1,147	−1,179	−1,233	−1,290	−4,437	−10,382
Tax gain from the sale of a partnership interest on look-through basis	....	−139	−241	−253	−265	−279	−293	−307	−323	−339	−356	−1,177	−2,795
Prevent use of leveraged distributions from related foreign corporations to avoid dividend treatment	....	−188	−318	−331	−345	−358	−371	−386	−401	−417	−433	−1,540	−3,548
Extend section 338(h)(16) to certain asset acquisitions	....	−60	−100	−100	−100	−100	−100	−100	−100	−100	−100	−460	−960
Remove foreign taxes from a section 902 corporation's foreign tax pool when earnings are eliminated	....	−13	−27	−36	−46	−50	−50	−50	−50	−50	−51	−172	−423
Create a new category of Subpart F income for transactions involving digital goods or services	....	−585	−1,004	−1,055	−1,107	−1,163	−1,221	−1,282	−1,346	−1,413	−1,484	−4,914	−11,660
Prevent avoidance of foreign base company sales income through manufacturing service arrangements	....	−1,235	−2,120	−2,226	−2,337	−2,454	−2,576	−2,705	−2,840	−2,983	−3,132	−10,372	−24,608
Restrict the use of hybrid arrangements that create stateless income	....	−38	−66	−73	−80	−88	−97	−107	−117	−129	−142	−345	−937
Limit the application of exceptions under Subpart F to certain transactions that use reverse hybrids to create stateless income	....	−67	−115	−121	−127	−133	−140	−147	−154	−162	−170	−563	−1,336

Table S–9. Mandatory and Receipt Proposals—Continued

(Deficit increases (+) or decreases (−) in millions of dollars)

	2014	2015	2016	2017	2018	2019	2020	2021	2022	2023	2024	Totals 2015–2019	Totals 2015–2024
Limit the ability of domestic entities to expatriate	......	−150	−415	−706	−1,025	−1,375	−1,756	−2,173	−2,627	−3,120	−3,657	−3,671	−17,004
Total, reform U.S. international tax system	......	−13,900	−23,933	−25,444	−27,045	−28,595	−30,197	−29,923	−30,398	−32,348	−34,522	−118,917	−276,305
Reform treatment of financial and insurance industry institutions and products:													
Require that derivative contracts be marked to market with resulting gain or loss treated as ordinary	......	−2,583	−4,674	−3,900	−2,600	−1,655	−1,132	−697	−506	−528	−529	−15,412	−18,804
Modify rules that apply to sales of life insurance contracts		−14	−42	−46	−48	−50	−54	−56	−58	−62	−65	−200	−495
Modify proration rules for life insurance company general and separate accounts	......	−353	−607	−652	−682	−691	−688	−676	−668	−657	−643	−2,985	−6,317
Expand pro rata interest expense disallowance for corporate-owned life insurance		−32	−91	−168	−268	−392	−540	−706	−900	−1,109	−1,340	−951	−5,546
Total, reform treatment of financial and insurance industry institutions and products	......	−2,982	−5,414	−4,766	−3,598	−2,788	−2,414	−2,135	−2,132	−2,356	−2,577	−19,548	−31,162
Eliminate fossil fuel preferences:													
Eliminate oil and natural gas preferences:													
Repeal enhanced oil recovery credit [7]		......	......	......	......	......	......	......	......	......	......	......	......
Repeal credit for oil and natural gas produced from marginal wells [7]		......	......	......	......	......	......	......	......	......	......	......	......
Repeal expensing of intangible drilling costs		−2,317	−3,244	−2,348	−1,803	−1,469	−1,110	−665	463	464	467	−11,181	−14,350
Repeal deduction for tertiary injectants		−10	−10	−10	−10	−10	−10	−10	−10	−10	−10	−50	−100
Repeal exception to passive loss limitations for working interests in oil and natural gas properties		−5	−7	−7	−7	−6	−6	−6	−5	−5	−5	−32	−59
Repeal percentage depletion for oil and natural gas wells		−1,502	−1,568	−1,469	−1,375	−1,306	−1,261	−1,219	−1,181	−1,089	−1,060	−7,220	−13,030
Repeal domestic manufacturing deduction for oil and natural gas production		−963	−1,614	−1,585	−1,522	−1,453	−1,421	−1,410	−1,408	−1,416	−1,426	−7,137	−14,218
Increase geological and geophysical amortization period for independent producers to seven years		−103	−382	−596	−581	−463	−337	−224	−144	−123	−128	−2,125	−3,081
Subtotal, eliminate oil and natural gas preferences		−4,900	−6,825	−6,015	−5,298	−4,707	−4,145	−3,534	−3,211	−3,107	−3,096	−27,745	−44,838
Eliminate coal preferences:													
Repeal expensing of exploration and development costs		−39	−66	−69	−73	−77	−77	−75	−73	−70	−60	−324	−679
Repeal percentage depletion for hard mineral fossil fuels		−167	−173	−182	−195	−203	−211	−218	−225	−234	−244	−920	−2,052
Repeal capital gains treatment for royalties		−20	−43	−47	−49	−52	−55	−58	−61	−61	−62	−211	−508

Table S–9. Mandatory and Receipt Proposals—Continued

(Deficit increases (+) or decreases (−) in millions of dollars)

	2014	2015	2016	2017	2018	2019	2020	2021	2022	2023	2024	Totals 2015–2019	Totals 2015–2024
Repeal domestic manufacturing deduction for the production of coal and other hard mineral fuels	....	−36	−63	−67	−70	−73	−77	−80	−83	−87	−90	−309	−726
Subtotal, eliminate coal preferences ...	....	−262	−345	−365	−387	−405	−420	−431	−442	−452	−456	−1,764	−3,965
Total, eliminate fossil fuel preferences	....	−5,162	−7,170	−6,380	−5,685	−5,112	−4,565	−3,965	−3,653	−3,559	−3,552	−29,509	−48,803
Other revenue changes and loophole closers:													
Repeal the excise tax credit for distilled spirits with flavor and wine additives [2]	....	−85	−112	−112	−112	−112	−112	−112	−112	−112	−112	−533	−1,093
Repeal LIFO method of accounting for inventories	....	−4,151	−7,823	−8,786	−8,965	−8,850	−8,778	−8,818	−8,917	−8,770	−8,850	−38,575	−82,708
Repeal lower-of-cost-or-market inventory accounting method	....	−644	−1,404	−1,526	−1,537	−903	−270	−283	−296	−309	−323	−6,014	−7,495
Modify depreciation rules for purchases of general aviation passenger aircraft	....	−87	−273	−411	−456	−532	−549	−385	−209	−155	−153	−1,759	−3,210
Repeal gain limitation for dividends received in reorganization exchanges	....	−153	−263	−276	−290	−305	−319	−335	−352	−370	−388	−1,287	−3,051
Expand the definition of substantial built-in loss for purposes of partnership loss transfers	....	−5	−7	−7	−7	−7	−7	−8	−8	−10	−10	−33	−76
Extend partnership basis limitation rules to nondeductible expenditures	....	−63	−90	−97	−102	−105	−108	−110	−112	−114	−116	−457	−1,017
Limit the importation of losses under related party loss limitation rules	....	−56	−81	−87	−92	−95	−97	−99	−100	−102	−104	−411	−913
Deny deduction for punitive damages	....	....	−25	−36	−37	−38	−38	−40	−40	−41	−43	−136	−338
Modify like-kind exchange rules for real property	....	−616	−1,875	−1,894	−1,914	−1,936	−1,958	−1,981	−2,006	−2,031	−2,059	−8,235	−18,270
Conform corporate ownership standards	....	−24	−48	−51	−54	−57	−60	−63	−66	−69	−72	−234	−564
Prevent elimination of earnings and profits through distributions of certain stock	−2	−22	−33	−35	−37	−39	−41	−43	−45	−47	−49	−166	−391
Total, other revenue changes and loophole closers	−2	−5,906	−12,034	−13,318	−13,603	−12,979	−12,337	−12,277	−12,263	−12,130	−12,279	−57,840	−119,126
Total, reserve for long-run revenue-neutral business tax reform[8]	10,648	−10,035	−30,686	−31,412	−30,580	−28,891	−27,166	−23,970	−21,945	−21,658	−21,910	−131,604	−248,253

Note: For receipt effects, positive figures indicate lower receipts. For outlay effects, positive figures indicate higher outlays. For net costs, positive figures indicate higher deficits.

[1] The estimates for this proposal include effects on revenues. The revenue effects included in the totals above are as follows:

	2014	2015	2016	2017	2018	2019	2020	2021	2022	2023	2024	Totals 2015–2019	Totals 2015–2024
Offset DI benefits for period of concurrent UI receipt	....	....	....	....	2	11	17	23	27	33	81	13	194
Reauthorize special assessment from domestic nuclear utilities	....	−200	−204	−209	−213	−218	−223	−229	−234	−239	−245	−1,044	−2,214

Table S–9. Mandatory and Receipt Proposals—Continued

(Deficit increases (+) or decreases (−) in millions of dollars)

	2014	2015	2016	2017	2018	2019	2020	2021	2022	2023	2024	Totals 2015–2019	Totals 2015–2024
Permanently extend and reallocate the travel promotion surcharge	......	......	−114	−118	−123	−126	−129	−132	−135	−139	−142	−481	−1,158
Establish an AML hardrock reclamation fund	......	......	−200	−200	−200	−200	−200	−200	−200	−200	−200	−800	−1,800
Increase coal AML fee to pre–2006 levels	......	−52	−48	−50	−51	−53	−54	−54	......	......	......	−254	−362
Increase duck stamp fees	......	−14	−14	−14	−14	−14	−14	−14	−14	−14	−14	−70	−140
Enhance UI program integrity	......	......	......	1	2	3	5	6	6	6	8	6	37
Implement cap adjustments for UI program integrity	......	......	1	4	10	22	31	42	49	58	104	37	321
Strengthen UI system solvency	......	2,662	3,118	−9,344	−10,818	−6,987	−7,295	−8,081	−7,154	−8,036	−7,047	−21,369	−58,982
Provide the Secretary of the Treasury authority to access and disclose prisoner data to prevent and identify improper payments	......	......	......	......	1	2	2	3	4	4	5	3	21
Establish a mandatory surcharge for air traffic services	......	−725	−756	−787	−816	−844	−870	−894	−921	−947	−973	−3,928	−8,533
Increase levy authority for payments to Medicare providers with delinquent tax debt	......	−50	−71	−74	−76	−76	−77	−78	−80	−80	−81	−347	−743
Implement tax enforcement program integrity cap adjustment	......	−370	−1,265	−2,584	−3,978	−5,426	−6,620	−7,431	−7,850	−8,137	−8,343	−13,623	−52,004
Reform inland waterways funding	......	−82	−113	−113	−113	−113	−113	−113	−113	−113	−114	−534	−1,100
Enact immigration reform	......	−2,000	−12,000	−28,000	−39,000	−45,000	−47,000	−55,000	−64,000	−77,000	−87,000	−126,000	−456,000
Total revenue effects of mandatory proposals	−2,000	−831	−11,666	−41,488	−55,387	−59,019	−62,540	−72,152	−80,615	−94,804	−103,961	−168,391	−582,463

2 Net of income offsets.

3 The estimates for this proposal include effects on outlays. The outlay effects included in the totals above are as follows:

	2014	2015	2016	2017	2018	2019	2020	2021	2022	2023	2024	Totals 2015–2019	Totals 2015–2024
Expand EITC for workers without qualifying children	......	272	5,436	5,457	5,476	5,545	5,623	5,722	5,811	5,900	5,981	22,186	51,223
Designate Promise Zones	......	11	23	23	25	26	28	30	31	33	36	108	266
Provide America Fast Forward Bonds and expand eligible uses	......	216	966	2,051	3,221	4,505	5,878	7,325	8,826	10,360	11,914	10,959	55,262
Allow eligible uses of America Fast Forward Bonds to include financing all qualified private activity bond categories	......	50	227	489	765	1,054	1,356	1,668	1,990	2,319	2,651	2,585	12,569
Provide for automatic enrollment in IRAs, including a small employer tax credit, and double the tax credit for small employer plan start-up costs	......	......	96	148	150	152	153	156	160	164	168	546	1,347
Expand child and dependent care tax credit	......	......	347	342	348	352	362	368	374	382	392	1,389	3,267
Make Pell Grants excludable from income	......	......	547	959	906	862	824	793	764	735	704	3,274	7,094
Modify reporting of tuition expenses and scholarships on Form 1098-T	......	......	−20	−20	−20	−20	−20	−20	−20	−21	−21	−80	−182

Table S-9. Mandatory and Receipt Proposals—Continued

(Deficit increases (+) or decreases (–) in millions of dollars)

	2014	2015	2016	2017	2018	2019	2020	2021	2022	2023	2024	Totals 2015–2019	Totals 2015–2024
Provide the IRS with greater flexibility to address correctable errors	....	–3	–6	–7	–7	–7	–8	–8	–8	–9	–9	–30	–72
Rationalize tax return filing due dates so they are staggered	....	–28	–28	–28	–29	–29	–30	–30	–31	–32	–33	–142	–298
Simplify the rules for claiming the EITC for workers without qualifying children	....	26	516	526	538	526	536	546	556	526	536	2,132	4,832
Total outlay effects of tax proposals	....	544	8,104	9,940	11,373	12,966	14,702	16,550	18,453	20,357	22,319	42,927	135,308
Addendum, reserve for long-run revenue-neutral business tax reform:													
Modify and permanently extend renewable electricity production tax credit	....	28	120	241	382	523	661	811	978	1,158	1,349	1,294	6,251
Expand and simplify the tax credit provided to qualified small employers for non-elective contributions to employee health insurance ...	11	50	47	41	23	13	10	6	5	7	5	174	207

[4] This proposal costs $1 million over 2015–2019 and $3 million over 2015–2024.
[5] This proposal costs less than $500,000 in each year and over 5 and 10 years.
[6] This proposal saves $1 million over 2015–2019 and $4 million over 2015–2024.
[7] The provision is estimated to have zero revenue effect under the Administration's current economic projections.
[8] Because the Administration believes that these proposals should be enacted in the context of comprehensive business tax reform, the amounts are not reflected in the budget estimates of receipts and are not counted toward meeting the Administration's deficit reduction goals. The budget estimates do include $150 billion in temporary revenues that would be generated by the transition to a reformed business tax system, shown as part of the proposal to reauthorize surface transportation above.

Table S–10. Funding Levels for Appropriated ("Discretionary") Programs by Category

(Budget authority in billions of dollars)

	Actual 2013	Enacted 2014	Request 2015	Outyears									Totals	
				2016	2017	2018	2019	2020	2021	2022	2023	2024	2015-2019	2015-2024
Discretionary Adjusted Baseline by Category:[1]														
Defense Category	518	521	521	523	536	549	562	576	590	660	677	693	2,691	5,887
Non-Defense Category	479	512	492	492	504	516	530	543	556	605	620	635	2,534	5,492
Total, Base Discretionary Funding	997	1,033	1,014	1,015	1,040	1,065	1,092	1,119	1,146	1,265	1,296	1,328	5,225	11,379
Discretionary Policy Changes to Baseline Caps:														
2015 Opportunity, Growth, and Security Initiative and Outyear Cap Changes:[2]														
Defense Category			+28	+38	+33	+29	+24	+19	+14	–46	–48	–47	+152	+44
Non-Defense Category			+28	+38	+33	+29	+24	+19	+14	–25	–25	–23	+152	+113
Non-Defense Category Reclassifications:[3]														
Surface Transportation Programs	–4	–4	–4	–4	–4	–5	–5	–5	–5	–5	–5	–5	–22	–47
Program Integrity				–1	–1	–1	–1	–1	–1	–1	–1	–1	–2	–5
Proposed Discretionary Policy by Category:														
Defense Category	518	521	549	561	569	578	586	595	604	614	629	646	2,843	5,931
Non-Defense Category	475	508	516	525	532	540	549	557	565	574	589	606	2,661	5,553
Total, Base Discretionary Funding	993	1,029	1,065	1,086	1,101	1,118	1,135	1,152	1,169	1,188	1,218	1,252	5,504	11,484
Discretionary Cap Adjustments and Other Funding (not included above):[3]														
Overseas Contingency Operations[4,5]	93	92	85	30	30	30	30	30	30				205	265
Disaster Relief	11	6	7	7									7	7
Program Integrity	*	1	2	1	1	2	2	2	2	2	2	2	7	19
Wildfire Suppression			1	1	1	1	1	1	1	1	1	1	6	13
Other Emergency/Supplemental Funding	39													
Total, Cap Adjustments and Other	143	98	95	32	32	33	33	33	33	4	4	4	225	303
Grand Total, Discretionary Budget Authority	1,136	1,127	1,159	1,118	1,133	1,151	1,168	1,185	1,202	1,192	1,222	1,256	5,730	11,787

Table S–10. Funding Levels for Appropriated ("Discretionary") Programs by Category—Continued

(Budget authority in billions of dollars)

* $500 million or less.

[1] The discretionary funding levels from OMB's adjusted baseline are consistent with the caps in the Balanced Budget and Emergency Deficit Control Act of 1985 (BBEDCA), as amended, with separate categories of funding for "defense" (or Function 050) and "non-defense" for 2014–2021. These baseline levels assume Joint Committee enforcement cap reductions are in effect through 2021. For 2022 through 2024, programs are assumed to grow at current services with Joint Committee enforcement no longer in effect, consistent with current law. The levels shown here for the non-defense category do not include the reclassification of surface transportation programs shown later in the table.

[2] The 2015 Budget provides a detailed request for 2015 at the cap levels provided in the Bipartisan Budget Act of 2013 (BBA). The Budget also proposes for 2015 an Opportunity, Growth, and Security Initiative to provide investments in both defense and non-defense programs; these amounts are not programmatically allocated.

[3] Where applicable, amounts in 2013 through 2024 are existing or proposed cap adjustments designated pursuant to Section 251(b)(2) of BBEDCA, as amended. The 2015 Budget proposes new cap adjustments for program integrity and wildfire suppression activities. For 2016 through 2024, the cap adjustment levels for wildfire suppression are a placeholder that increase at the policy growth rates in the President's Budget. The existing disaster relief cap adjustment ceiling (which is determined one year at a time) would be reduced by the amount provided for wildfire suppression activities under the cap adjustment for the preceding fiscal year. The amounts will be refined in subsequent Budgets as data on the average costs for wildfire suppression are updated annually.

[4] Because the Administration has not yet made final decisions about an enduring presence in Afghanistan after calendar year 2014, the Budget includes a placeholder for the Department of Defense's 2015 OCO funding, equivalent to the amount requested in the 2014 Budget. Once DOD's OCO needs for 2015 are determined, the Administration will transmit a budget amendment package.

[5] The 2015 Budget includes placeholder amounts of nearly $30 billion per year for Government-wide OCO funding from 2016 to 2021. These amounts reflect the Administration's proposal to cap total OCO budget authority from 2013 to 2021 at $450 billion but do not reflect any specific decisions or assumptions about OCO funding in any particular year.

Table S–11. Funding Levels for Appropriated ("Discretionary") Programs by Agency

(Budget authority in billions of dollars)

	Actual 2013	Enacted 2014	Request 2015	Outyears 2016	2017	2018	2019	2020	2021	2022	2023	2024	Totals 2015-2019	2015-2024
Base Discretionary Funding by Agency:[1]														
Agriculture	23.0	24.1	22.2	23.6	24.1	24.6	25.1	25.7	26.3	26.9	27.6	28.3	119.6	254.4
Commerce	7.3	8.3	8.8	9.2	9.6	10.6	11.7	18.0	10.1	9.9	10.1	10.1	49.8	108.0
Census Bureau	*0.8*	*0.9*	*1.2*	*1.5*	*1.7*	*2.5*	*3.5*	*9.6*	*1.5*	*1.1*	*1.1*	*0.9*	*10.5*	*24.6*
Defense[2]	495.5	496.0	495.6	535.1	543.7	551.4	559.0	567.6	576.3	585.9	600.6	616.9	2,684.9	5,632.2
Education	65.7	67.3	68.6	69.5	70.5	71.6	72.7	73.8	74.9	76.2	77.5	78.8	352.8	733.9
Energy	25.2	27.2	27.9	27.5	28.2	28.8	29.4	30.0	30.7	31.4	32.2	33.0	141.8	299.2
National Nuclear Security Administration[2]	*10.6*	*11.2*	*11.7*	*10.8*	*11.1*	*11.3*	*11.5*	*11.8*	*12.1*	*12.4*	*12.7*	*13.0*	*56.4*	*118.3*
Health & Human Services[3]	74.3	79.8	73.7	80.1	81.9	83.7	85.6	87.4	89.3	91.6	93.8	96.2	404.9	863.3
Homeland Security	38.1	39.3	38.2	38.2	38.9	39.6	40.6	41.4	42.3	43.4	44.5	45.4	195.4	412.6
Housing and Urban Development	22.8	33.7	32.6	33.2	33.9	34.5	35.2	35.9	36.6	37.5	38.3	39.2	169.5	356.9
Interior	10.9	11.5	11.5	11.8	12.0	12.3	12.6	12.9	13.1	13.5	13.8	14.1	60.3	127.7
Justice	25.4	27.2	16.7	28.1	28.7	29.4	30.0	30.7	31.3	32.1	32.9	33.7	132.9	293.8
Labor	11.8	12.0	11.8	11.9	11.3	11.5	11.8	12.0	12.2	12.5	12.8	13.1	58.3	120.8
State and Other International Programs	39.6	42.7	42.6	43.5	44.4	45.4	46.4	47.4	48.4	49.5	50.8	52.0	222.3	470.3
Transportation	13.1	13.7	14.0	14.1	14.4	14.7	15.1	15.4	15.7	16.1	16.5	16.9	72.3	153.0
Treasury	12.3	12.6	12.4	13.5	13.8	14.2	14.6	15.0	15.5	15.9	16.4	16.8	68.5	148.1
Veterans Affairs	61.1	63.4	65.3	68.4	69.8	71.4	73.0	74.6	76.2	78.1	80.1	82.1	347.8	738.9
Corps of Engineers	8.1	5.5	4.5	4.7	4.7	4.9	5.0	5.1	5.2	5.3	5.4	5.6	23.7	50.3
Environmental Protection Agency	7.9	8.2	7.9	8.0	8.2	8.4	8.6	8.8	9.0	9.2	9.4	9.7	41.2	87.2
General Services Administration	-1.2	1.8	0.2	0.2	0.3	0.3	0.3	0.3	0.3	0.3	0.3	0.3	1.3	2.7
National Aeronautics & Space Administration	16.9	17.6	17.5	17.8	18.2	18.6	19.0	19.4	19.8	20.3	20.8	21.4	91.0	192.8
National Science Foundation	6.9	7.2	7.3	7.4	7.6	7.7	7.9	8.1	8.2	8.4	8.7	8.9	37.8	80.1
Small Business Administration	1.0	0.9	0.7	0.7	0.7	0.8	0.8	0.8	0.8	0.8	0.8	0.9	3.7	7.8
Social Security Administration[3]	8.6	8.9	9.1	9.0	9.2	9.4	9.6	9.8	10.0	10.2	10.5	10.8	46.2	97.6
Corporation for National & Community Service	1.0	1.1	1.1	1.1	1.1	1.1	1.1	1.2	1.2	1.2	1.3	1.3	5.5	11.6
Other Agencies	17.9	18.7	19.2	19.2	19.6	20.0	20.5	20.9	21.3	21.8	22.4	22.9	98.5	207.8
2015 Opportunity, Growth, and Security Initiative[4]	......	......	55.4	......	......	......	......	......	......	......	......	......	55.4	55.4
Allowances[5]	......	......	......	10.3	6.2	3.1	-0.6	-10.4	-6.1	-9.7	-9.2	-6.0	19.0	-22.4
Subtotal, Base Discretionary Funding	993.0	1,028.9	1,064.7	1,086.1	1,101.0	1,117.9	1,134.8	1,151.7	1,168.6	1,185.5	1,218.4	1,252.3	5,504.4	11,483.9

Table S–11. Funding Levels for Appropriated ("Discretionary") Programs by Agency—Continued

(Budget authority in billions of dollars)

	Actual 2013	Enacted 2014	Request 2015	Outyears 2016	2017	2018	2019	2020	2021	2022	2023	2024	Totals 2015-2019	2015-2024
Discretionary Cap Adjustments and Other Funding (not included above):[6]														
Overseas Contingency Operations	93.0	91.9	85.4	29.9	29.9	29.9	29.9	29.9	29.9	......	......	......	205.1	265.0
Defense[7]	82.0	85.2	79.4	......	......	......	......	......	......	......	......	......	79.4	79.4
Homeland Security	0.2	0.2	......											
State and Other International Programs	10.8	6.5	5.9	......	......	......	......	......	......	......	......	......	5.9	5.9
Overseas Contingency Operations Outyears[8]	......	......	......	29.9	29.9	29.9	29.9	29.9	29.9	......	......	......	119.8	179.7
Program Integrity	0.5	0.9	1.6	0.9	1.3	1.6	2.0	2.1	2.2	2.2	2.3	2.4	7.5	18.7
Treasury	......	......	0.5	0.9	1.2	1.6	2.0	2.1	2.1	2.2	2.2	2.3	6.2	17.1
Labor and SSA	0.5	0.9	1.1	*	*	*	*	*	*	*	*	*	1.1	1.1
Disaster Relief	11.2	5.6	6.6	......	......	......	......	......	......	......	......	......	6.6	6.6
Homeland Security	11.2	5.6	6.4	......	......	......	......	......	......	......	......	......	6.4	6.4
Small Business Administration	......	......	0.2	......	......	......	......	......	......	......	......	......	0.2	0.2
Wildfire Suppression[9]	......	......	1.2	1.2	1.2	1.3	1.3	1.3	1.4	1.4	1.4	1.5	6.2	13.2
Agriculture	......	......	1.0	1.0	1.0	1.0	1.0	1.1	1.1	1.1	1.1	1.2	5.0	10.5
Interior	......	......	0.2	0.2	0.3	0.3	0.3	0.3	0.3	0.3	0.3	0.3	1.3	2.7
Other Emergency/Supplemental Funding	38.6	......	......	......	......	......	......	......	......	......	......	......	......	......
Agriculture	0.2													
Commerce	0.3													
Energy	-0.5													
Health & Human Services	0.3													
Homeland Security	6.4													
Housing and Urban Development	15.2													
Interior	0.8													
Transportation	12.4													
Veterans Affairs	0.2													
Corps of Engineers	1.8													
Environmental Protection Agency	0.6													
Small Business Administration	0.8													
Other Agencies	0.1													
Grand Total, Discretionary Funding	1,136.3	1,127.4	1,159.5	1,118.1	1,133.4	1,150.7	1,168.1	1,185.1	1,202.1	1,192.1	1,222.1	1,256.1	5,729.8	11,787.3

Table S–11. Funding Levels for Appropriated ("Discretionary") Programs by Agency—Continued

(Budget authority in billions of dollars)

* $50 million or less.

[1] Amounts in the actual and enacted years of 2013 and 2014 exclude changes in mandatory programs enacted in appropriations bills since those amounts have been rebased as mandatory, whereas amounts in 2015 are net of these proposals. In addition, 2013 levels include the effects of the March 1, 2013 Joint Committee sequestration reductions.

[2] The Department of Defense (DOD) levels in 2016–2024 include funding that will be allocated, in annual increments, to the National Nuclear Security Administration (NNSA). Current estimates by which DOD's budget authority will decrease and NNSA's will increase are, in millions of dollars: 2016: $1,444; 2017: $1,602; 2018: $1,665; 2019: $1,698; 2020: $1,735; 2016–2024: $15,507. DOD and NNSA are reviewing NNSA's outyear requirements and these will be included in future reports to the Congress.

[3] Funding from the Hospital Insurance and Supplementary Medical Insurance trust funds for administrative expenses incurred by the Social Security Administration that support the Medicare program are included in the Health and Human Services total and not in the Social Security Administration total.

[4] The 2015 Budget provides a detailed request for 2015 at the cap levels provided in the Bipartisan Budget Act of 2013 (BBA). The Budget also proposes for 2015 an Opportunity, Growth, and Security Initiative to provide investments in both defense and non-defense programs; these amounts are not programmatically allocated.

[5] The 2015 Budget includes allowances, similar to the Function 920 allowances used in Budget Resolutions, to represent amounts to be allocated among the respective agencies to reach the proposed defense and non-defense caps for 2016 and beyond. These levels are determined for illustrative purposes but do not reflect specific policy decisions.

[6] Where applicable, amounts in 2013 through 2024 are existing or proposed cap adjustments designated pursuant to Section 251(b)(2) of the BBEDCA, as amended.

[7] Because the Administration has not yet made final decisions about an enduring presence in Afghanistan after calendar year 2014, the Budget includes a placeholder for the Department of Defense's 2015 OCO funding, equivalent to the amount requested in the 2014 Budget. Once DOD's OCO needs for 2015 are determined, the Administration will transmit a budget amendment package.

[8] The 2015 Budget includes placeholder amounts of $29.9 billion per year for Government-wide OCO funding from 2016 to 2021. These amounts reflect the Administration's proposal to cap total OCO budget authority from 2013 to 2021 at $450 billion but do not reflect any specific decisions or assumptions about OCO funding in any particular year.

[9] For 2016 through 2024, the cap adjustment levels are a placeholder that increase at the policy growth rates in the President's Budget. The existing disaster relief cap adjustment ceiling (which is determined one year at a time) would be reduced by the amount provided for wildfire suppression activities under the cap adjustment for the preceding fiscal year. Those amounts will be refined in subsequent Budgets as data on the average costs for wildfire suppression are updated annually.

Table S-12.　Economic Assumptions[1]

(Calendar years)

	Actual 2012	Projections											
		2013	2014	2015	2016	2017	2018	2019	2020	2021	2022	2023	2024
Gross Domestic Product (GDP):													
Nominal level, billions of dollars	16,245	16,768	17,544	18,454	19,432	20,460	21,459	22,445	23,454	24,484	25,551	26,664	27,826
Percent change, nominal GDP, year/year	4.6	3.2	4.6	5.2	5.3	5.3	4.9	4.6	4.5	4.4	4.4	4.4	4.4
Real GDP, percent change, year/year	2.8	1.7	3.1	3.4	3.3	3.2	2.8	2.5	2.4	2.3	2.3	2.3	2.3
Real GDP, percent change, Q4/Q4	2.0	2.3	3.3	3.4	3.3	3.2	2.6	2.5	2.4	2.3	2.3	2.3	2.3
GDP chained price index, percent change, year/year	1.7	1.4	1.6	1.8	1.9	2.0	2.0	2.0	2.0	2.0	2.0	2.0	2.0
Consumer Price Index,[2] percent change, year/year	2.1	1.4	1.6	2.0	2.1	2.2	2.3	2.3	2.3	2.3	2.3	2.3	2.3
Interest rates, percent:[3]													
91-day Treasury bills[4]	0.1	0.1	0.1	0.3	1.2	2.3	3.2	3.6	3.7	3.7	3.7	3.7	3.7
10-year Treasury notes	1.8	2.3	3.0	3.5	4.0	4.3	4.6	4.7	4.9	5.0	5.1	5.1	5.1
Unemployment rate, civilian, percent[3]	8.1	7.5	6.9	6.4	6.0	5.6	5.4	5.4	5.4	5.4	5.4	5.4	5.4

Note: A more detailed table of economic assumptions appears in Chapter 2, "Economic Assumptions and Interactions with the Budget," in the *Analytical Perspectives* volume of the Budget.

[1] Based on information available as of mid-November 2013.

[2] Seasonally adjusted CPI for all urban consumers.

[3] Annual average.

[4] Average rate, secondary market (bank discount basis).

Table S–13. Federal Government Financing and Debt

(Dollar amounts in billions)

	Actual 2013	Estimate 2014	2015	2016	2017	2018	2019	2020	2021	2022	2023	2024
Financing:												
Unified budget deficit:												
Primary deficit (+)/surplus (−)	459	425	312	214	66	−60	−48	−103	−166	−191	−290	−379
Net interest	221	223	252	318	392	474	551	616	669	721	772	812
Unified budget deficit	680	649	564	531	458	413	503	512	504	530	482	434
As a percent of GDP	4.1%	3.7%	3.1%	2.8%	2.3%	1.9%	2.3%	2.2%	2.1%	2.1%	1.8%	1.6%
Other transactions affecting borrowing from the public:												
Changes in financial assets and liabilities:[1]												
Change in Treasury operating cash balance	3	2	......	......	......	......	......	......	......	......	......	......
Net disbursements of credit financing accounts:												
Direct loan accounts	139	126	121	127	123	109	102	103	104	106	111	114
Guaranteed loan accounts	−1	26	10	8	8	6	8	7	4	1	−1	−2
Troubled Asset Relief Program (TARP) equity purchase accounts	−7	−2	−4	−*	−*	−*	−*	−*	−*	−*	−*	−*
Net purchases of non-Federal securities by the National Railroad Retirement Investment Trust (NRRIT)	1	−*	−1	−1	−1	−1	−1	−1	−1	−1	−1	−1
Net change in other financial assets and liabilities[2]	−114	120										
Subtotal, changes in financial assets and liabilities	22	271	126	134	129	114	109	109	107	106	110	112
Seigniorage on coins	−*	−*	−*	−*	−*	−*	−*	−*	−*	−*	−*	−*
Total, other transactions affecting borrowing from the public	22	271	126	134	129	114	109	109	107	106	109	112
Total, requirement to borrow from the public (equals change in debt held by the public)	701	920	689	665	587	527	611	621	611	636	591	545
Changes in Debt Subject to Statutory Limitation:												
Change in debt held by the public	701	920	689	665	587	527	611	621	611	636	591	545
Change in debt held by Government accounts	−33	253	132	133	163	172	98	85	78	47	49	52
Change in other factors	4	−8	1	2	2	2	3	3	2	2	3	3
Total, change in debt subject to statutory limitation	672	1,165	822	801	753	701	712	709	691	686	643	600
Debt Subject to Statutory Limitation, End of Year:												
Debt issued by Treasury	16,692	17,864	18,684	19,483	20,234	20,934	21,645	22,352	23,042	23,726	24,368	24,967
Adjustment for discount, premium, and coverage[3]	8	−*	2	4	5	6	8	9	10	12	13	14
Total, debt subject to statutory limitation[4]	16,699	17,864	18,686	19,487	20,239	20,941	21,653	22,362	23,052	23,738	24,381	24,981

Table S–13. Federal Government Financing and Debt—Continued

(Dollar amounts in billions)

	Actual	Estimate										
	2013	2014	2015	2016	2017	2018	2019	2020	2021	2022	2023	2024
Debt Outstanding, End of Year:												
Gross Federal debt:[5]												
Debt issued by Treasury	16,692	17,864	18,684	19,483	20,234	20,934	21,645	22,352	23,042	23,726	24,368	24,967
Debt issued by other agencies	28	29	29	29	28	27	26	25	24	23	21	19
Total, gross Federal debt	16,719	17,893	18,713	19,512	20,262	20,961	21,671	22,377	23,065	23,749	24,389	24,986
Held by:												
Debt held by Government accounts	4,737	4,990	5,122	5,255	5,418	5,591	5,689	5,774	5,852	5,899	5,948	6,000
Debt held by the public[6]	11,983	12,903	13,592	14,257	14,843	15,370	15,982	16,603	17,213	17,850	18,441	18,986
As a percent of GDP	72.1%	74.4%	74.6%	74.3%	73.5%	72.4%	72.0%	71.6%	71.1%	70.6%	69.9%	69.0%
Debt Held by the Public Net of Financial Assets:												
Debt held by the public	11,983	12,903	13,592	14,257	14,843	15,370	15,982	16,603	17,213	17,850	18,441	18,986
Less financial assets net of liabilities:												
Treasury operating cash balance	88	90	90	90	90	90	90	90	90	90	90	90
Credit financing account balances:												
Direct loan accounts	944	1,069	1,190	1,318	1,440	1,549	1,651	1,754	1,858	1,964	2,075	2,189
Guaranteed loan accounts	–10	16	25	33	41	47	55	62	65	67	66	64
TARP equity purchase accounts	7	5	1	1	1	*	*	*	*	*	*	*
Government-sponsored enterprise preferred stock	140	140	140	140	140	140	140	140	140	140	140	140
Non-Federal securities held by NRRIT	24	24	23	22	21	20	19	19	18	17	16	16
Other assets net of liabilities	–137	–17	–17	–17	–17	–17	–17	–17	–17	–17	–17	–17
Total, financial assets net of liabilities	1,056	1,328	1,453	1,587	1,716	1,830	1,939	2,048	2,155	2,261	2,371	2,483
Debt held by the public net of financial assets	10,926	11,575	12,138	12,669	13,127	13,540	14,043	14,555	15,058	15,588	16,070	16,503
As a percent of GDP	65.7%	66.8%	66.6%	66.1%	65.0%	63.8%	63.3%	62.7%	62.2%	61.7%	60.9%	59.9%

* $500 million or less.

[1] A decrease in the Treasury operating cash balance (which is an asset) is a means of financing a deficit and therefore has a negative sign. An increase in checks outstanding (which is a liability) is also a means of financing a deficit and therefore also has a negative sign.

[2] Includes checks outstanding, accrued interest payable on Treasury debt, uninvested deposit fund balances, allocations of special drawing rights, and other liability accounts; and, as an offset, cash and monetary assets (other than the Treasury operating cash balance), other asset accounts, and profit on sale of gold.

[3] Consists mainly of debt issued by the Federal Financing Bank (which is not subject to limit), Treasury securities held by the Federal Financing Bank, the unamortized discount (less premium) on public issues of Treasury notes and bonds (other than zero-coupon bonds), and the unrealized discount on Government account series securities.

[4] Legislation enacted February 15, 2014, (P.L. 113-83) temporarily suspends the debt limit through March 15, 2015.

[5] Treasury securities held by the public and zero-coupon bonds held by Government accounts are almost all measured at sales price plus amortized discount or less amortized premium. Agency debt securities are almost all measured at face value. Treasury securities in the Government account series are otherwise measured at face value less unrealized discount (if any).

[6] At the end of 2013, the Federal Reserve Banks held $2,072.3 billion of Federal securities and the rest of the public held $9,910.3 billion. Debt held by the Federal Reserve Banks is not estimated for future years.

OMB CONTRIBUTORS TO THE 2015 BUDGET

The following personnel contributed to the preparation of this publication. Hundreds, perhaps thousands, of others throughout the Government also deserve credit for their valuable contributions.

A

Andrew Abrams
Brenda Aguilar
Shagufta Ahmed
Steven Aitken
Jameela Raja Akbari
Matthew H. Akridge
David W. Alekson
Victoria L. Allred
Lois E. Altoft
Aaron K. Ampaw
Scott J. Anchin
Linda Angstadt
Kevin M. Arnwine
Aviva R. Aron-Dine
Anna R. Arroyo
Emily E. Askew
Ari I. Astles
Lisa L. August
Renee Austin

B

Peter Babb
Susan E. Badgett
Jessie W. Bailey
Paul W. Baker
Carol A. Bales
Avital Bar-Shalom
Bethanne Barnes
Patti A. Barnett
Leslie D. Barrack
Jody M. Barringer
Mary Barth
Thomas A.
  Bartholomew
Jennifer Wagner Bell

Frank J. Benenati
Kheira Z. Benkreira
Daniel L. Berger
Samuel K. Berger
Benjamin R.
  Bergersen
Lindsey Berman
Scott A. Bernard
Elizabeth Bernhard
Roberto C. Berrios
Matthew F. Blazek
Mathew C. Blum
Quan Myles Boatman
James Boden
Erin Boeke Burke
Melissa B. Bomberger
Cole A. Borders
Gitanjali G. Borkar
Katherine Bowman
William J. Boyd
Chantel M. Boyens
Brianna A. Bradford-
  Benesh
Bing Bradshaw
Michael Branson
Denise Bray
Shannon C. Bregman
Joseph F. Breighner
Julie A. Brewer
Andrea Brian
Erik G. Brine
Candice M. Bronack
Jonathan M. Brooks
Christopher R. Broome
Calla R. Brown
Dustin S. Brown
Jamal T. Brown
James A. Brown

Kelly D. Brown
Melissa Brown
Rachel E. H. Brown
Michael T. Brunetto
Paul Bugg
Tom D. Bullers
Robert Bullock
Ben Burnett
Ryan M. Burnette
John D. Burnim
John C. Burton
Sylvia M. Burwell
Mark Bussow
Cinnamon L. Butler

C

Kathleen D. Cahill
Steven Cahill
Emily E. Cain
Jhaval Cain
Erica L. Cameron
Mark F. Cancian
Eric Cardoza
Todd S. Carolin
J. Kevin Carroll
William S. S. Carroll
Scott D. Carson
Mary I. Cassell
David Cassidy
Joseph R. Castle
Ben Chan
Daniel E. Chandler
James Chase
Anita Chellaraj
Michael Clark
Beth F. Cobert
Matthew W. Collier

Victoria W. Collin
Debra M. Collins
Kelly T. Colyar
Nicole E. Comisky
Jaclyn Corona
Martha B. Coven
Claire E. Cramer
Catherine E. Crato
Joseph Crilley
Rose Crow
Albert T. Crowley
Juliana Crump
Craig Crutchfield
Edna Falk Curtin
Tyler Curtis
William Curtis

D

D. Michael Daly
Neil B. Danberg
Matthew Dantas-
  McCutcheon
Alexander J. Daumit
Joanne Chow
  Davenport
Kenneth L. Davis
Margaret B. Davis-
  Christian
Chad J. Day
Kirsten S. Day
Brian C. Deese
David M. Diamond
John H. Dick
Vernon T. Dickerson
Julie Allen Dingley
James R. Dishaw
Jason C. Dixson

Derek M. Donahoo
Angela M. Donatelli
Norman S. Dong
Paul S. Donohue
Bridget C. Dooling
Shamera A. Dorsey
Lisa Cash Driskill
Francis J. DuFrayne
Laura E. Duke
Matthew S. Dunn

E

Jacqueline A. Easley
Jeanette Edwards
Emily M. Eelman
Christopher J. Elliott
Noah Engelberg
Michelle A. Enger
Sally Ericsson
Mark T. Erwin
Edward V. Etzkorn
Haig L. Evans-
  Kavaldjian
Rowe Ewell
Laura J. Eyester

F

Chris Fairhall
Robert Fairweather
Michael C. Falkenheim
Kara L. Farley-Cahill
Christine E.
  Farquharson
Kira R. Fatherree
Andrew R. Feldman
Patricia Ferrell

Lesley A. Field
Daren H. Firestone
Mary S. Fischietto
E Holly Fitter
John Joseph
  Fitzpatrick
Darlene B. Fleming
Tera L. Fong
Kelsey J. Foster
Nicholas A. Fraser

Elizabeth A. Frederick
Marc P. Freiman
Farrah B. Freis
Nathan J. Frey

G

Marc Garufi
Thomas O. Gates
Benjamin P. Geare
Jeremy Gelb
Brian Gillis
Joshua S. Glazer
Ja'Cia D. Goins
Melanie Goldberg
Jeff Goldstein
Oscar Gonzalez
Thomas W.
  Grannemann
Kathleen A. Gravelle
Jennifer E. Gray
Richard E. Green
Andrei M. Greenawalt
Aron Greenberg
Liam E. Grimley
Hester C. Grippando
Rebecca Grusky

H

Michael B. Hagan
Christopher C. Hall
Erika S. Hamalainen
Christina L. Hansen
Linda W. Hardin
Dionne Hardy
David Harmon
Julian J. Harris
Patsy W. Harris
Brian A. Harris-
  Kojetin

Nicholas R. Hart
Jelani Harvey
Paul Harvey
Ryan Bensussan
  Harvey
Tomer Hasson
David Haun

Laurel S. Havas
Mark Hazelgren
Jeffrey K. Hendrickson
John David Henson
Kevin W. Herms
Jennifer M. Hesch
Alexander G.
  Hettinger
Gretchen T. Hickey
Michael J. Hickey
Cortney Higgins
Rebecca A. Higgins
Mary Lou Hildreth
Andrew Hire
Thomas E. Hitter
Jennifer E. Hoef
Joanne C. Hoff
Adam Hoffberg
Stuart Hoffman
Troy L. Holland
James S. Holm
Peter M. Holm
Daniel Hornung
Lynette Hornung-
  Kobes
Grace Hu
Kathy M. Hudgins
Jeremy D. Hulick
Alexander T. Hunt
Lorraine D. Hunt
James C. Hurban
Jaki Mayer Hurwitz
Dana J. Hyde

I

Eric G. Iacobucci
Robert Ikoku
Tae H. Im
Janet E. Irwin
Paul Iwugo

J

Laurence R. Jacobson
Varun M. Jain
Carol Jenkins
Aaron D. Joachim
Barbara A. Johnson

Carol S. Johnson
Kim I. Johnson
Michael D. Johnson
Bobby Jones
Bryant A. Jones
Danielle Yvonne Jones
Lisa M. Jones
Othni A. Jones
Joseph G. Jordan
Reshma Joshi
Hee Jun

K

Paul A. Kagan
Richard E. Kane
Jacob H. Kaplan
Jenifer Karwoski
Molly M. Kawahata
Regina L. Kearney
Dan J. Keenaghan
Matt J. Keeneth
Grace Kelemen
Hunter S. Kellett
Jack Kelly
Ann Kendrall
Nancy B. Kenly
Amanda R. Kepko
Alper A. Kerman
Paul E. Kilbride
Cristina F.
  Killingsworth
James H. Kim
Barry King
Kelly Kinneen
Carole Kitti
Ben Klay
Sarah B. Klein
Kevin E. Kobee
Steve Kosiak
John Kraemer
Lori Krauss
Aaron T. Krupkin
Joydip Kundu

L

Christopher D. LaBaw
Leonard L. Lainhart
Lawrence L. Lambert
Daniel LaPlaca
Janisa S. LaSalle
Eric P. Lauer
Jerry R.
   Lautenschlager
Jessie L. LaVine
Jessica K. Lee
Karen F. Lee
Malcolm Lee
Susan E. Leetmaa
Clarissa E. Leonard
Andrea Leung
Malissa C. Levesque
Eli L. Levine
Shoshana M. Lew
Lauren N. Lewis
Sheila Lewis
Bryan León
Jeremy L. León
Wendy L. Liberante
Richard Alan
   Lichtenberger
Sara Rose Lichtenstein
Kristina E. Lilac
Jennifer M. Lipiew
Lin C. Liu
Patrick Locke
Aaron M. Lopata
Alexander W. Louie
Adrienne Lucas
Kimberley S.
   Luczynski
Gideon F. Lukens
Sarah Lyberg
Laura E. Lynch

M

Chi T. Mac
Deborah L. Macaulay
Brendan P. Mackesey
Ryan J. MacMaster
John S. MacNeil
Natalia Mahmud

Claire A. Mahoney
Kathryn A. Malague
Margaret A. Malanoski
Dominic J. Mancini
Robert G. Mann
Sharon Mar
Anne-Louise Marquis
Celinda A. Marsh
Brendan A. Martin
Kathryn E. Martin
Rochelle W. Martinez
J. Kevin Maskornick
Surujpat (Adrian) J.
   Mathura
Andrew Mayock
Shelly McAllister
George H. McArdle
Alexander J.
   McClelland
Jeremy McCrary
Timothy D. McCrosson
Anthony W. McDonald
Christine A. McDonald
Katrina A. McDonald
Renford A. McDonald
Luther C. McGinty
Christopher McLaren
Robin J. McLaughry
Colleen McLoughlin
William J. McQuaid
William J. Mea
Inna L. Melamed
Patrick J. Mellon
Barbara A. Menard
Flavio Menasce
Jose A. Mendez
Jessica Menter
P. Thaddeus
   Messenger
William L. Metzger
Julie L. Miller
Kimberly Miller
Asma Mirza
Mirghani S. Mohamed
Joseph E. Montoni
Cindy H. Moon
Laura S. Morton
Bruno Muscolino
Christian G. Music

N

Jennifer M. Nading
Jeptha E. Nafziger
Larry J. Nagl
Barry Napear
Ashley M. Nathanson
Allie R. Neill
Melissa K. Neuman
Betsy A. Newcomer
Joanie F. Newhart
John D. Newman
Kimberly Armstrong
   Newman
Teresa O. Nguyen
Eric Ngwa
Alexander M. Niejelow
Tige D. Nishimoto
Abigail P. Norris
Tim H. Nusraty

O

Erin O'Brien
Devin L. O'Connor
Megan M. O'Doherty
Matthew J. O'Kane
Benjamin J. Ossoff
Jared L. Ostermiller
Tyler J. Overstreet
D. Brooke Owens
Adeniran O. Oyebade

P

Benjamin J. Page
Heather C. Pajak
Jennifer E. Park
Sangkyun Park
John C. Pasquantino
Arati N. Patel
Terri B. Payne
Jacqueline M. Peay
Falisa Peoples-Tittle
Andrew B. Perraut
Michael A. Perz
Andrea M. Petro
Stacey Que-Chi Pham
Carolyn R. Phelps

Karen A. Pica
Joseph Pipan
Alisa M. Ple-Plakon
Kimberly A. Pohland
Rachel C. Pollock
Aaron W. Pollon
Ruxandra I. Pond
Steven C. Posner
Celestine M. Pressley
Larrimer S. Prestosa
Nina M. Preuss
Marguerite E. Pridgen
Timothy W. Puetz
Robert Purdy

Q

John P. Quinlan

R

Jonathan E. Rackoff
Lucas R. Radzinschi
Latonda Glass Raft
Louis M. Rager
Angelo Ramilo
Maria S. Raphael
Jeff Reczek
Dexter Reece
Rudolph G. Regner
Paul B. Rehmus
Sean Reilly
Thomas M. Reilly
Scott D. Renda
Richard J. Renomeron
Keri A. Rice
Shannon A. Richter
Justin R. Riordan
Emma K. Roach
Benjamin T. Roberts
Beth Higa Roberts
Catherine Robinson
Donovan Robinson
Marshall J. Rodgers
Cynthia S. Rodriguez-
   Knox
Alexandra N. Rogers
Rodolfo Rojas
Meredith B. Romley

Dan T. Rosenbaum
Eric M. Rosiere
Adam J. Ross
David J. Rowe
Mario Roy
Trevor H. Rudolph
Ryan D. Rusnak
Latisha M. Russell
Kristin C. Rzeczkowski

S

Fouad P. Saad
Sonya E. Sackner-
  Bernstein
John Asa Saldivar
Dominic K. Sale
Mark S. Sandy
Kristen J. Sarri
Mary Scheuermann
Lisa Schlosser
Tricia Schmitt
Andrew M. Schoenbach
Daniel K. Schory
Margo Schwab
Nancy Schwartz
Jasmeet K. Seehra
Richard Segal
Will Sellheim
Shahid N. Shah
Dianne Shaughnessy
Paul Shawcross
Howard A. Shelanski
Amy L. Shlossman
Gary F. Shortencarrier
Sara R. Sills
Samantha E.
  Silverberg
Jeffrey S. Simms
John L. S. Simpkins
Benjamin J. Skidmore
Jack Smalligan
Christopher B. Smith

Curtina O. Smith
Nikolis R. Smith
Stephen A. Sola
Silvana Solano
Rod Solomon
Kathryn Stack
Scott R. Stambaugh
Spencer G. Stanfield
Melanie A. Stansbury
Nora Stein
Joseph W. Stekli
Ryan J. Stelzer
Lamar R. Stewart
Gary R. Stofko
Carla B. Stone
Shayna L. Strom
Thomas J. Suarez
Kevin J. Sullivan
Jessica L. Sun
Harry K. Swann
Jennifer A. Swartz
Ben Sweezy

T

Teresa A. Tancre
Naomi S. Taransky
Benjamin K. Taylor
Myra Taylor
Emma K. Tessier
Raina Thiele
Judith F. Thomas
Latina D. Thomas
Will Thomas
Edith R. Thompson
Courtney B.
  Timberlake
Thomas Tobasko
Toinita Tolson
Richard W. Toner
Taryn H. Toyama
Hai M. Tran
James (Trey) D.
  Treadwell, III

Raya B. Treiser
Susan M. Truslow
Donald L. Tuck
Heather K. Turner
Melissa H. Turner
Benjamin J. Turpen
Sara A. Twyman

U

Nicholas A. Uchalik
Darrell J. Upshaw

V

Matthew J. Vaeth
Ofelia M. Valeriano
Amanda Valerio
Cynthia Vallina
Haley L. Van Dyck
Samuel C. Van Kopp
Sarita Vanka
Steven L. VanRoekel
David W. Varvel
Areletha L. Venson
Alexandra Ventura
Patricia A. Vinkenes
Dean R. Vonk
David A. Vorhaus
Ann M. Vrabel

W

James A. Wade
James R. Walker
Katherine K. Wallman
Heather V. Walsh
Mary E. Walsh
Tim Wang
Sharon A. Warner
Geovette E.
  Washington
Gary Waxman
Mark A. Weatherly

Bess Weaver
Jeffrey A. Weinberg
Philip R. Wenger
Michael S. Wetklow
Arnette C. White
Kamela G. White
Kim S. White
Sherron R. White
Chad S. Whiteman
Carrie L. Wibben
Sarah M. Widor
Mary Ellen Wiggins
Shimika N. Wilder
Calvin L. Williams
Debra (Debbie) L.
  Williams
Monique C. Williams
Terrill M. Williams
Gregory Wilson
Jennifer Winkler
Melanie J. Winston
Julia Wise
Julie Wise
Raymond Wong
Lauren Wright
Sophia M. Wright
Michael J. Wrona
William Wu
Steven N. Wynands

Y

Abra S. Yeh
Melany N. Yeung

Z

Eliana M. Zavala
Lisa Ziehmann
Gail S Zimmerman
Rita R. Zota